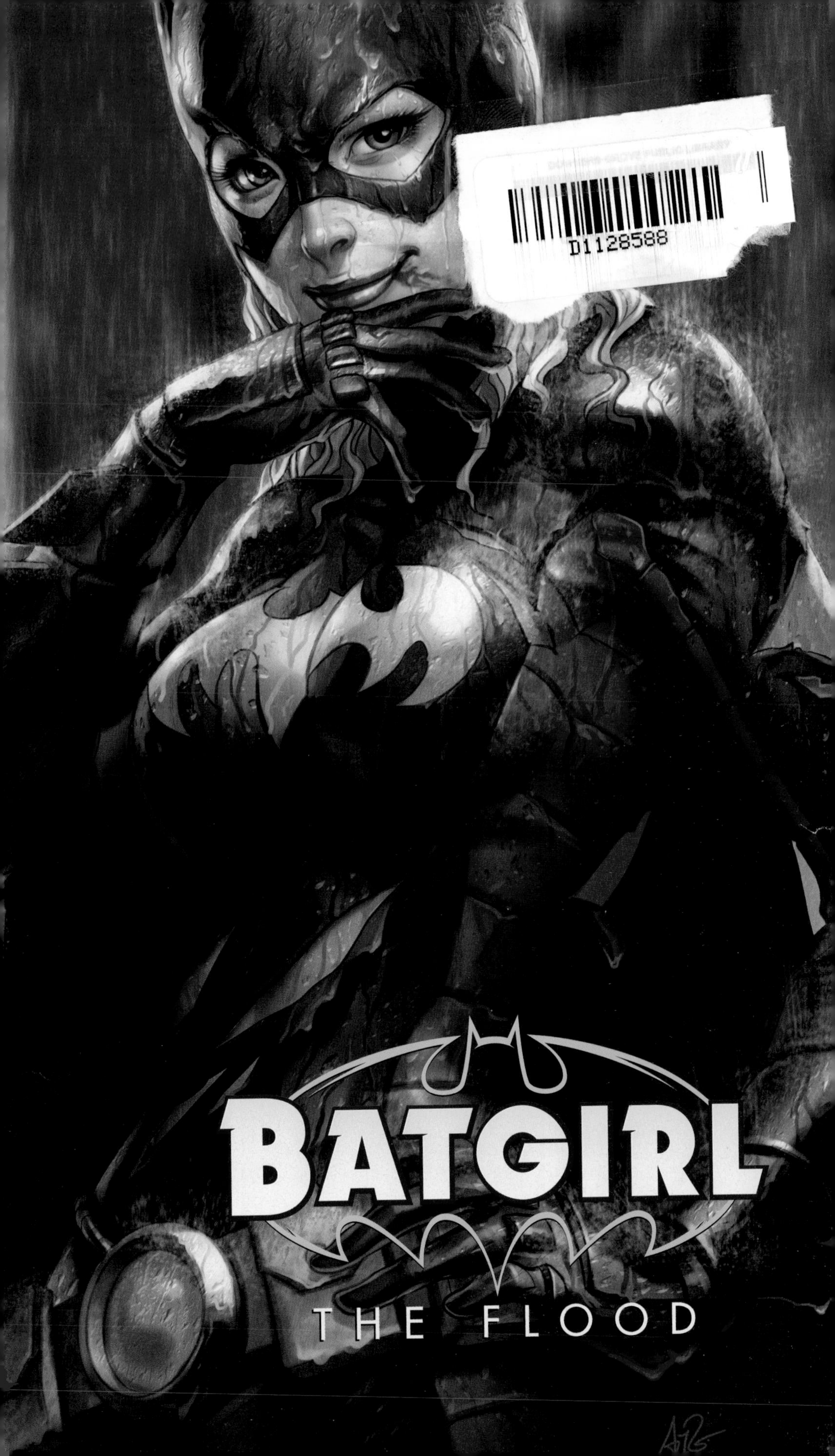
BATGIRL
THE FLOOD

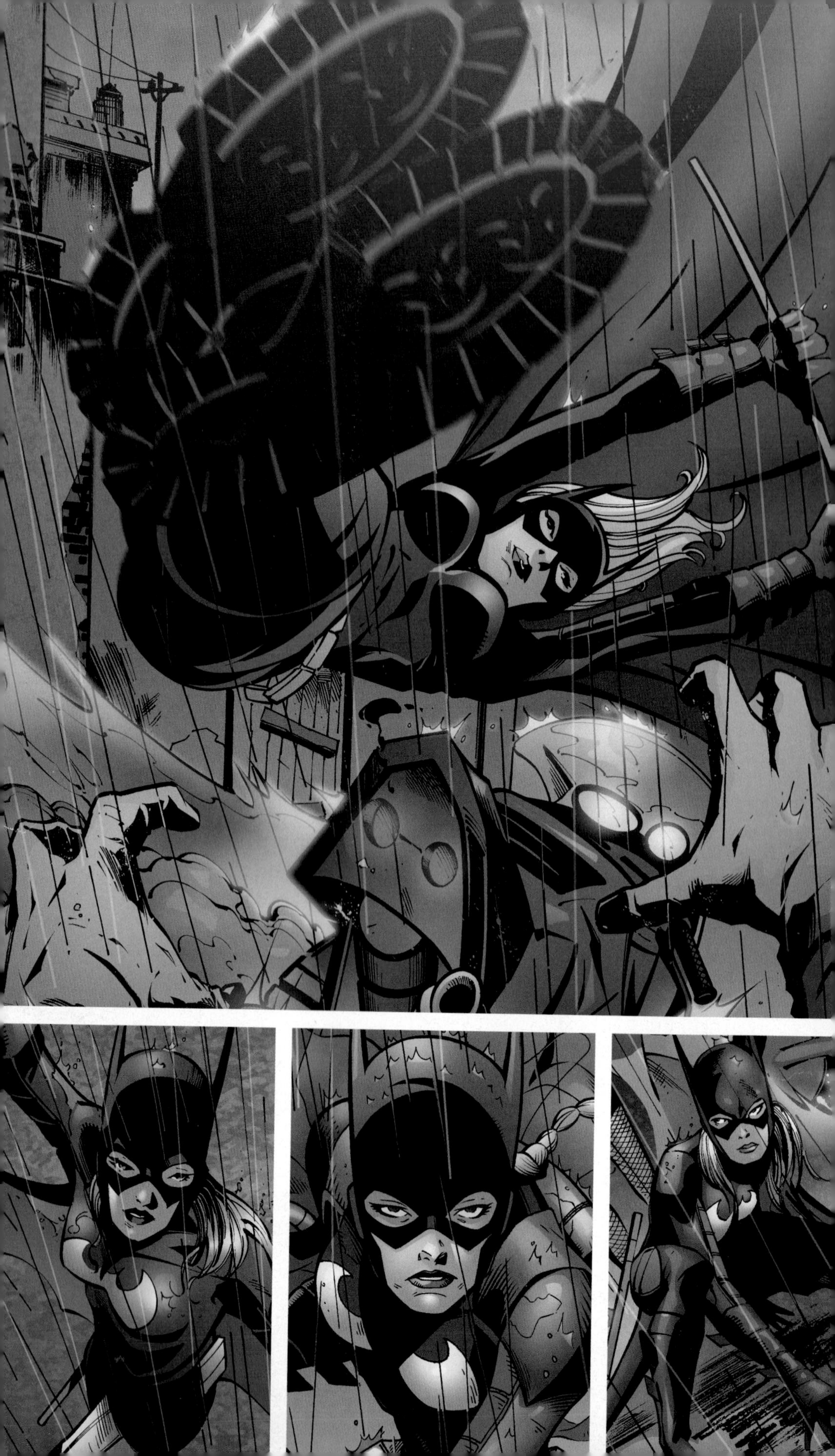

BATGIRL

THE FLOOD

BRYAN Q. MILLER
WRITER

LEE GARBETT PERE PEREZ
PENCILLERS

**JONATHAN GLAPION RICHARD FRIEND
RODNEY RAMOS PERE PEREZ
WALDEN WONG TREVOR SCOTT**
INKERS

GUY MAJOR
COLORIST

PAT BROSSEAU TRAVIS LANHAM JOHN J. HILL
LETTERERS

STANLEY "ARTGERM" LAU
COVER ARTIST

BATMAN CREATED BY **BOB KANE**

SEAN RYAN MICHAEL SIGLAIN Editors-original series
HARVEY RICHARDS Assistant Editor-original series
BOB HARRAS Group Editor-Collected Editions
ROBBIN BROSTERMAN Design Director-Books

DC COMICS
DIANE NELSON President
DAN DIDIO and JIM LEE Co-Publishers
GEOFF JOHNS Chief Creative Officer
PATRICK CALDON EVP-Finance and Administration
JOHN ROOD EVP-Sales, Marketing and Business Development
AMY GENKINS SVP-Business and Legal Affairs
STEVE ROTTERDAM SVP-Sales and Marketing
JOHN CUNNINGHAM VP-Marketing
TERRI CUNNINGHAM VP-Managing Editor
ALISON GILL VP-Manufacturing
DAVID HYDE VP-Publicity
SUE POHJA VP-Book Trade Sales
ALYSSE SOLL VP-Advertising and Custom Publishing
BOB WAYNE VP-Sales
MARK CHIARELLO Art Director

DC Comics, 1700 Broadway, New York, NY 10019
A Warner Bros. Entertainment Company
Printed by Quad/Graphics, Dubuque, IA, USA. 4/15/11.
First printing.
ISBN: 978-1-4012-3142-2

LIBRARY OF CONGRESS CATALOGING-IN-PUBLICATION DATA

MILLER, BRYAN Q.
   BATGIRL : FLOOD / WRITER, BRYAN Q. MILLER ; PENCILS, LEE GARBETT.
      P. CM.
   "ORIGINALLY PUBLISHED IN SINGLE MAGAZINE FORM IN BATGIRL 9-14 (2010)."
   ISBN 978-1-4012-3142-2 (SOFTCOVER)
   1. BATGIRL (FICTITIOUS CHARACTER)--COMIC BOOKS, STRIPS, ETC. 2.
GRAPHIC NOVELS. I. GARBETT, LEE. II. TITLE.
   PN6728.B358M5 2011
   741.5'973--DC22
                    2011008694

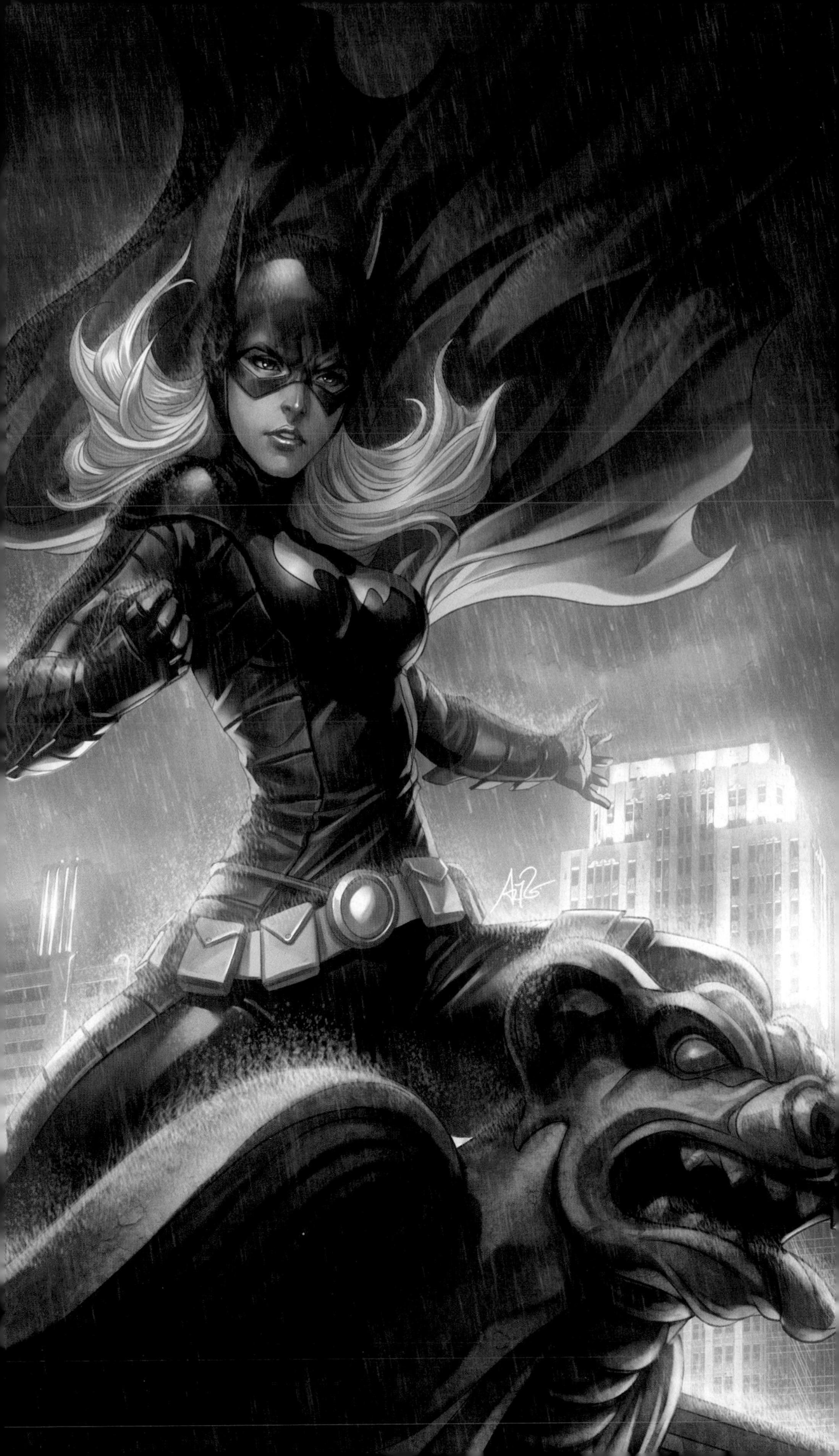

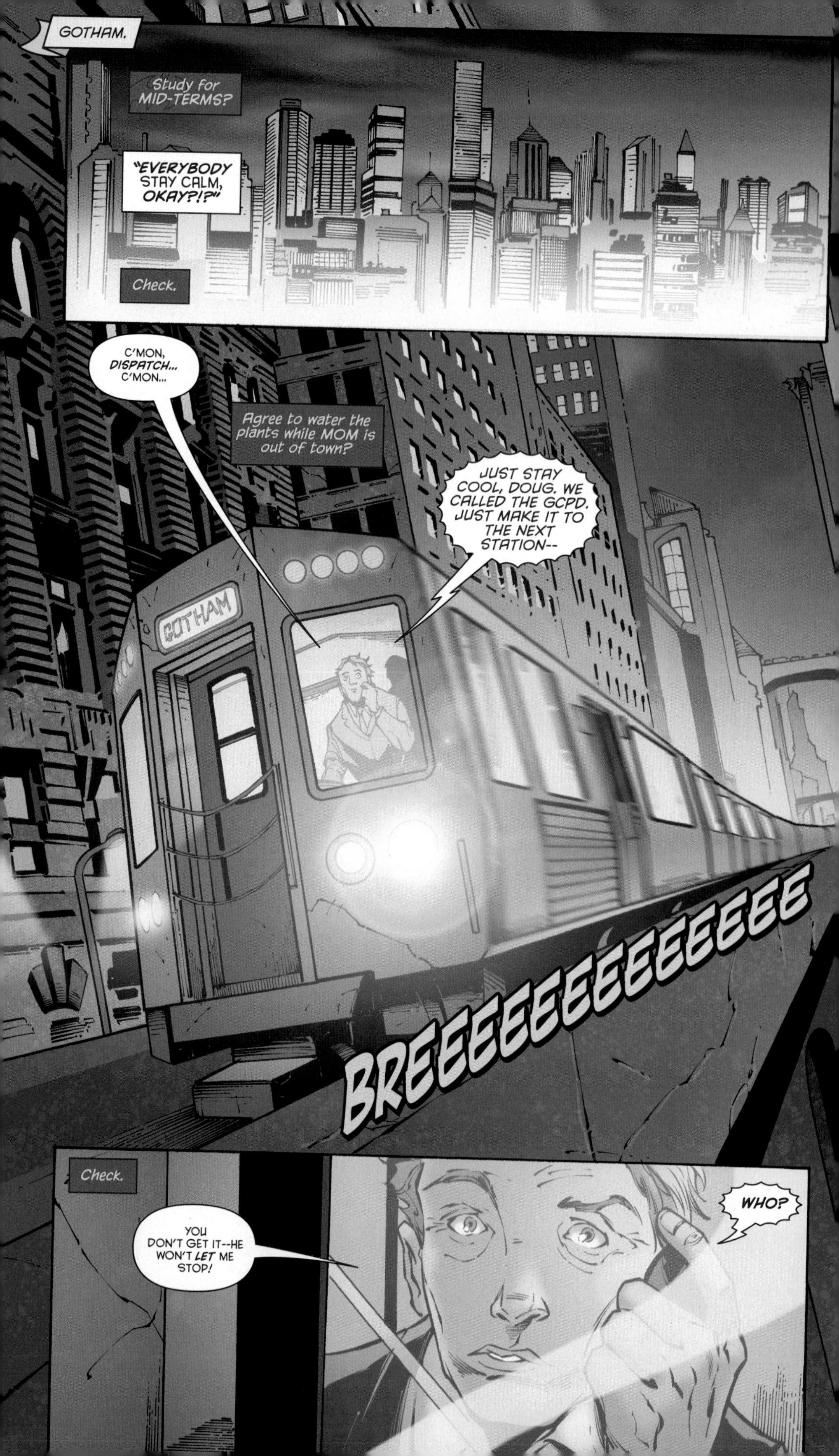
GOTHAM.
Study for MID-TERMS?
"EVERYBODY STAY CALM, OKAY?!?"
Check.
C'MON, DISPATCH... C'MON...
Agree to water the plants while MOM is out of town?
JUST STAY COOL, DOUG. WE CALLED THE GCPD. JUST MAKE IT TO THE NEXT STATION--
GOTHAM
BREEEEEEEEEEEEEEE
Check.
YOU DON'T GET IT--HE WON'T LET ME STOP!
WHO?

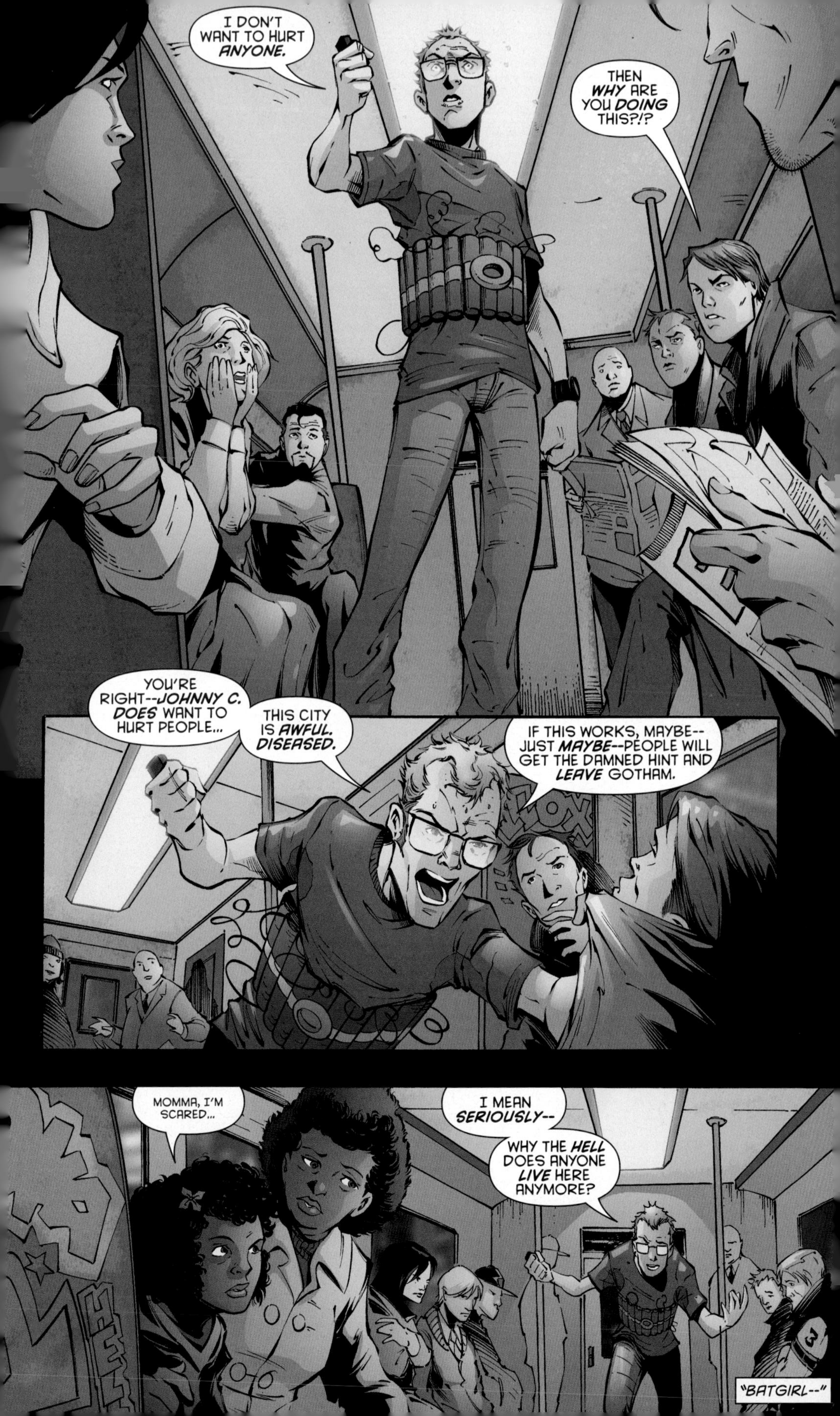
I DON'T WANT TO HURT ANYONE.
THEN WHY ARE YOU DOING THIS?!?
YOU'RE RIGHT--JOHNNY C. DOES WANT TO HURT PEOPLE...
THIS CITY IS AWFUL. DISEASED.
IF THIS WORKS, MAYBE--JUST MAYBE--PEOPLE WILL GET THE DAMNED HINT AND LEAVE GOTHAM.
MOMMA, I'M SCARED...
I MEAN SERIOUSLY--
WHY THE HELL DOES ANYONE LIVE HERE ANYMORE?
"BATGIRL--"

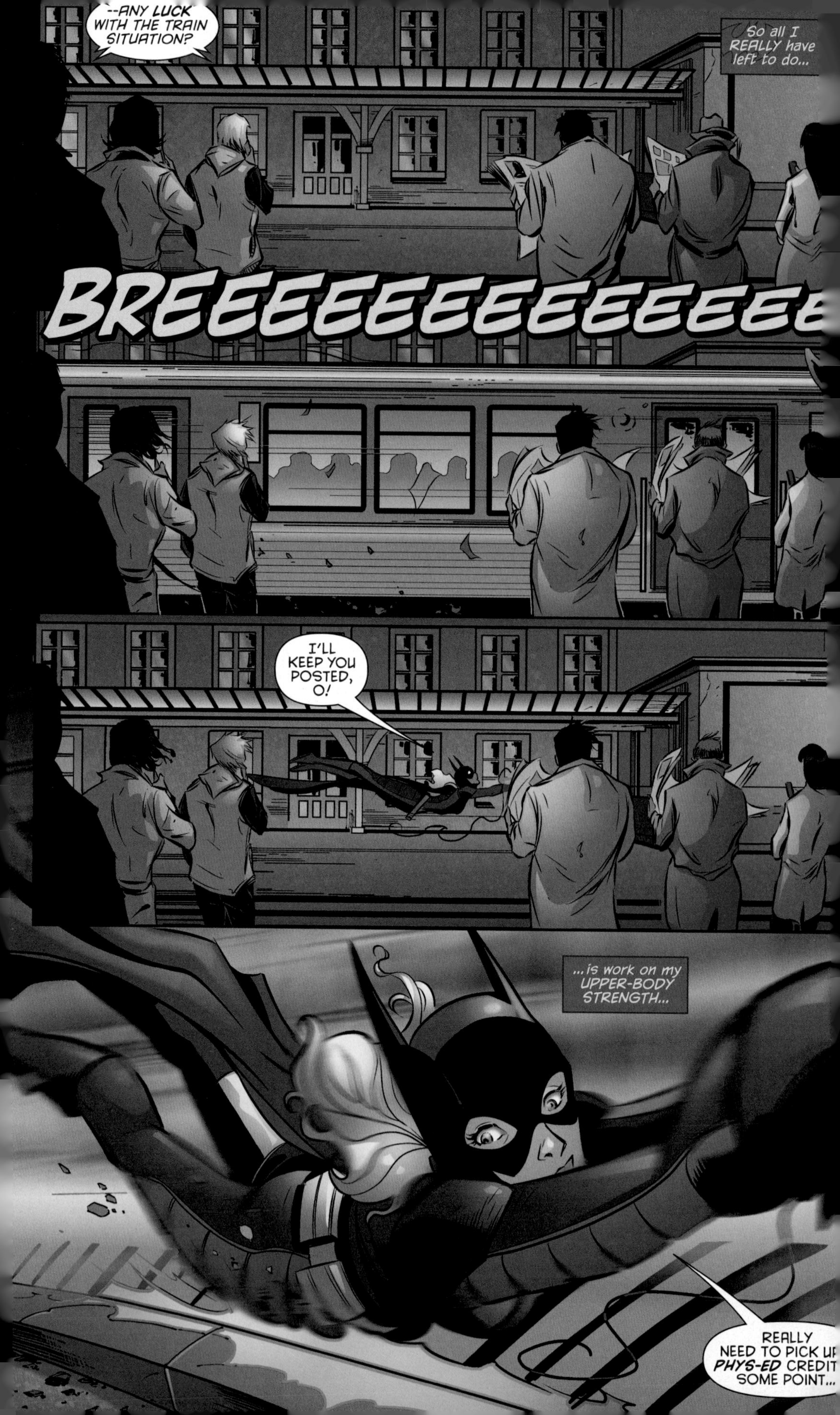
--ANY LUCK WITH THE TRAIN SITUATION?
So all I REALLY have left to do...
BREEEEEEEEEEEEEE
I'LL KEEP YOU POSTED, O!
...is work on my UPPER-BODY STRENGTH...
REALLY NEED TO PICK UP PHYS-ED CREDIT SOME POINT...

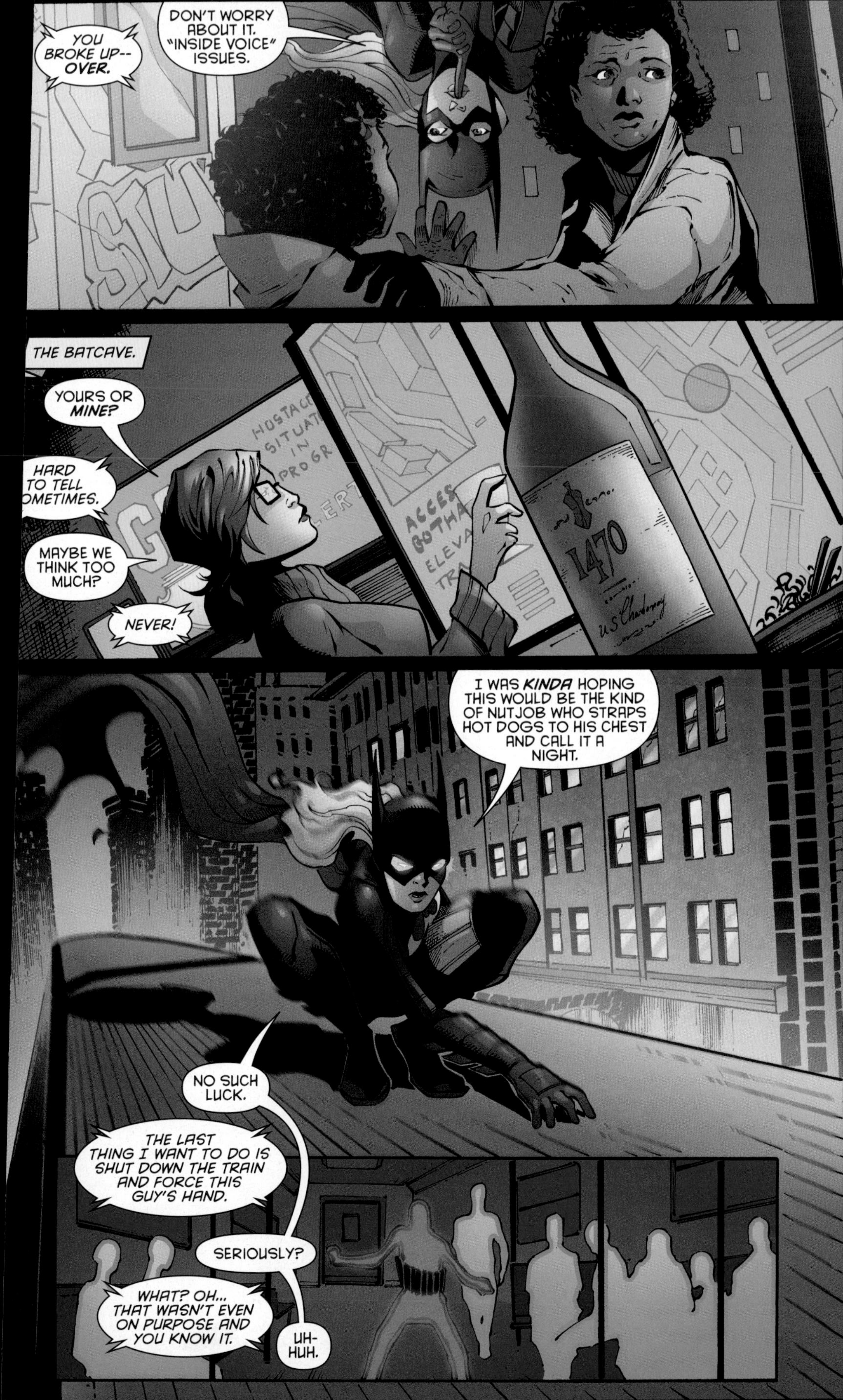

YOU BROKE UP-- OVER.
DON'T WORRY ABOUT IT. "INSIDE VOICE" ISSUES.
THE BATCAVE.
YOURS OR MINE?
HARD TO TELL OMETIMES.
MAYBE WE THINK TOO MUCH?
NEVER!
HOSTAG SITUAT IN PROGR
ACCES GOTHA ELEVA TRA
1470
U.S Chardonnay
I WAS KINDA HOPING THIS WOULD BE THE KIND OF NUTJOB WHO STRAPS HOT DOGS TO HIS CHEST AND CALL IT A NIGHT.
NO SUCH LUCK.
THE LAST THING I WANT TO DO IS SHUT DOWN THE TRAIN AND FORCE THIS GUY'S HAND.
SERIOUSLY?
WHAT? OH... THAT WASN'T EVEN ON PURPOSE AND YOU KNOW IT.
UH-HUH.

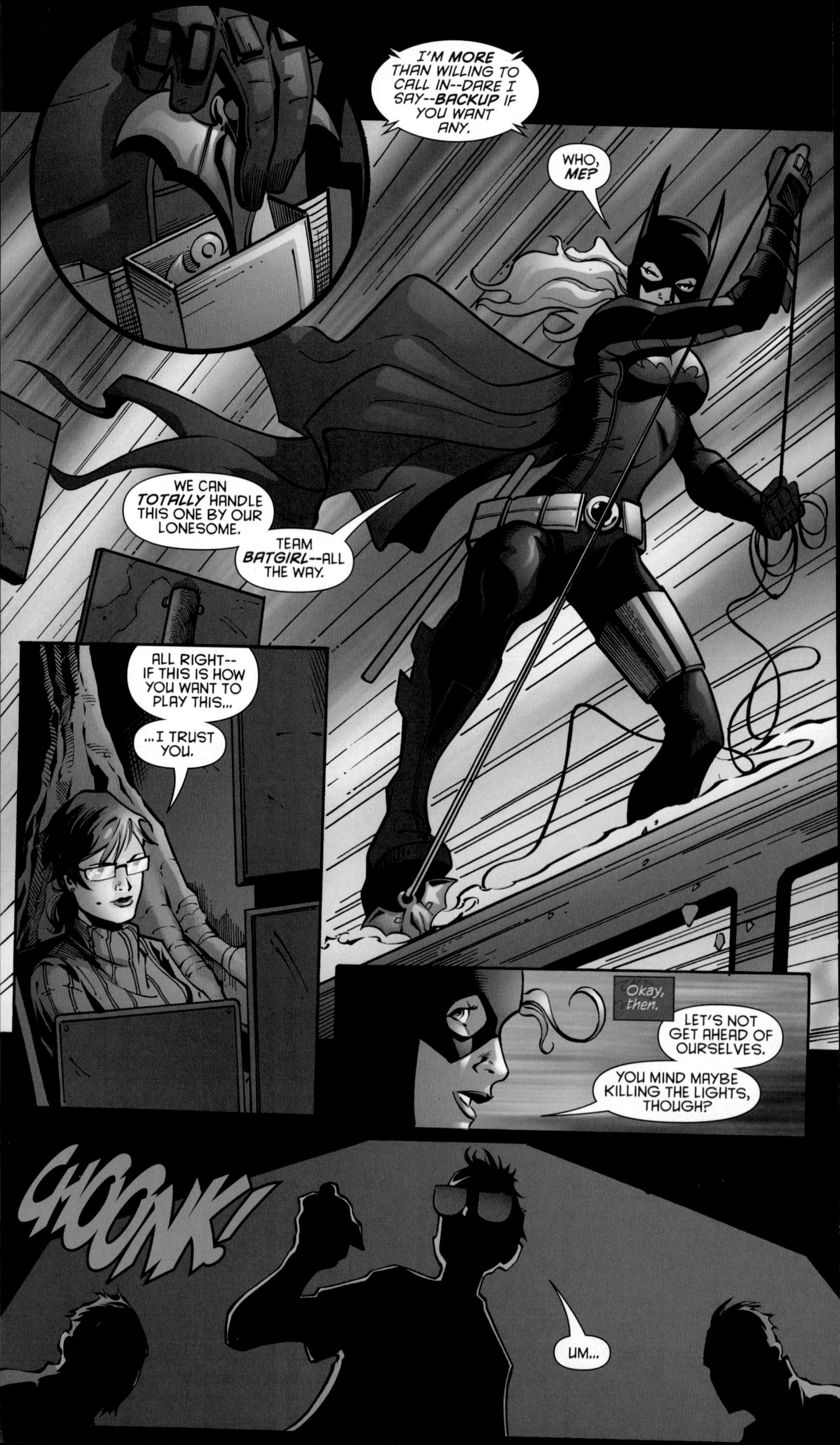
I'M MORE THAN WILLING TO CALL IN--DARE I SAY--BACKUP IF YOU WANT ANY.
WHO, ME?
WE CAN TOTALLY HANDLE THIS ONE BY OUR LONESOME.
TEAM BATGIRL--ALL THE WAY.
ALL RIGHT-- IF THIS IS HOW YOU WANT TO PLAY THIS...
...I TRUST YOU.
Okay, then.
LET'S NOT GET AHEAD OF OURSELVES.
YOU MIND MAYBE KILLING THE LIGHTS, THOUGH?
CHOONK!
UM...

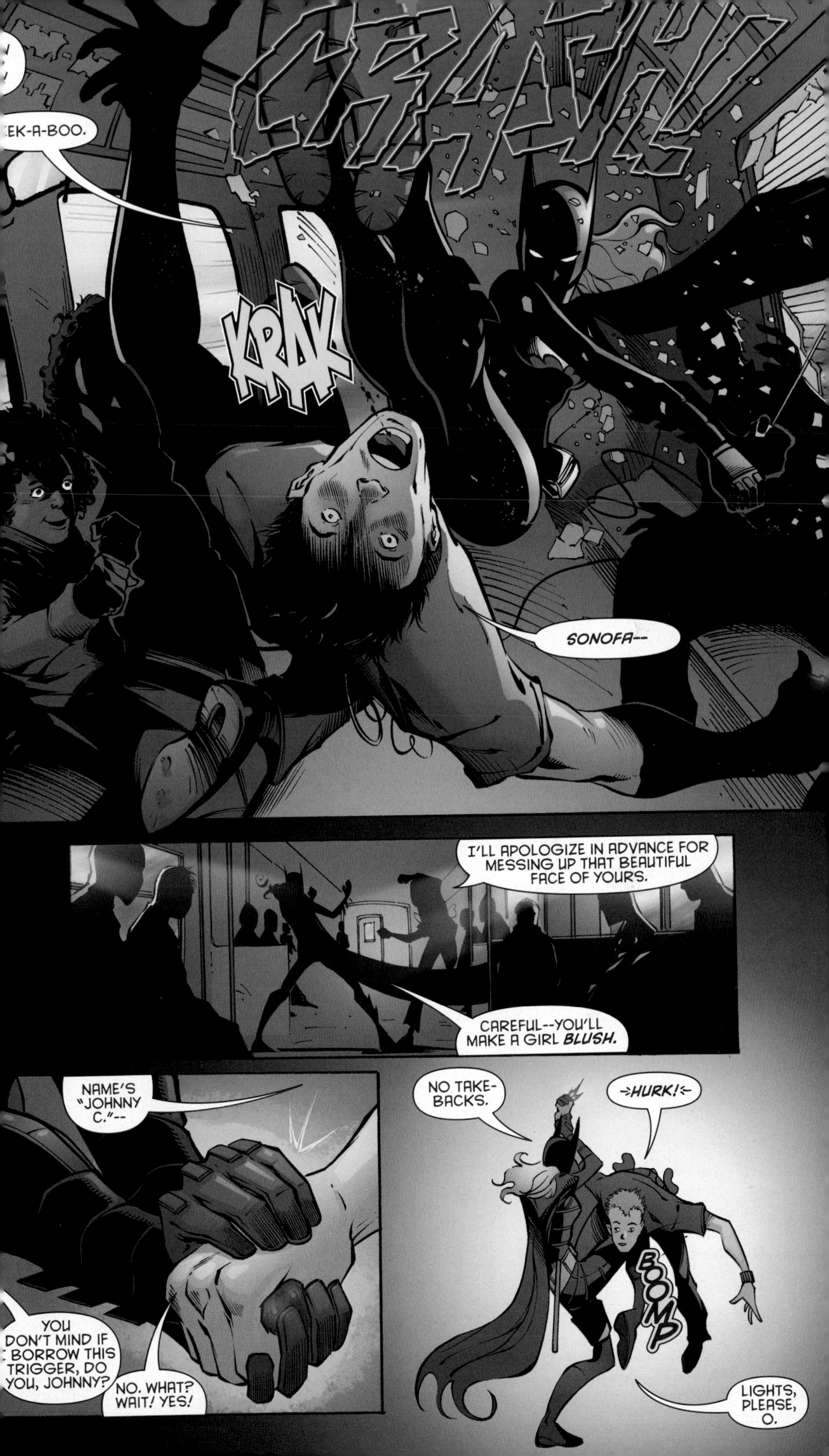
EK-A-BOO.
CRASH!
KRAK
SONOFA--
I'LL APOLOGIZE IN ADVANCE FOR MESSING UP THAT BEAUTIFUL FACE OF YOURS.
CAREFUL--YOU'LL MAKE A GIRL *BLUSH.*
NAME'S "JOHNNY C."--
YOU DON'T MIND IF BORROW THIS TRIGGER, DO YOU, JOHNNY?
NO. WHAT? WAIT! YES!
NO TAKE-BACKS.
HURK!
BOOMP
LIGHTS, PLEASE, O.

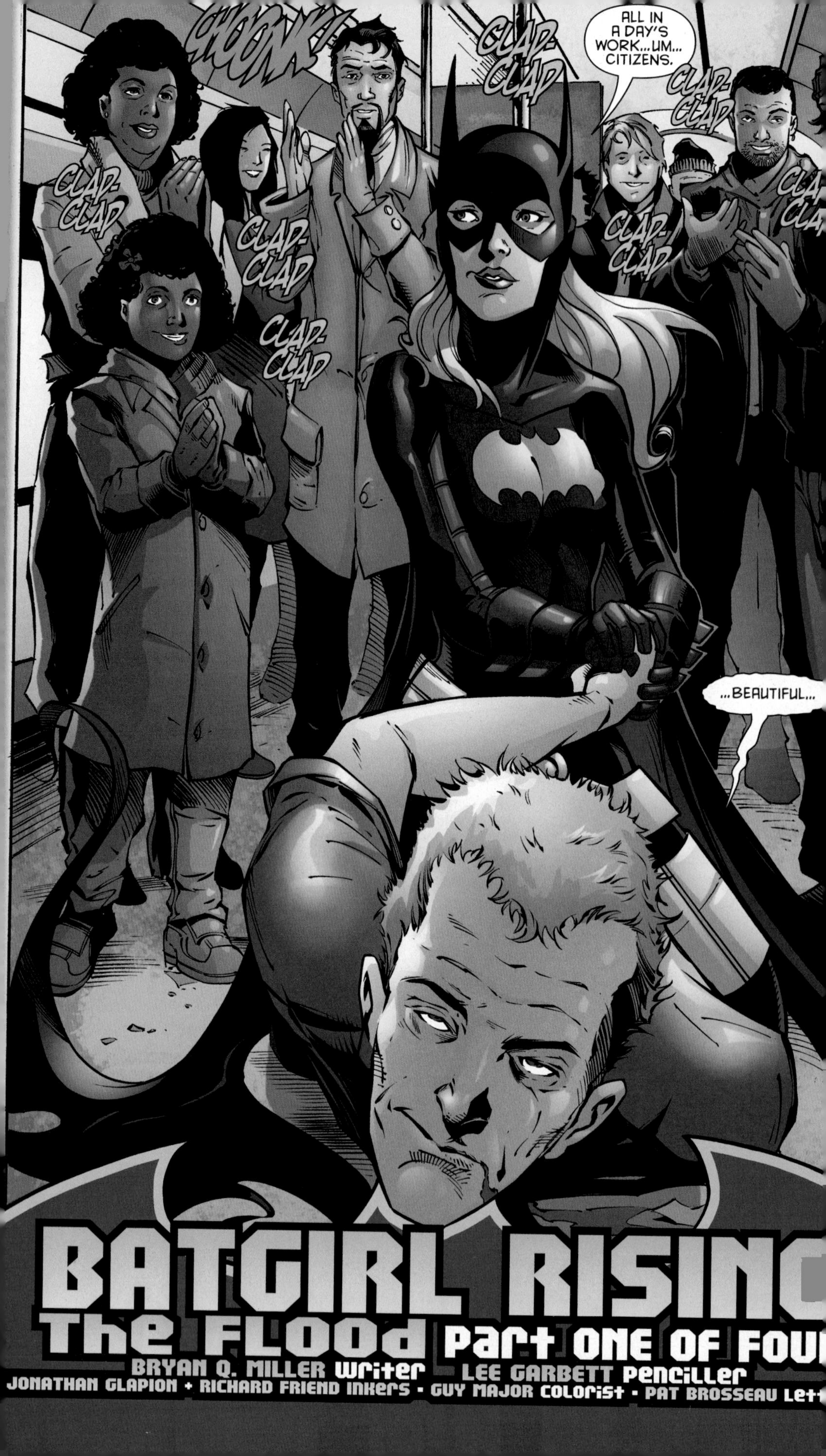
CHOONK!
CLAP-CLAP
ALL IN A DAY'S WORK...UM... CITIZENS.
CLAP-CLAP
CLAP-CLAP
CLAP-CLAP
CLAP-CLAP
CLAP-CLAP
...BEAUTIFUL...
BATGIRL RISING
The FLOOD PART ONE OF FOUR
BRYAN Q. MILLER writer LEE GARBETT penciller
JONATHAN GLAPION + RICHARD FRIEND inkers • GUY MAJOR colorist • PAT BROSSEAU Lett

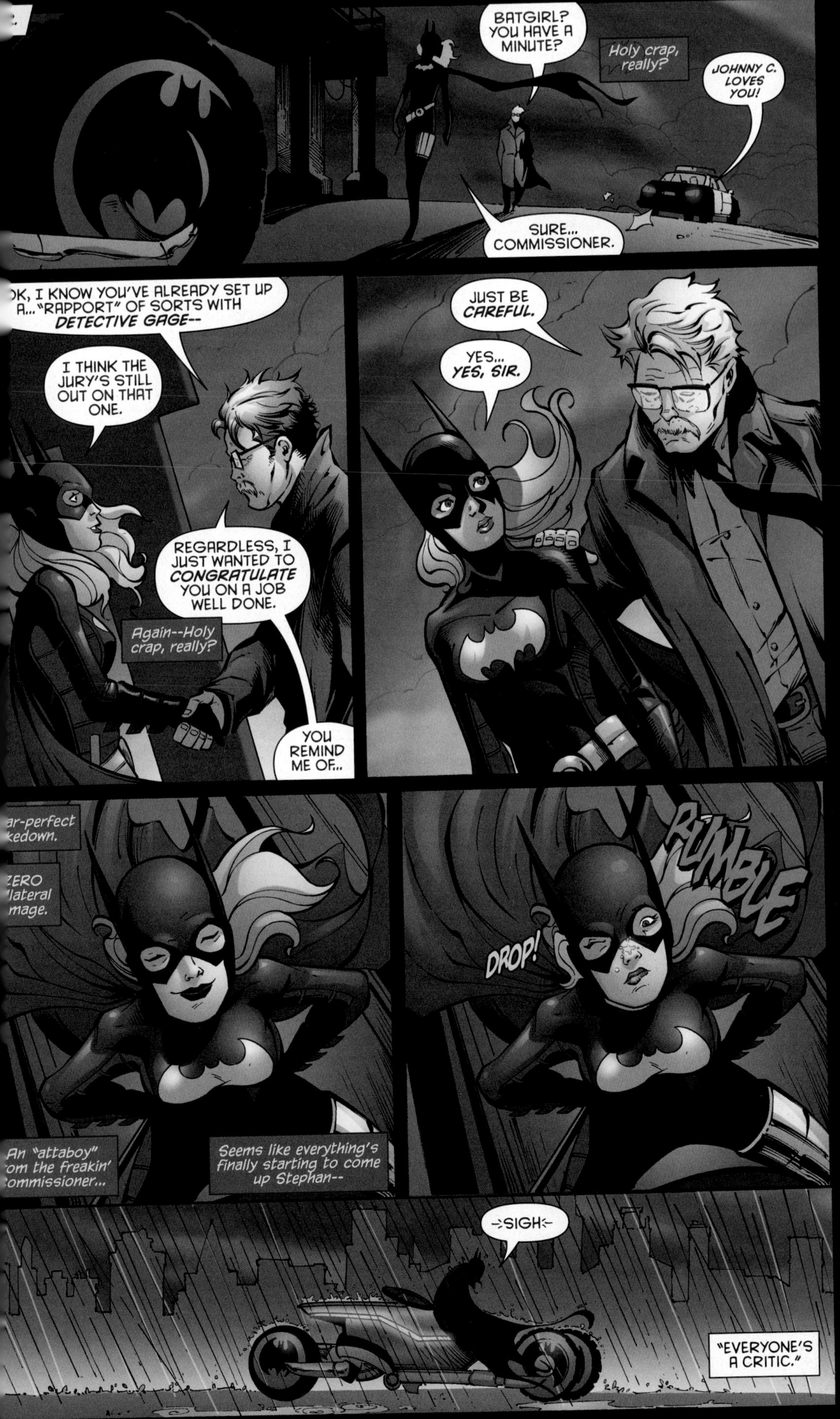

BATGIRL? YOU HAVE A MINUTE?
Holy crap, really?
JOHNNY C. LOVES YOU!
SURE... COMMISSIONER.
OK, I KNOW YOU'VE ALREADY SET UP A... "RAPPORT" OF SORTS WITH DETECTIVE GAGE--
I THINK THE JURY'S STILL OUT ON THAT ONE.
REGARDLESS, I JUST WANTED TO CONGRATULATE YOU ON A JOB WELL DONE.
Again--Holy crap, really?
YOU REMIND ME OF...
JUST BE CAREFUL.
YES... YES, SIR.
ar-perfect kedown.
ZERO llateral mage.
An "attaboy" om the freakin' ommissioner...
Seems like everything's finally starting to come up Stephan--
RUMBLE
DROP!
SIGH
"EVERYONE'S A CRITIC."

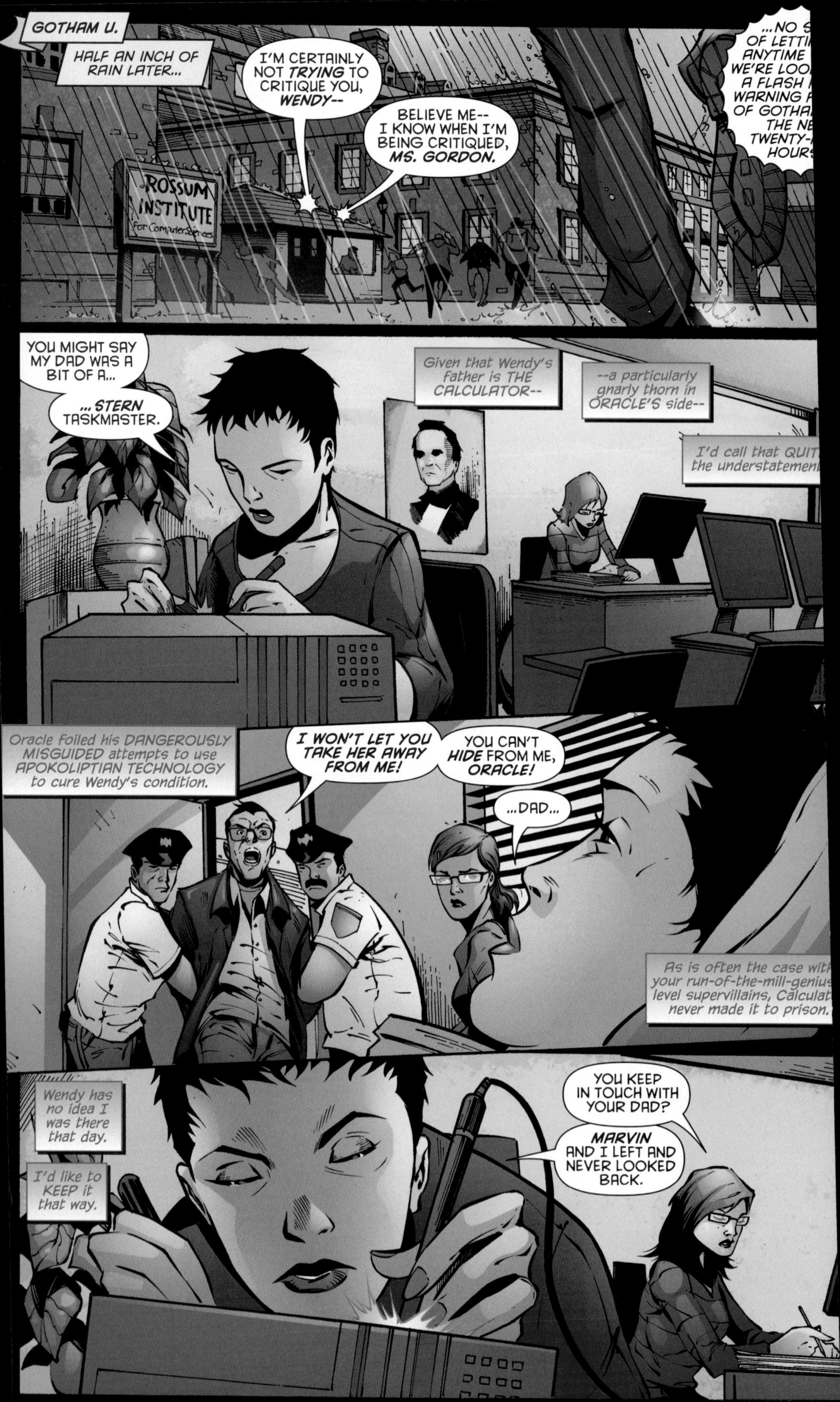

GOTHAM U.
HALF AN INCH OF RAIN LATER...
I'M CERTAINLY NOT TRYING TO CRITIQUE YOU, WENDY--
BELIEVE ME-- I KNOW WHEN I'M BEING CRITIQUED, MS. GORDON.
ROSSUM INSTITUTE For Computer Sciences
YOU MIGHT SAY MY DAD WAS A BIT OF A...
... STERN TASKMASTER.
Given that Wendy's father is THE CALCULATOR--
--a particularly gnarly thorn in ORACLE'S side--
Oracle foiled his DANGEROUSLY MISGUIDED attempts to use APOKOLIPTIAN TECHNOLOGY to cure Wendy's condition.
I WON'T LET YOU TAKE HER AWAY FROM ME!
YOU CAN'T HIDE FROM ME, ORACLE!
...DAD...
Wendy has no idea I was there that day.
I'd like to KEEP it that way.
YOU KEEP IN TOUCH WITH YOUR DAD?
MARVIN AND I LEFT AND NEVER LOOKED BACK.

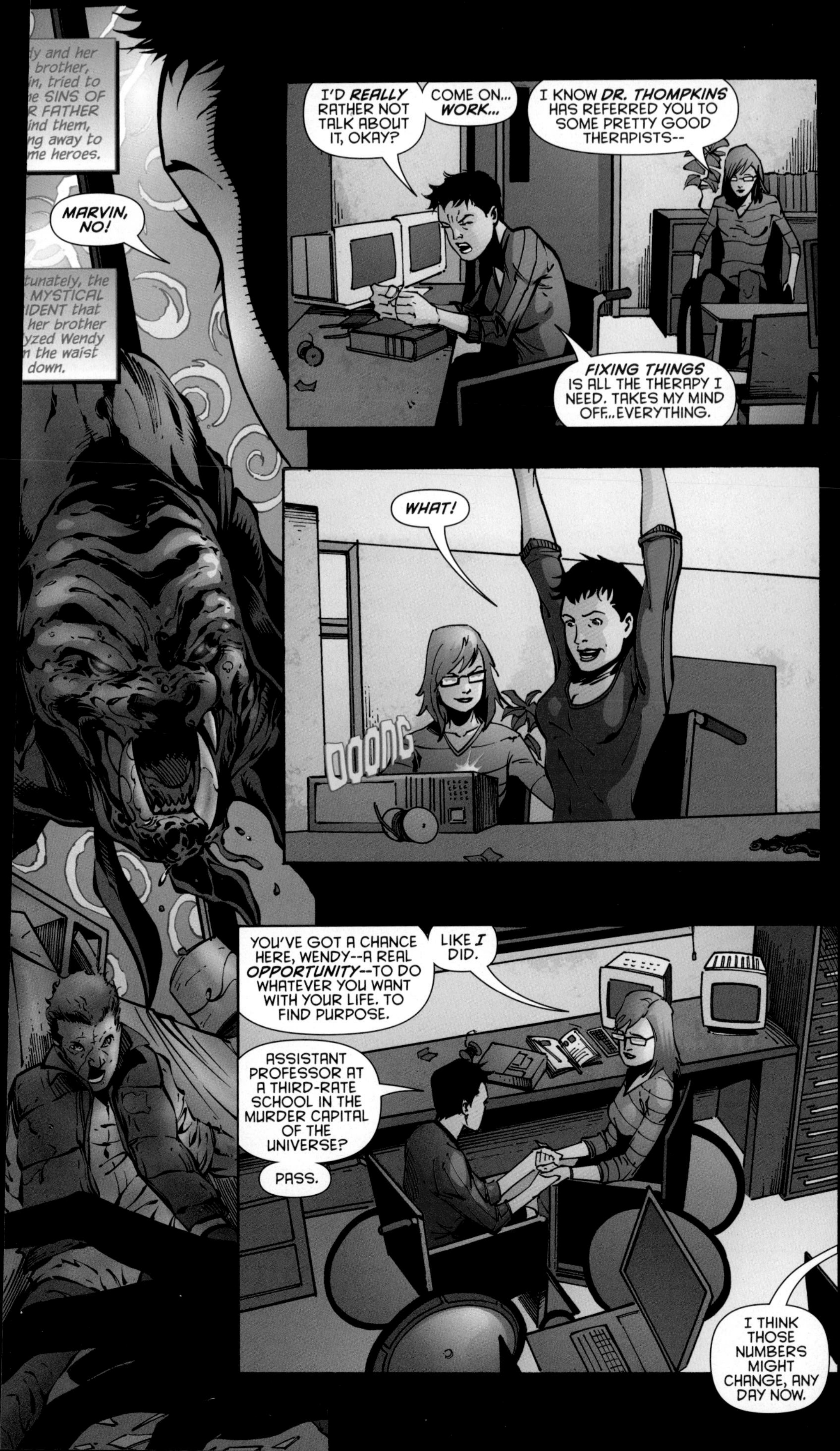
dy and her brother, in, tried to he SINS OF R FATHER ind them, ng away to me heroes.
MARVIN, NO!
tunately, the MYSTICAL IDENT that her brother yzed Wendy n the waist down.
I'D REALLY RATHER NOT TALK ABOUT IT, OKAY?
COME ON... WORK...
I KNOW DR. THOMPKINS HAS REFERRED YOU TO SOME PRETTY GOOD THERAPISTS--
FIXING THINGS IS ALL THE THERAPY I NEED. TAKES MY MIND OFF...EVERYTHING.
WHAT!
DOOONG
YOU'VE GOT A CHANCE HERE, WENDY--A REAL OPPORTUNITY--TO DO WHATEVER YOU WANT WITH YOUR LIFE. TO FIND PURPOSE.
LIKE I DID.
ASSISTANT PROFESSOR AT A THIRD-RATE SCHOOL IN THE MURDER CAPITAL OF THE UNIVERSE?
PASS.
I THINK THOSE NUMBERS MIGHT CHANGE, ANY DAY NOW.

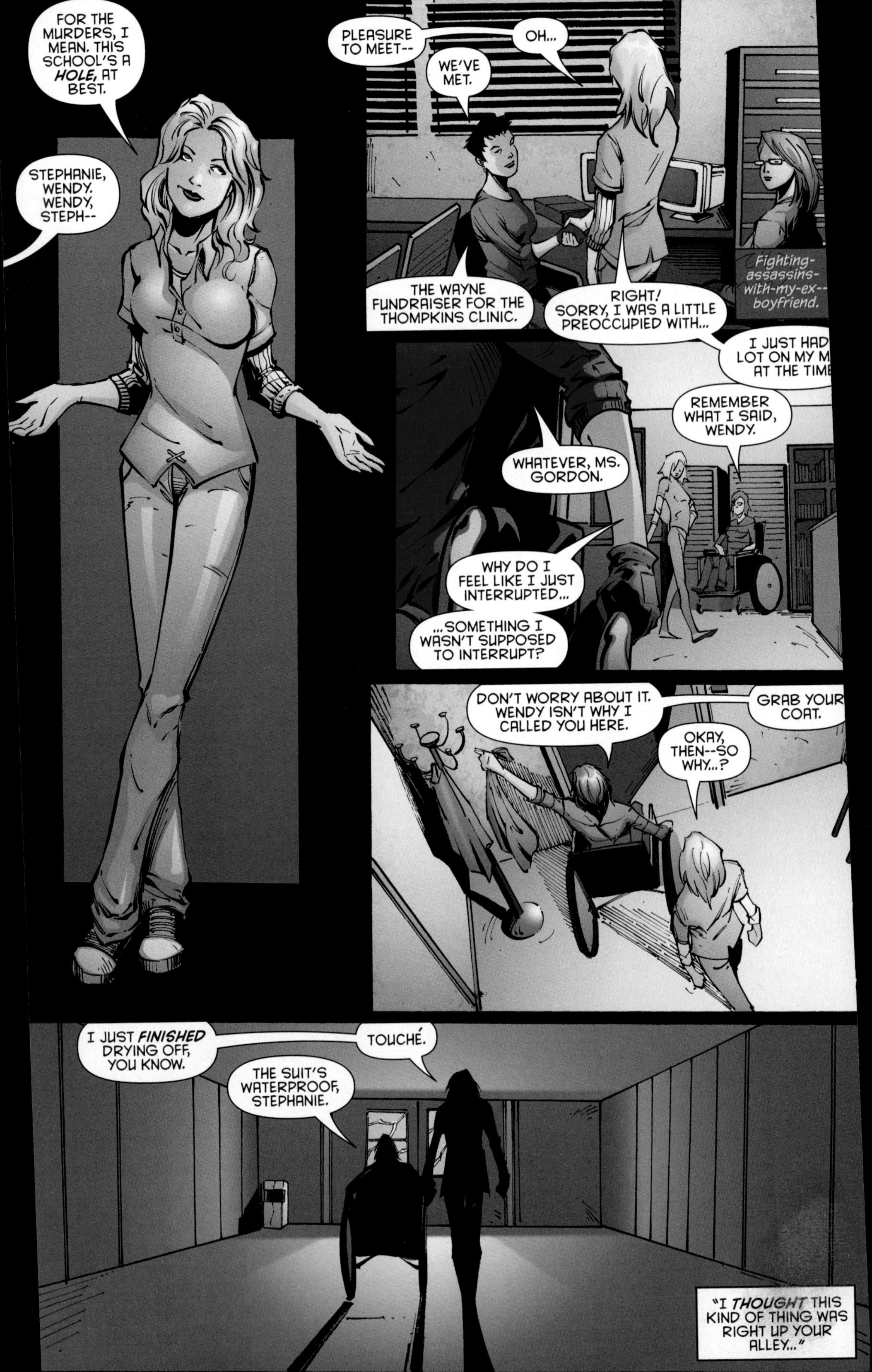
FOR THE MURDERS, I MEAN. THIS SCHOOL'S A *HOLE,* AT BEST.
STEPHANIE, WENDY. WENDY, STEPH--
PLEASURE TO MEET--
OH...
WE'VE MET.
THE WAYNE FUNDRAISER FOR THE THOMPKINS CLINIC.
RIGHT! SORRY, I WAS A LITTLE PREOCCUPIED WITH...
Fighting-assassins-with-my-ex--boyfriend.
I JUST HAD LOT ON MY M AT THE TIME
REMEMBER WHAT I SAID, WENDY.
WHATEVER, MS. GORDON.
WHY DO I FEEL LIKE I JUST INTERRUPTED...
...SOMETHING I WASN'T SUPPOSED TO INTERRUPT?
DON'T WORRY ABOUT IT. WENDY ISN'T WHY I CALLED YOU HERE.
GRAB YOUR COAT.
OKAY, THEN--SO WHY...?
I JUST *FINISHED* DRYING OFF, YOU KNOW.
TOUCHÉ.
THE SUIT'S WATERPROOF, STEPHANIE.
"I *THOUGHT* THIS KIND OF THING WAS RIGHT UP YOUR ALLEY..."

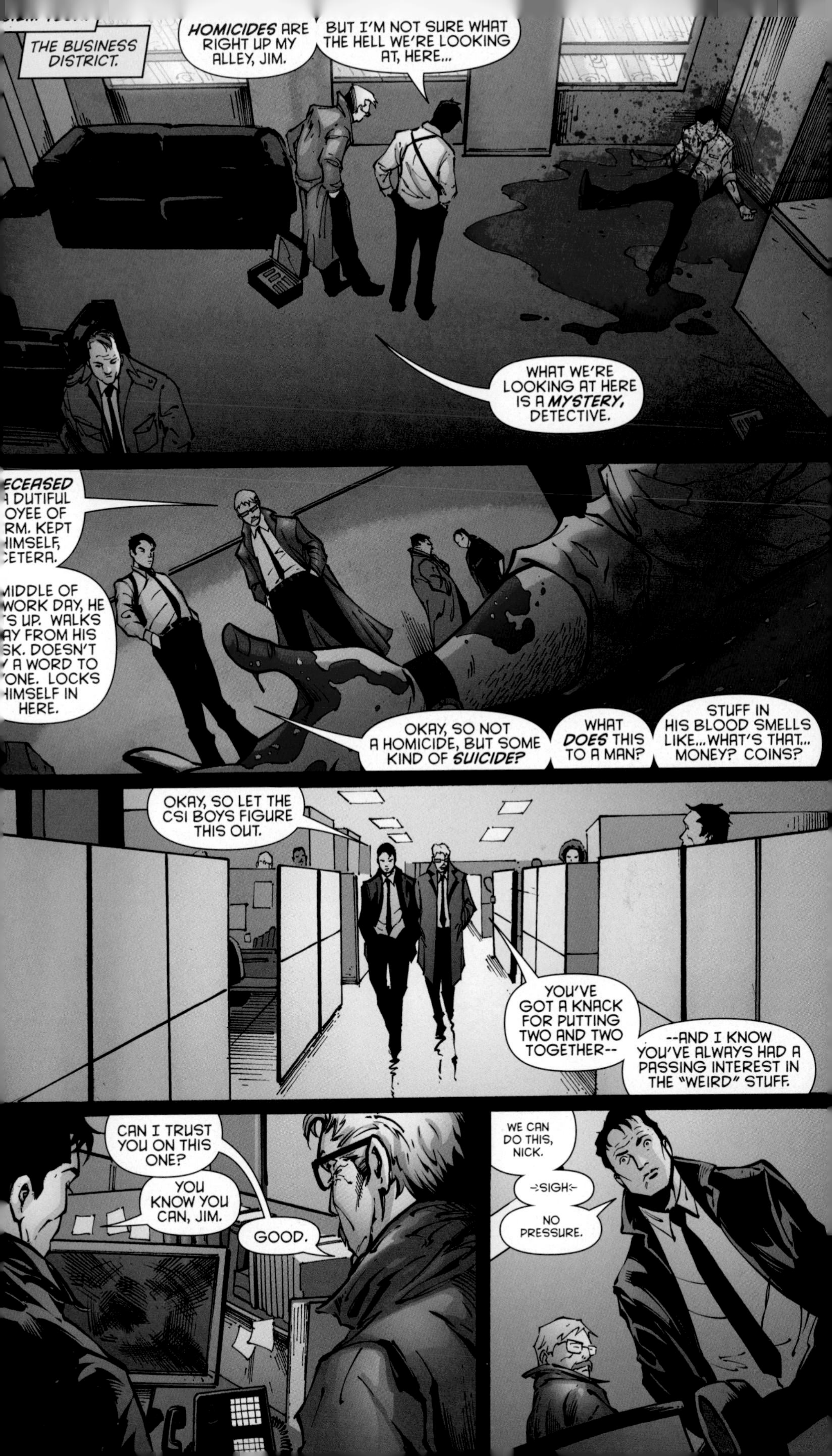
THE BUSINESS DISTRICT.
HOMICIDES ARE RIGHT UP MY ALLEY, JIM.
BUT I'M NOT SURE WHAT THE HELL WE'RE LOOKING AT, HERE...
WHAT WE'RE LOOKING AT HERE IS A MYSTERY, DETECTIVE.
ECEASED A DUTIFUL OYEE OF RM. KEPT HIMSELF, CETERA.
MIDDLE OF WORK DAY, HE 'S UP. WALKS AY FROM HIS SK. DOESN'T A WORD TO ONE. LOCKS HIMSELF IN HERE.
OKAY, SO NOT A HOMICIDE, BUT SOME KIND OF SUICIDE?
WHAT DOES THIS TO A MAN?
STUFF IN HIS BLOOD SMELLS LIKE... WHAT'S THAT... MONEY? COINS?
OKAY, SO LET THE CSI BOYS FIGURE THIS OUT.
YOU'VE GOT A KNACK FOR PUTTING TWO AND TWO TOGETHER--
--AND I KNOW YOU'VE ALWAYS HAD A PASSING INTEREST IN THE "WEIRD" STUFF.
CAN I TRUST YOU ON THIS ONE?
YOU KNOW YOU CAN, JIM.
GOOD.
WE CAN DO THIS, NICK.
SIGH
NO PRESSURE.

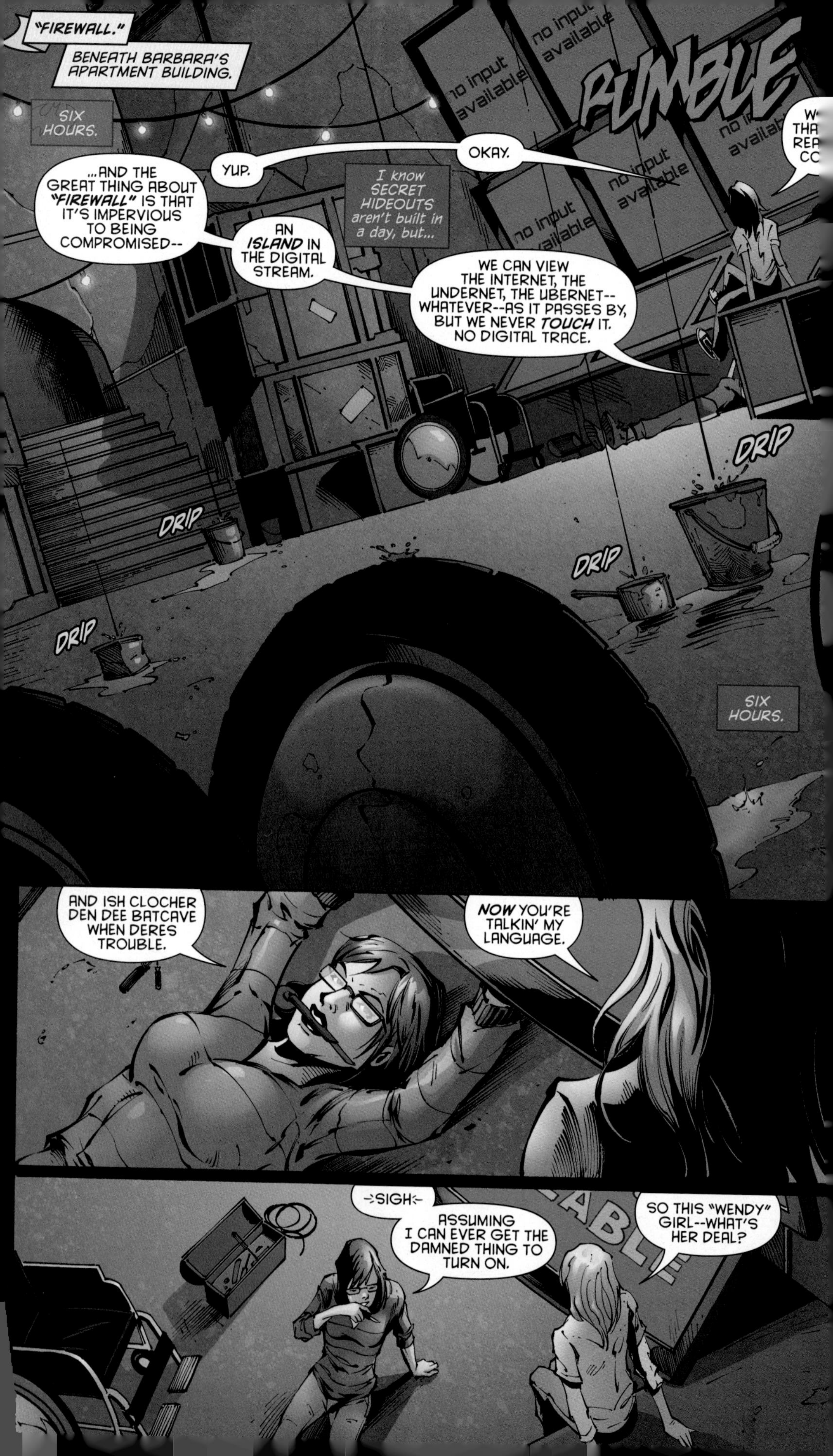
"FIREWALL."
BENEATH BARBARA'S APARTMENT BUILDING.
SIX HOURS.
no input available
RUMBLE
...AND THE GREAT THING ABOUT "FIREWALL" IS THAT IT'S IMPERVIOUS TO BEING COMPROMISED--
YUP.
AN ISLAND IN THE DIGITAL STREAM.
OKAY.
I know SECRET HIDEOUTS aren't built in a day, but...
WE CAN VIEW THE INTERNET, THE UNDERNET, THE UBERNET--WHATEVER--AS IT PASSES BY, BUT WE NEVER TOUCH IT. NO DIGITAL TRACE.
DRIP
DRIP
DRIP
DRIP
SIX HOURS.
AND ISH CLOCHER DEN DEE BATCAVE WHEN DERES TROUBLE.
NOW YOU'RE TALKIN' MY LANGUAGE.
-SIGH-
ASSUMING I CAN EVER GET THE DAMNED THING TO TURN ON.
SO THIS "WENDY" GIRL--WHAT'S HER DEAL?

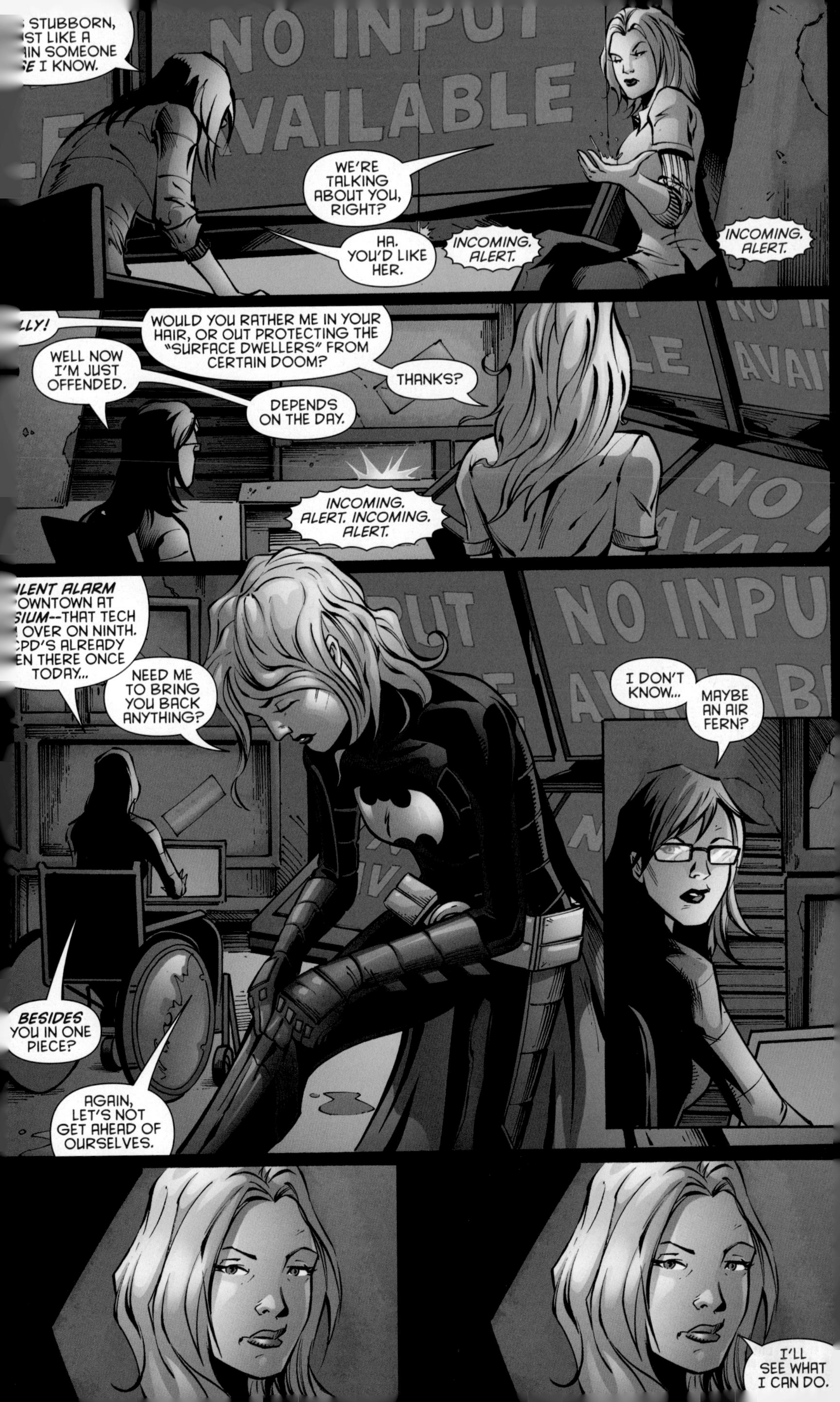
STUBBORN, ST LIKE A IN SOMEONE SE I KNOW.
WE'RE TALKING ABOUT YOU, RIGHT?
HA. YOU'D LIKE HER.
INCOMING. ALERT.
INCOMING. ALERT.
LLY!
WOULD YOU RATHER ME IN YOUR HAIR, OR OUT PROTECTING THE "SURFACE DWELLERS" FROM CERTAIN DOOM?
THANKS?
WELL NOW I'M JUST OFFENDED.
DEPENDS ON THE DAY.
INCOMING. ALERT. INCOMING. ALERT.
ILENT ALARM OWNTOWN AT SIUM--THAT TECH OVER ON NINTH. CPD'S ALREADY EN THERE ONCE TODAY...
NEED ME TO BRING YOU BACK ANYTHING?
I DON'T KNOW...
MAYBE AN AIR FERN?
BESIDES YOU IN ONE PIECE?
AGAIN, LET'S NOT GET AHEAD OF OURSELVES.
I'LL SEE WHAT I CAN DO.

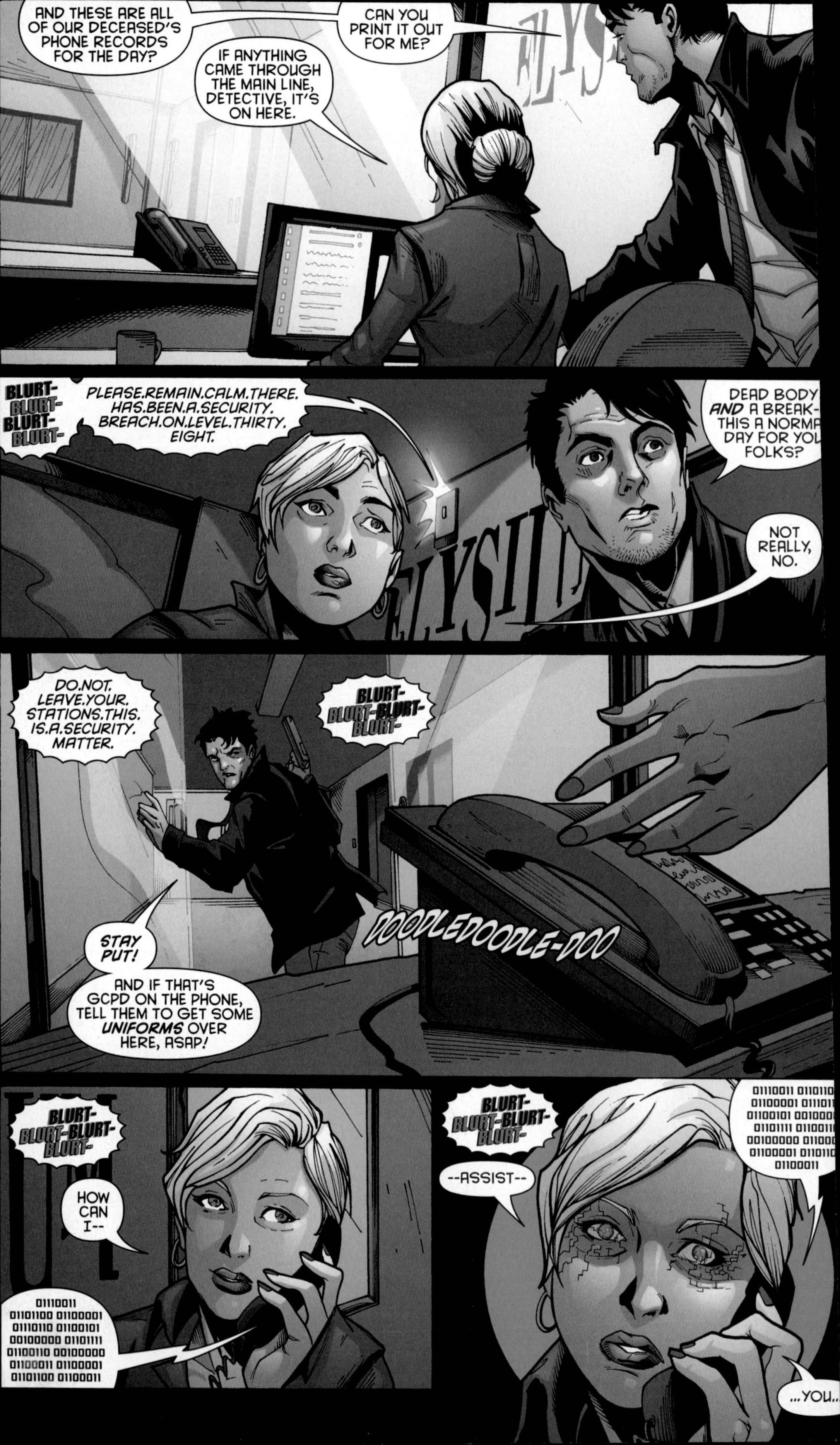
AND THESE ARE ALL OF OUR DECEASED'S PHONE RECORDS FOR THE DAY?
IF ANYTHING CAME THROUGH THE MAIN LINE, DETECTIVE, IT'S ON HERE.
CAN YOU PRINT IT OUT FOR ME?
BLURT- BLURT- BLURT- BLURT-
PLEASE.REMAIN.CALM.THERE. HAS.BEEN.A.SECURITY. BREACH.ON.LEVEL.THIRTY. EIGHT.
DEAD BODY AND A BREAK- THIS A NORMA DAY FOR YOU FOLKS?
NOT REALLY, NO.
DO.NOT. LEAVE.YOUR. STATIONS.THIS. IS.A.SECURITY. MATTER.
BLURT- BLURT-BLURT- BLURT-
DOODLEDOODLE-DOO
STAY PUT!
AND IF THAT'S GCPD ON THE PHONE, TELL THEM TO GET SOME UNIFORMS OVER HERE, ASAP!
BLURT- BLURT-BLURT- BLURT-
HOW CAN I--
01110011 01101100 01100001 01110110 01100101 00100000 01101111 01100110 00100000 01100011 01100001 01101100 01100011
BLURT- BLURT-BLURT- BLURT-
--ASSIST--
01110011 0110110 01100001 0111011 01100101 0010000 01101111 0110011 00100000 011000 01100001 0110110 01100011
...YOU...

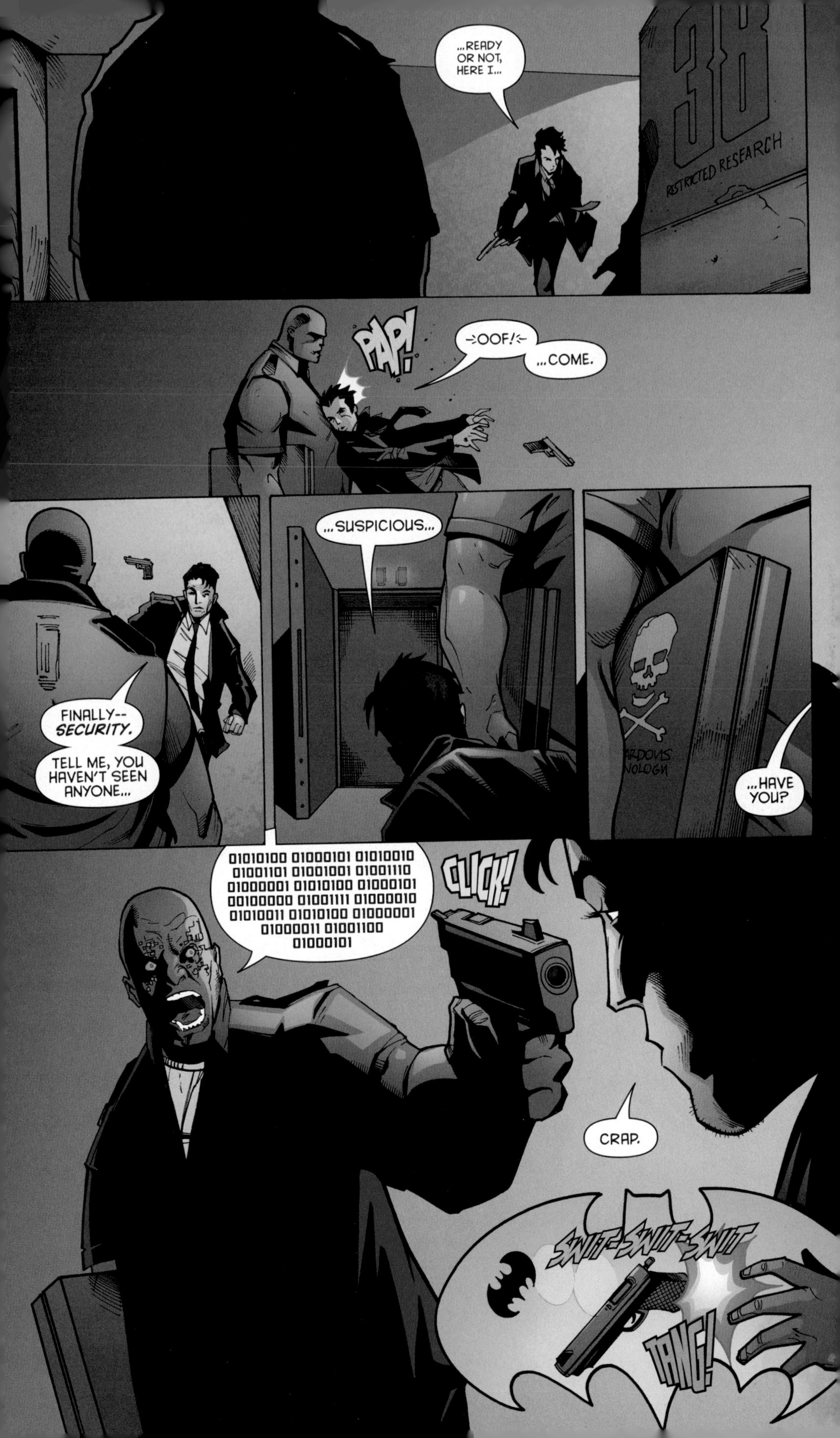
...READY OR NOT, HERE I...
38
RESTRICTED RESEARCH
PAP!
-OOF!-
...COME.
FINALLY-- SECURITY.
TELL ME, YOU HAVEN'T SEEN ANYONE...
...SUSPICIOUS...
...HAVE YOU?
01010100 01000101 01010010 01001101 01001001 01001110 01000001 01010100 01000101 00100000 01001111 01000010 01010011 01010100 01000001 01000011 01001100 01000101
CLICK!
CRAP.
SWIT-SWIT-SWIT
TANG!

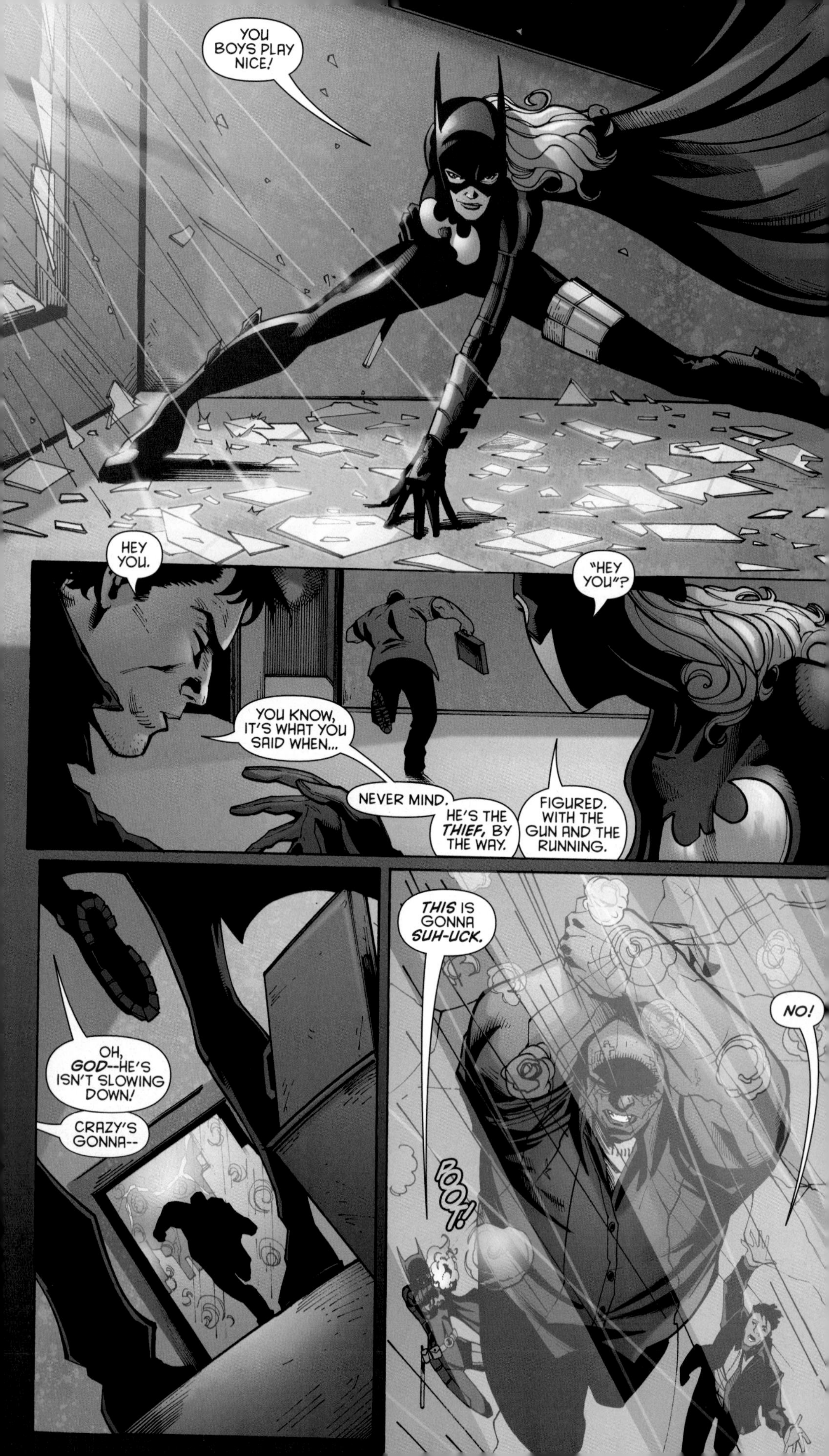

YOU BOYS PLAY NICE!
HEY YOU.
"HEY YOU"?
YOU KNOW, IT'S WHAT YOU SAID WHEN...
NEVER MIND.
HE'S THE *THIEF,* BY THE WAY.
FIGURED. WITH THE GUN AND THE RUNNING.
OH, *GOD*--HE'S ISN'T SLOWING DOWN!
CRAZY'S GONNA--
THIS IS GONNA *SUH-UCK.*
POOF!
NO!

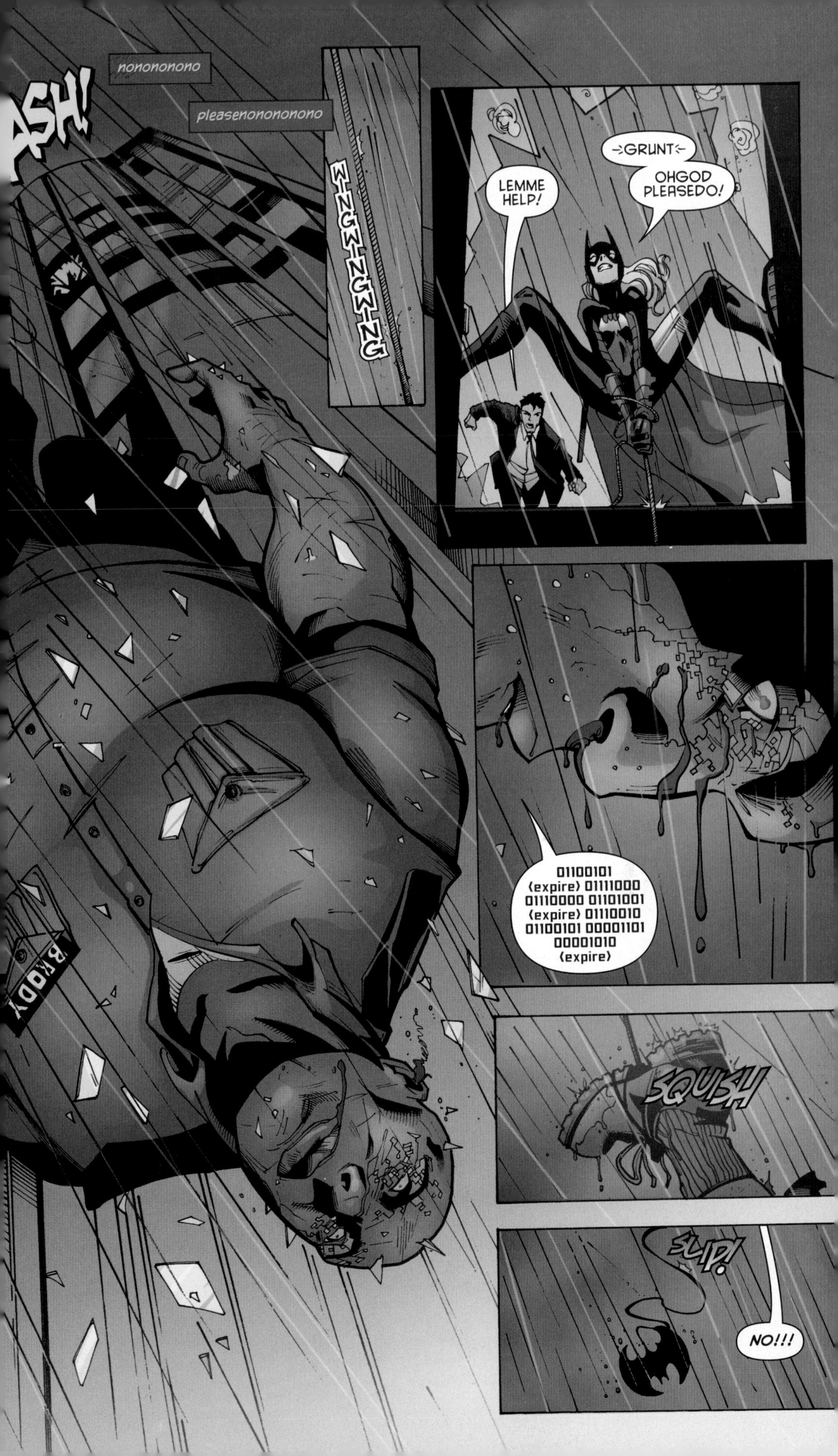
ASH!
nononononono
pleasenononononono
WINGWINGWING
LEMME HELP!
-GRUNT-
OHGOD PLEASEDO!
01100101 (expire) 01111000 01110000 01101001 (expire) 01110010 01100101 00001101 00001010 (expire)
SQUISH
SLIP!
NO!!!

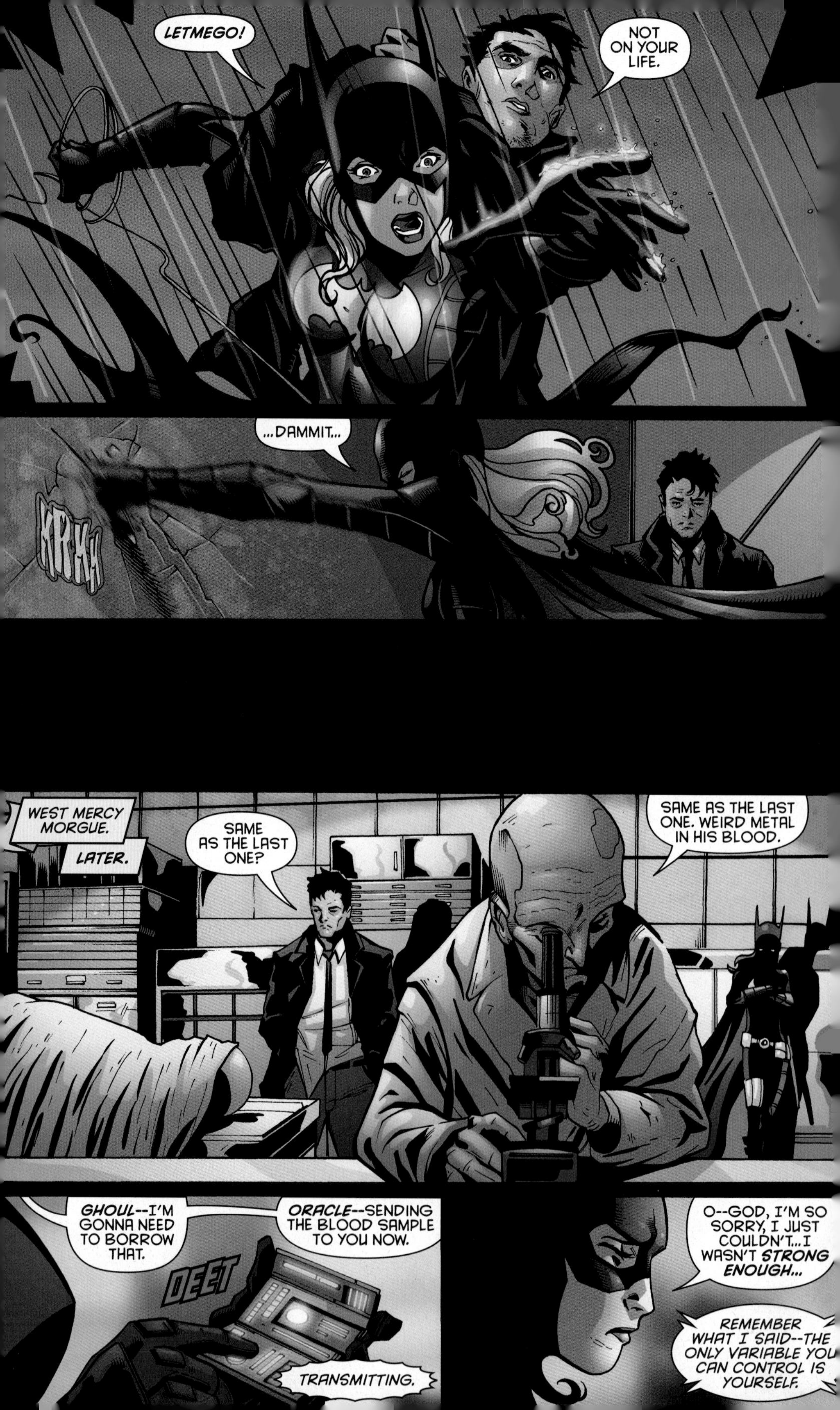
LETMEGO!
NOT ON YOUR LIFE.
...DAMMIT...
WEST MERCY MORGUE.
LATER.
SAME AS THE LAST ONE?
SAME AS THE LAST ONE. WEIRD METAL IN HIS BLOOD.
GHOUL--I'M GONNA NEED TO BORROW THAT.
ORACLE--SENDING THE BLOOD SAMPLE TO YOU NOW.
DEET
TRANSMITTING.
O--GOD, I'M SO SORRY, I JUST COULDN'T...I WASN'T STRONG ENOUGH...
REMEMBER WHAT I SAID--THE ONLY VARIABLE YOU CAN CONTROL IS YOURSELF.

BATCAVE.

Keep her focused. She can grieve later.

THE ONLY THING YOU CAN DO NOW IS FIND AND STOP WHOEVER DID THIS TO HIM.

ANY IDEA WHAT IT IS?

ONLINE

THE METAL, THE *SOLUTION* IN HIS BLOOD...

A COLONY OF *NANITES*...

There's a pit in my stomach, like I know what's coming...

THEY'RE PUTTING OUT A SUBTLE WIFI SIGNATURE...

HE *WASN'T* IN CONTROL OF HIS ACTIONS, BATGIRL.

Like LIGHTNING before THUNDER.

AND YOU DIDN'T RECOVER THE ITEM?

NO SIGN OF IT.

ANY IDEA WHAT WAS IN IT?

ELYSIUM. MANIFESTS. ACCESSED.

Babs sounds worried. I don't like that Babs sounds worried.

ELYSIUM'S BEEN HOARDING TECH FROM...

APOKOLIPS.

YOU'RE FREAKIN' ME OUT, O...

GET BACK TO THE CAVE.

WHY?

HE'S COMING.

ORACLE, WHO?

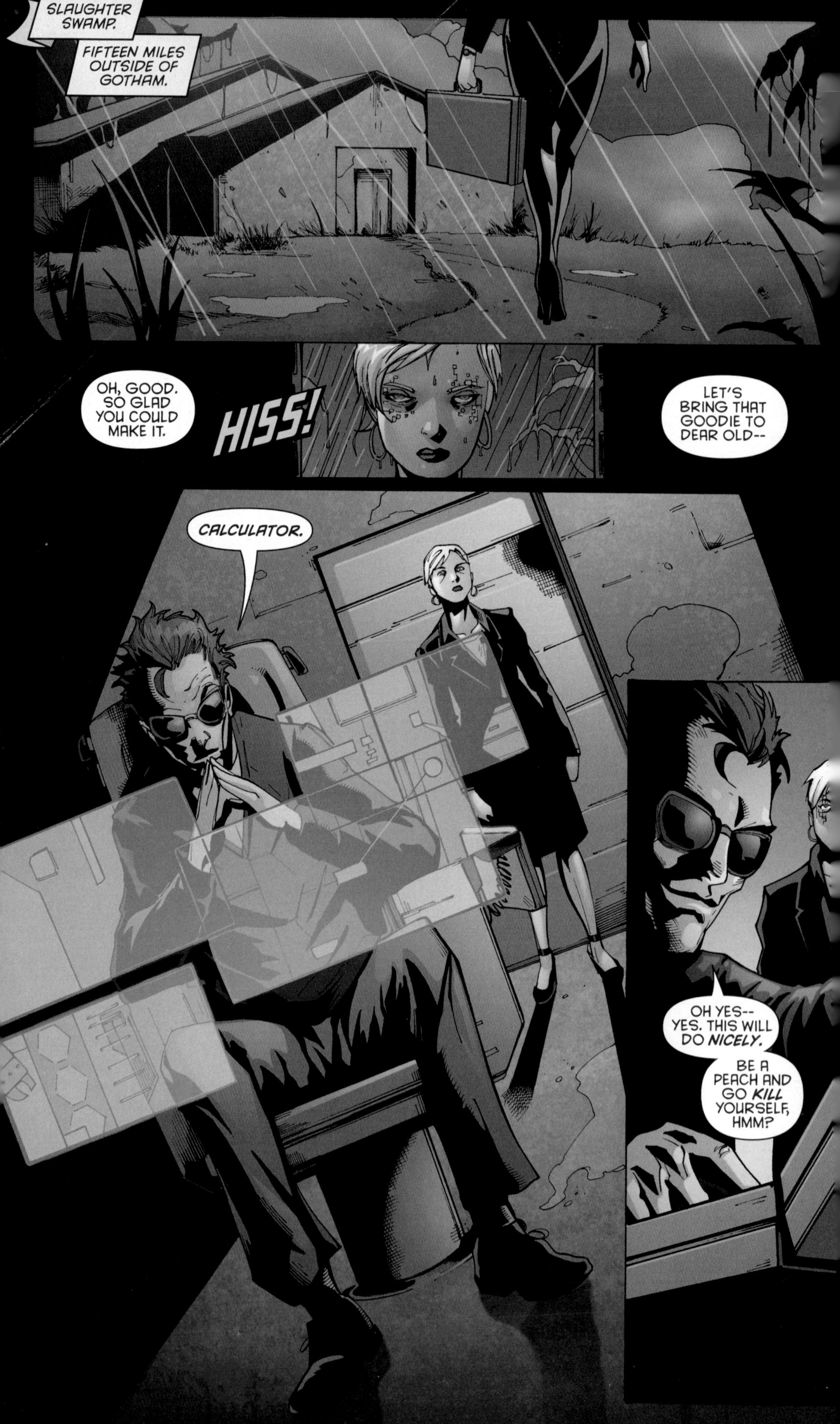
SLAUGHTER SWAMP.
FIFTEEN MILES OUTSIDE OF GOTHAM.
OH, GOOD. SO GLAD YOU COULD MAKE IT.
HISS!
LET'S BRING THAT GOODIE TO DEAR OLD--
CALCULATOR.
OH YES-- YES. THIS WILL DO NICELY.
BE A PEACH AND GO KILL YOURSELF, HMM?

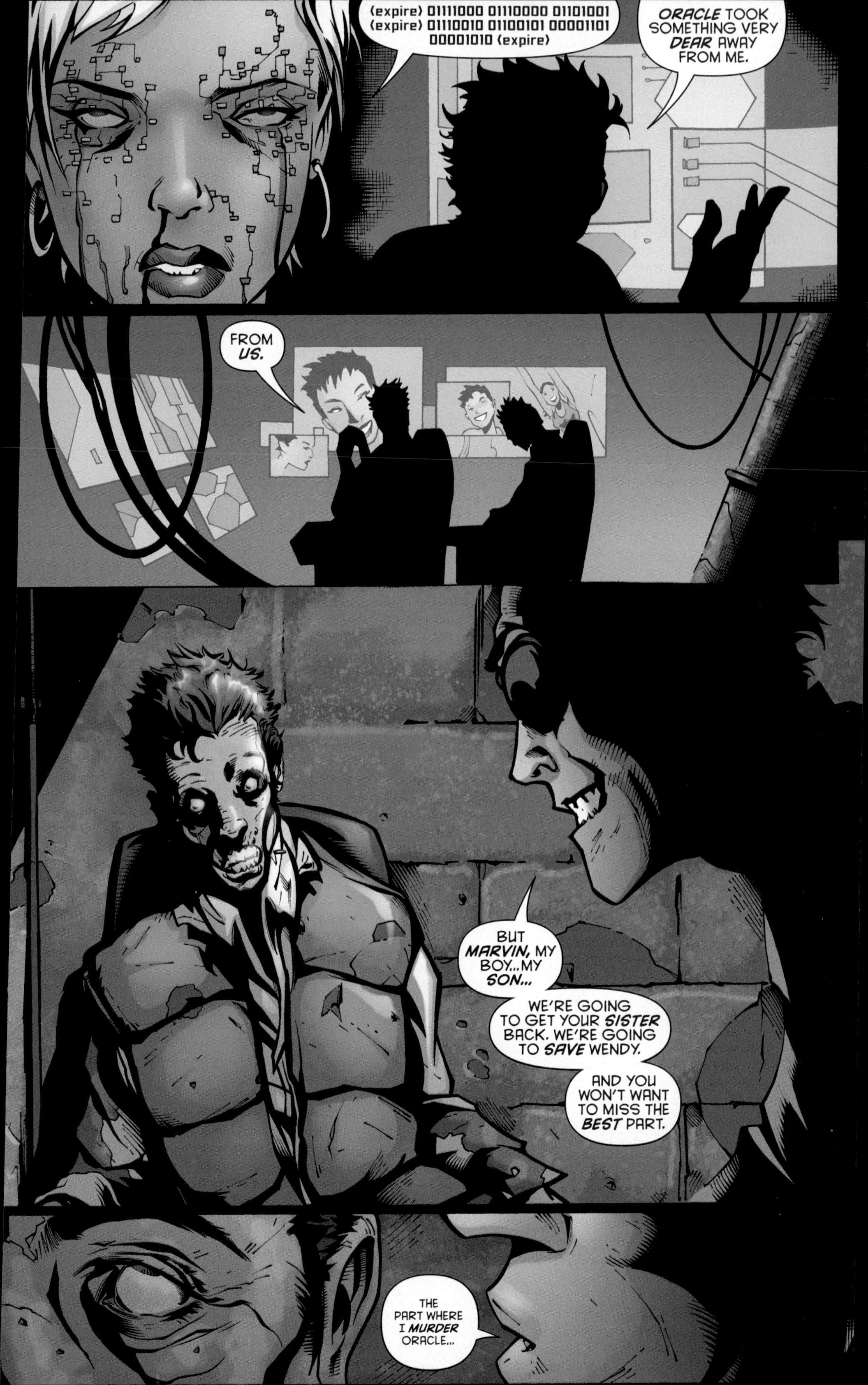
(expire) 01111000 01110000 01101001 (expire) 01110010 01100101 00001101 00001010 (expire)
ORACLE TOOK SOMETHING VERY DEAR AWAY FROM ME.
FROM US.
BUT MARVIN, MY BOY...MY SON...
WE'RE GOING TO GET YOUR SISTER BACK. WE'RE GOING TO SAVE WENDY.
AND YOU WON'T WANT TO MISS THE BEST PART.
THE PART WHERE I MURDER ORACLE...

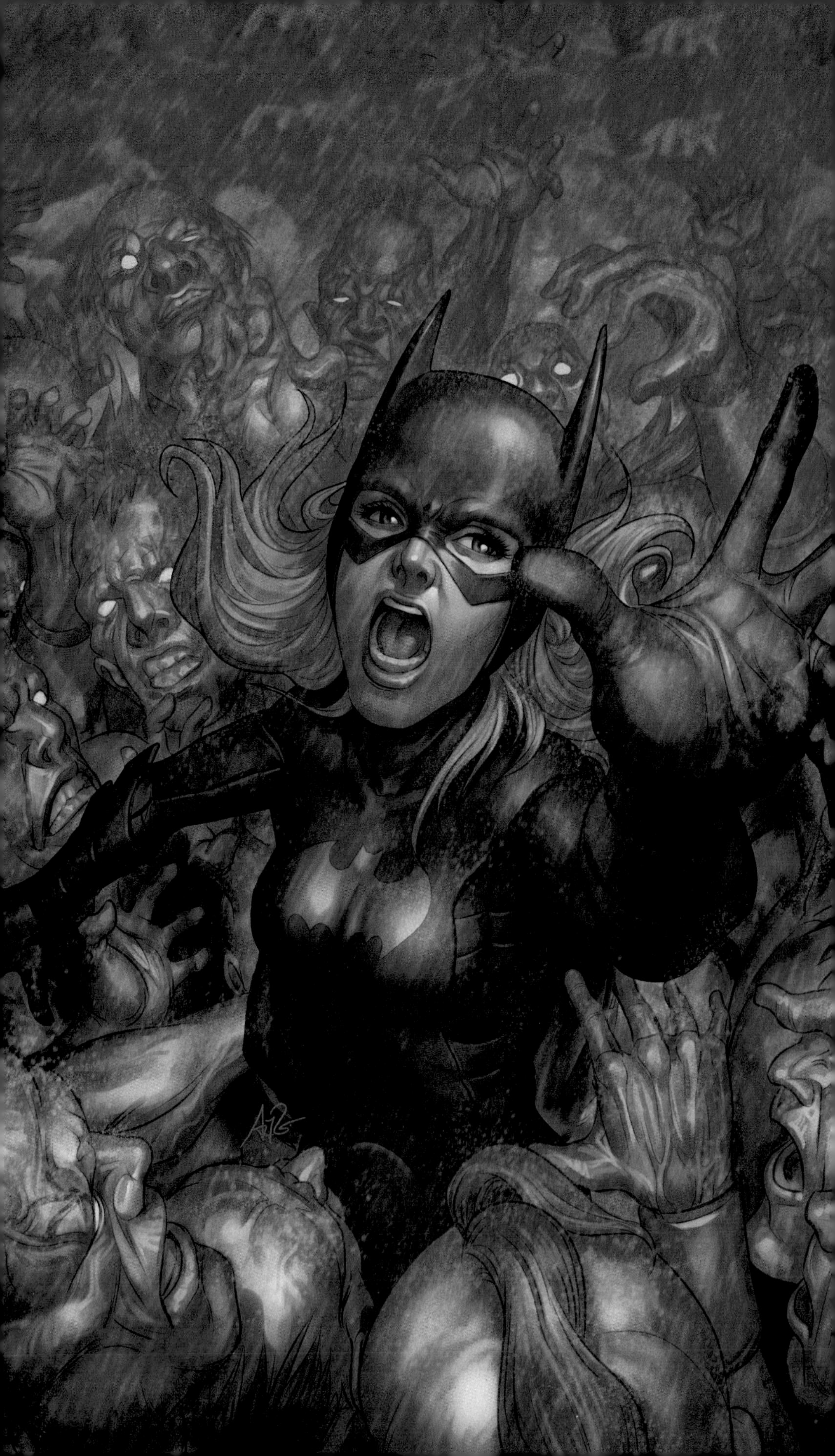

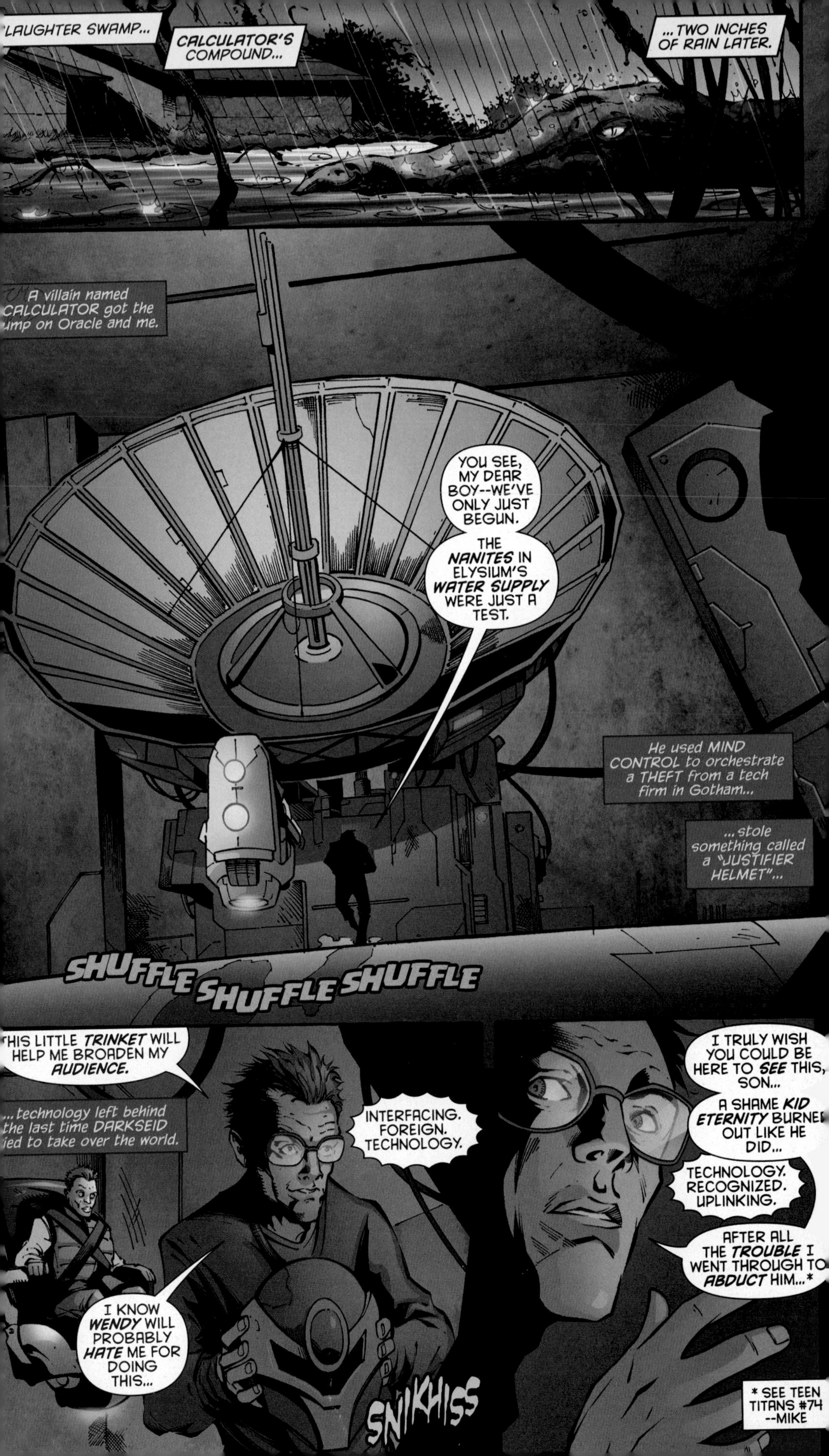

LAUGHTER SWAMP...
CALCULATOR'S COMPOUND...
...TWO INCHES OF RAIN LATER.
A villain named CALCULATOR got the ump on Oracle and me.
YOU SEE, MY DEAR BOY--WE'VE ONLY JUST BEGUN.
THE NANITES IN ELYSIUM'S WATER SUPPLY WERE JUST A TEST.
He used MIND CONTROL to orchestrate a THEFT from a tech firm in Gotham...
...stole something called a "JUSTIFIER HELMET"...
SHUFFLE SHUFFLE SHUFFLE
HIS LITTLE TRINKET WILL HELP ME BROADEN MY AUDIENCE.
...technology left behind the last time DARKSEID ied to take over the world.
INTERFACING. FOREIGN. TECHNOLOGY.
I TRULY WISH YOU COULD BE HERE TO SEE THIS, SON...
A SHAME KID ETERNITY BURNE OUT LIKE HE DID...
TECHNOLOGY. RECOGNIZED. UPLINKING.
AFTER ALL THE TROUBLE I WENT THROUGH TO ABDUCT HIM...*
I KNOW WENDY WILL PROBABLY HATE ME FOR DOING THIS...
SNIKHISS
* SEE TEEN TITANS #74 --MIKE

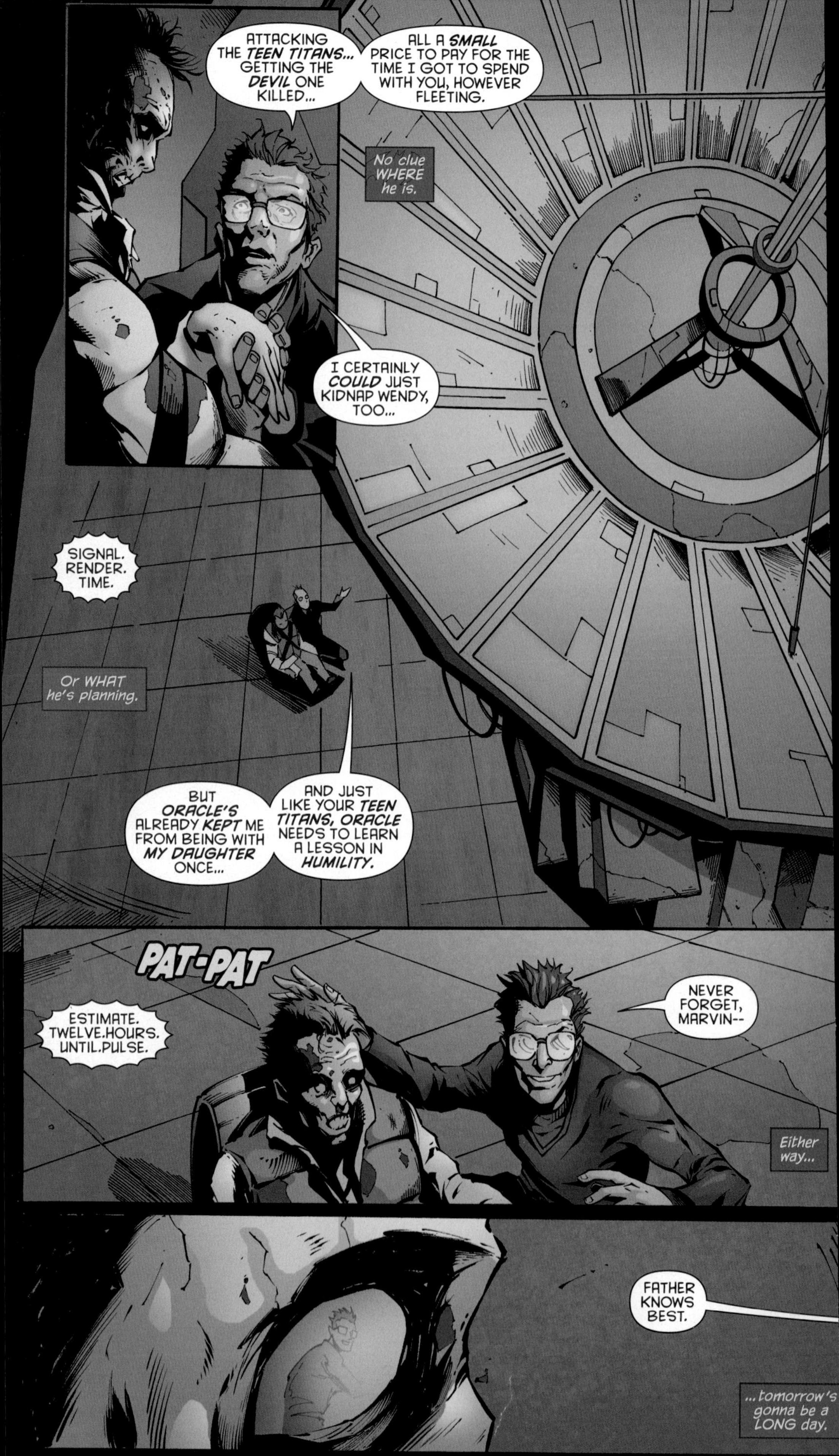
ATTACKING THE TEEN TITANS... GETTING THE DEVIL ONE KILLED...
ALL A SMALL PRICE TO PAY FOR THE TIME I GOT TO SPEND WITH YOU, HOWEVER FLEETING.
No clue WHERE he is.
I CERTAINLY COULD JUST KIDNAP WENDY, TOO...
SIGNAL. RENDER. TIME.
Or WHAT he's planning.
BUT ORACLE'S ALREADY KEPT ME FROM BEING WITH MY DAUGHTER ONCE...
AND JUST LIKE YOUR TEEN TITANS, ORACLE NEEDS TO LEARN A LESSON IN HUMILITY.
PAT-PAT
ESTIMATE. TWELVE.HOURS. UNTIL.PULSE.
NEVER FORGET, MARVIN--
Either way...
FATHER KNOWS BEST.
...tomorrow's gonna be a LONG day.

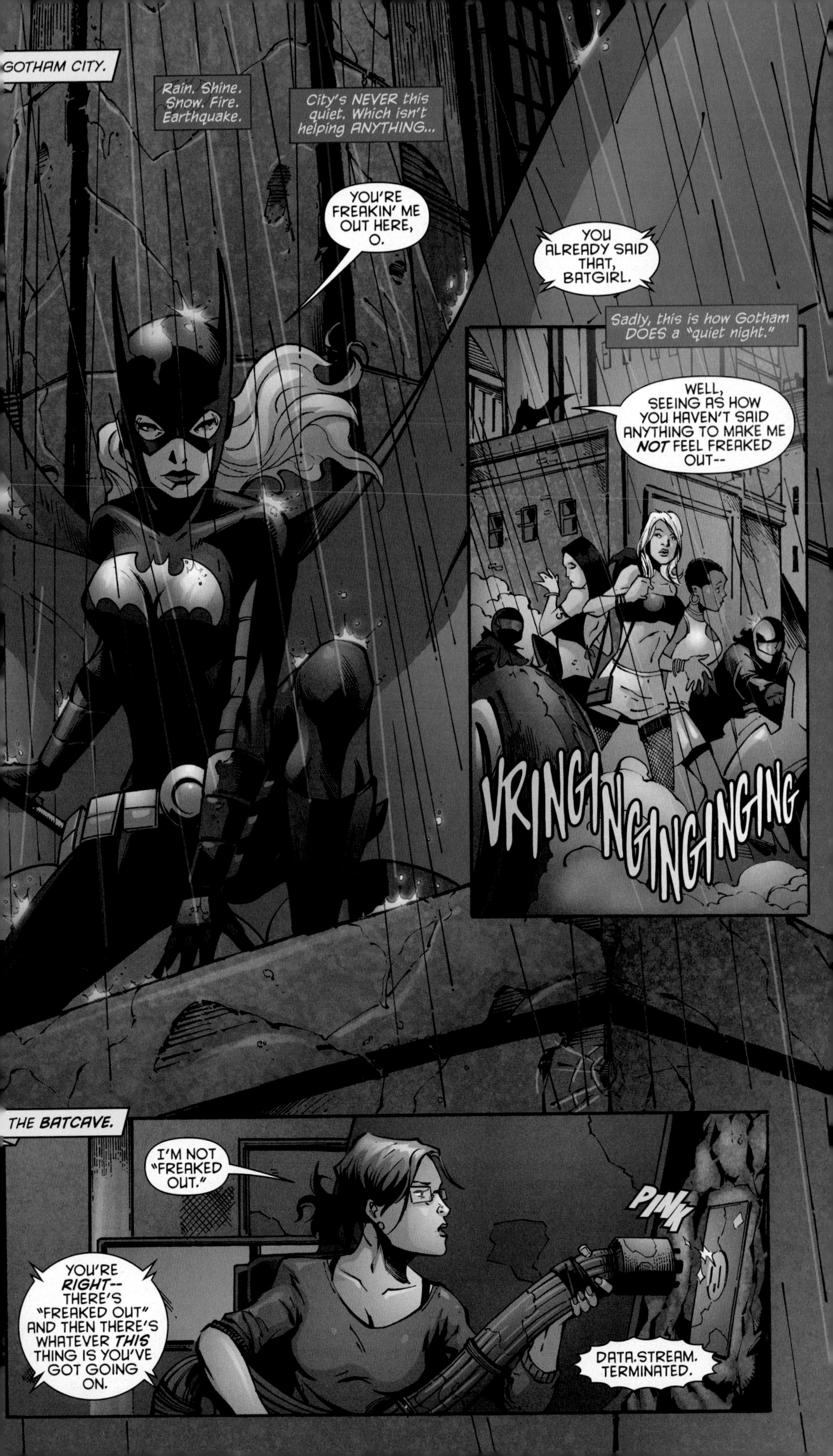
GOTHAM CITY.
Rain. Shine. Snow. Fire. Earthquake.
City's NEVER this quiet. Which isn't helping ANYTHING...
YOU'RE FREAKIN' ME OUT HERE, O.
YOU ALREADY SAID THAT, BATGIRL.
Sadly, this is how Gotham DOES a "quiet night."
WELL, SEEING AS HOW YOU HAVEN'T SAID ANYTHING TO MAKE ME NOT FEEL FREAKED OUT--
VRINGINGINGINGINGING
THE BATCAVE.
I'M NOT "FREAKED OUT."
PINK
YOU'RE RIGHT-- THERE'S "FREAKED OUT" AND THEN THERE'S WHATEVER THIS THING IS YOU'VE GOT GOING ON.
DATA.STREAM. TERMINATED.

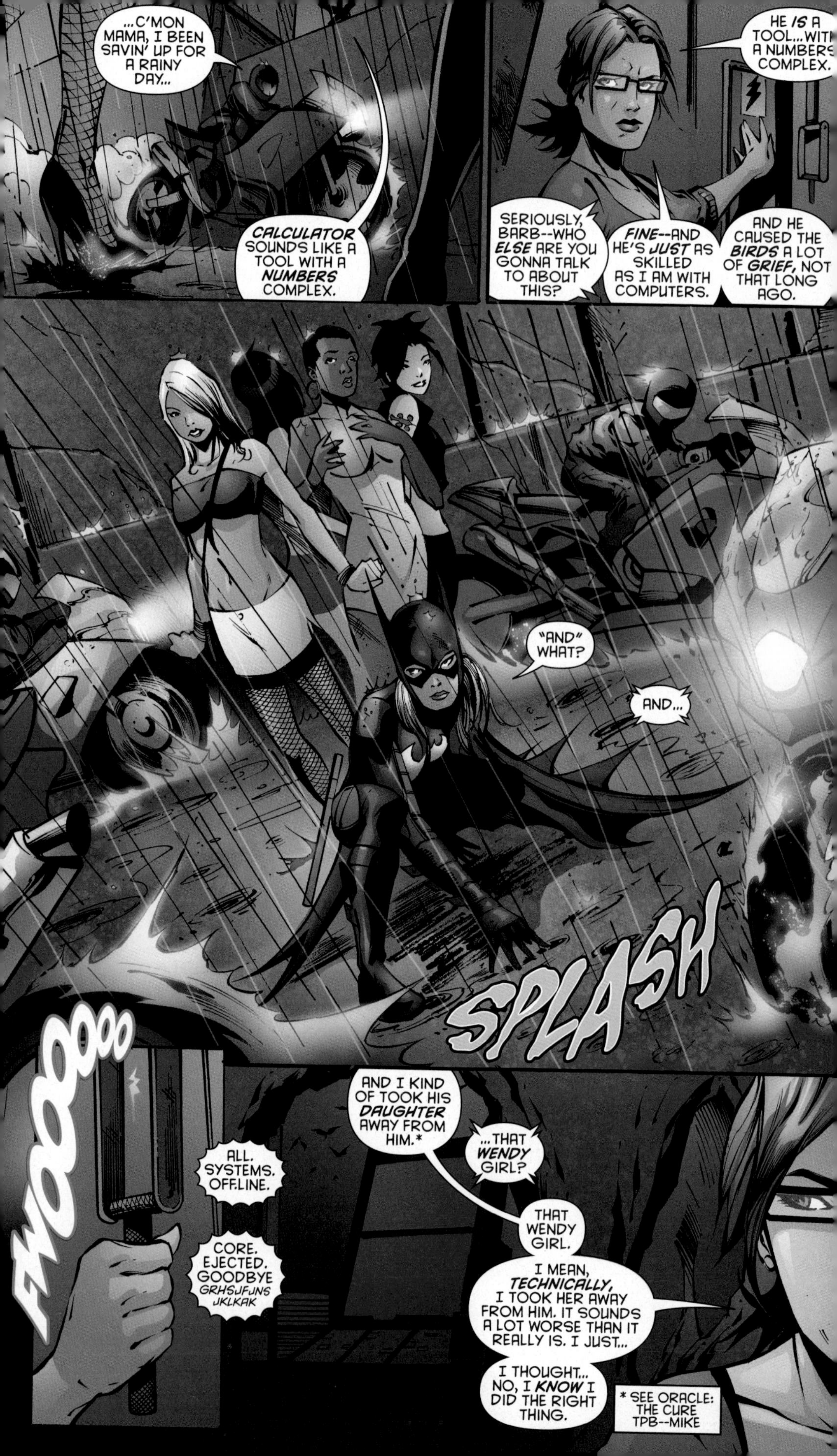

...C'MON MAMA, I BEEN SAVIN' UP FOR A RAINY DAY...
CALCULATOR SOUNDS LIKE A TOOL WITH A NUMBERS COMPLEX.
HE IS A TOOL...WITH A NUMBERS COMPLEX.
SERIOUSLY, BARB--WHO ELSE ARE YOU GONNA TALK TO ABOUT THIS?
FINE--AND HE'S JUST AS SKILLED AS I AM WITH COMPUTERS.
AND HE CAUSED THE BIRDS A LOT OF GRIEF, NOT THAT LONG AGO.
"AND" WHAT?
AND...
SPLASH
FWOOOOOO
AND I KIND OF TOOK HIS DAUGHTER AWAY FROM HIM.*
...THAT WENDY GIRL?
THAT WENDY GIRL.
ALL. SYSTEMS. OFF.LINE.
CORE. EJECTED. GOODBYE GRHSUFJNS JKLKAK
I MEAN, TECHNICALLY, I TOOK HER AWAY FROM HIM. IT SOUNDS A LOT WORSE THAN IT REALLY IS. I JUST...
I THOUGHT... NO, I KNOW I DID THE RIGHT THING.
* SEE ORACLE: THE CURE TPB--MIKE

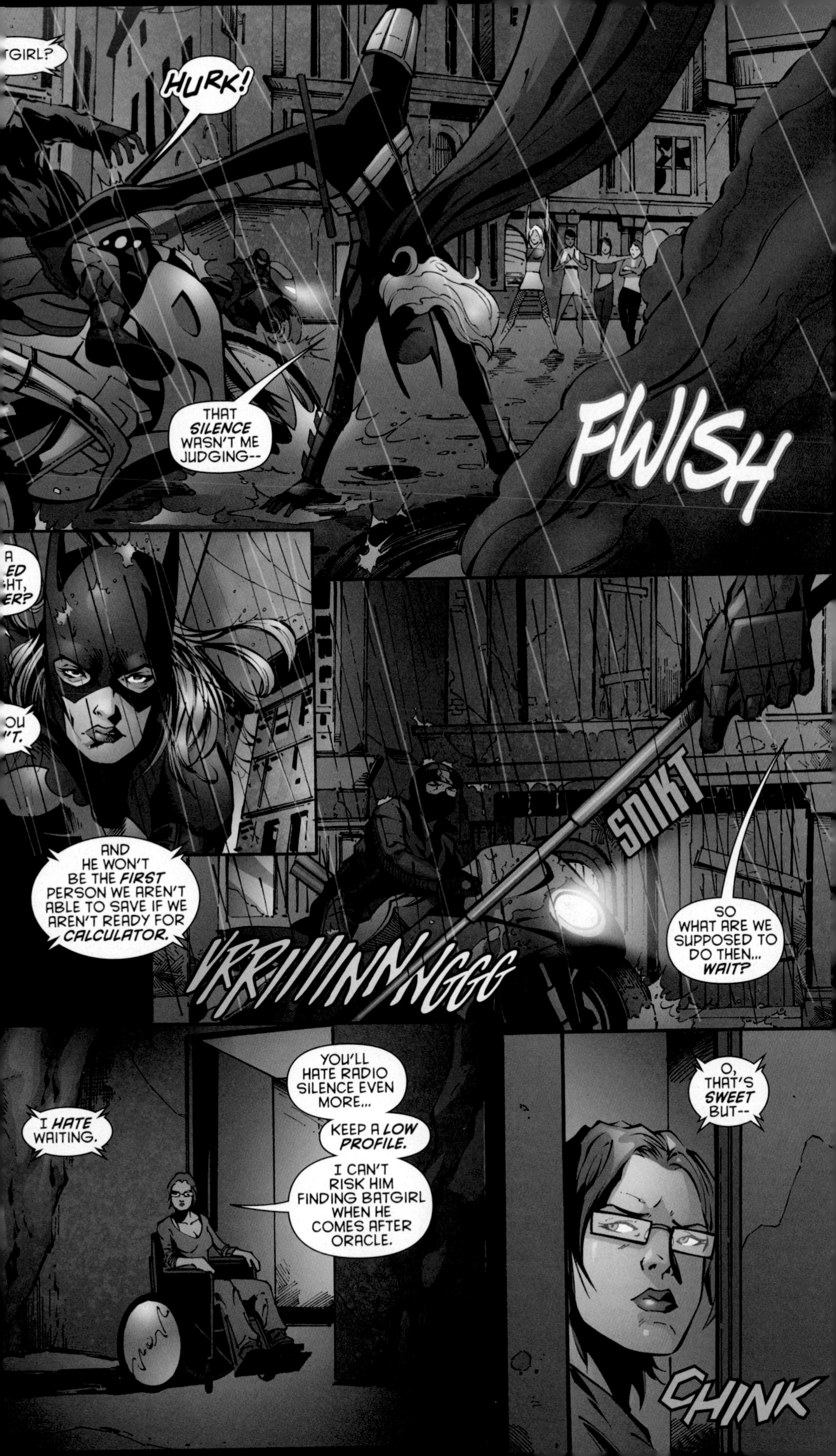
HURK!
THAT SILENCE WASN'T ME JUDGING--
FWISH
AND HE WON'T BE THE FIRST PERSON WE AREN'T ABLE TO SAVE IF WE AREN'T READY FOR CALCULATOR.
SNIKT
VRRIIIINNNGGG
SO WHAT ARE WE SUPPOSED TO DO THEN... WAIT?
I HATE WAITING.
YOU'LL HATE RADIO SILENCE EVEN MORE...
KEEP A LOW PROFILE.
I CAN'T RISK HIM FINDING BATGIRL WHEN HE COMES AFTER ORACLE.
O, THAT'S SWEET BUT--
CHINK

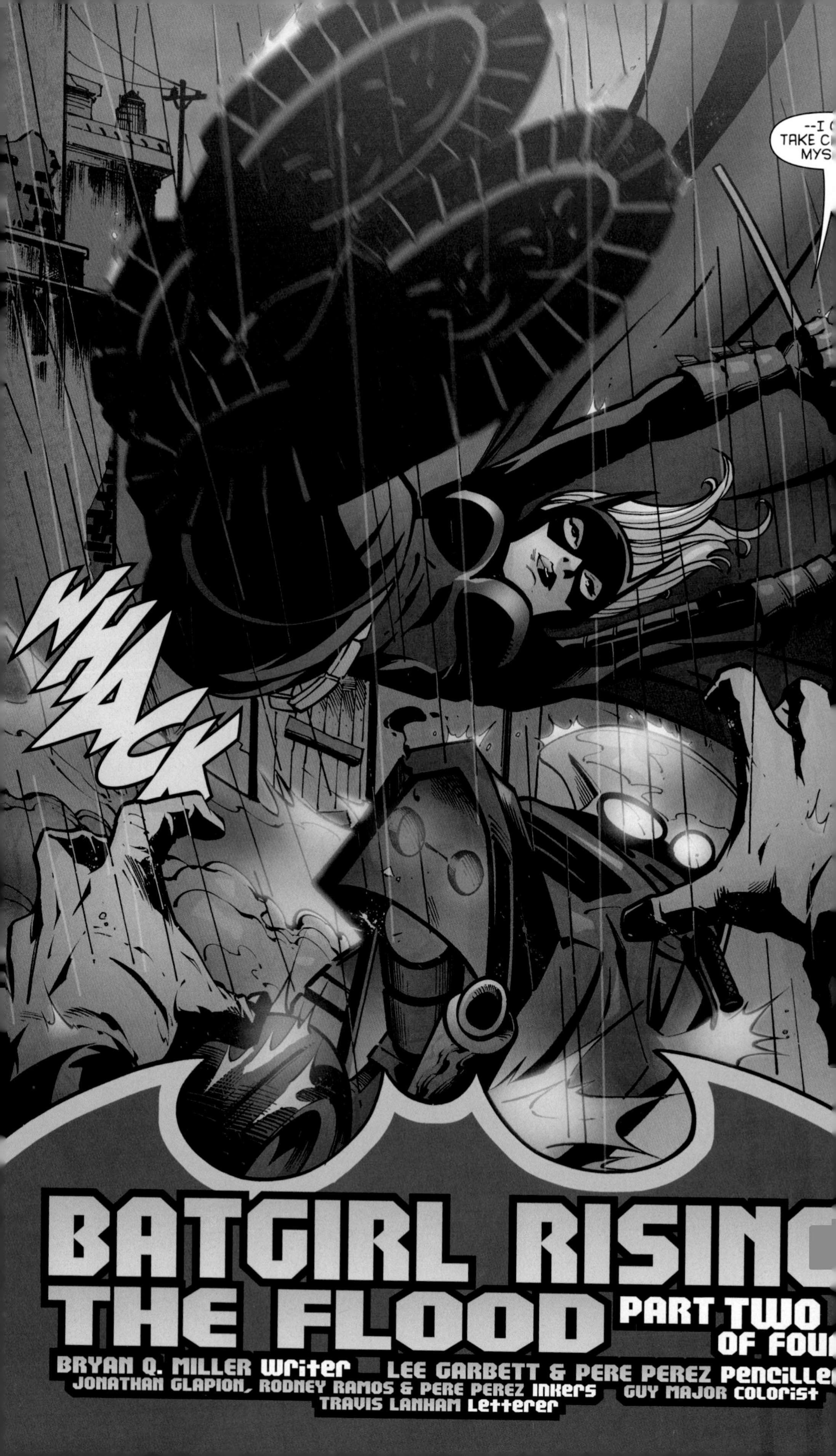

--I C
TAKE C
MYS
WHACK
BATGIRL RISING
THE FLOOD PART TWO
OF FOUR
BRYAN Q. MILLER writer LEE GARBETT & PERE PEREZ penciller
JONATHAN GLAPION, RODNEY RAMOS & PERE PEREZ inkers GUY MAJOR colorist
TRAVIS LANHAM letterer

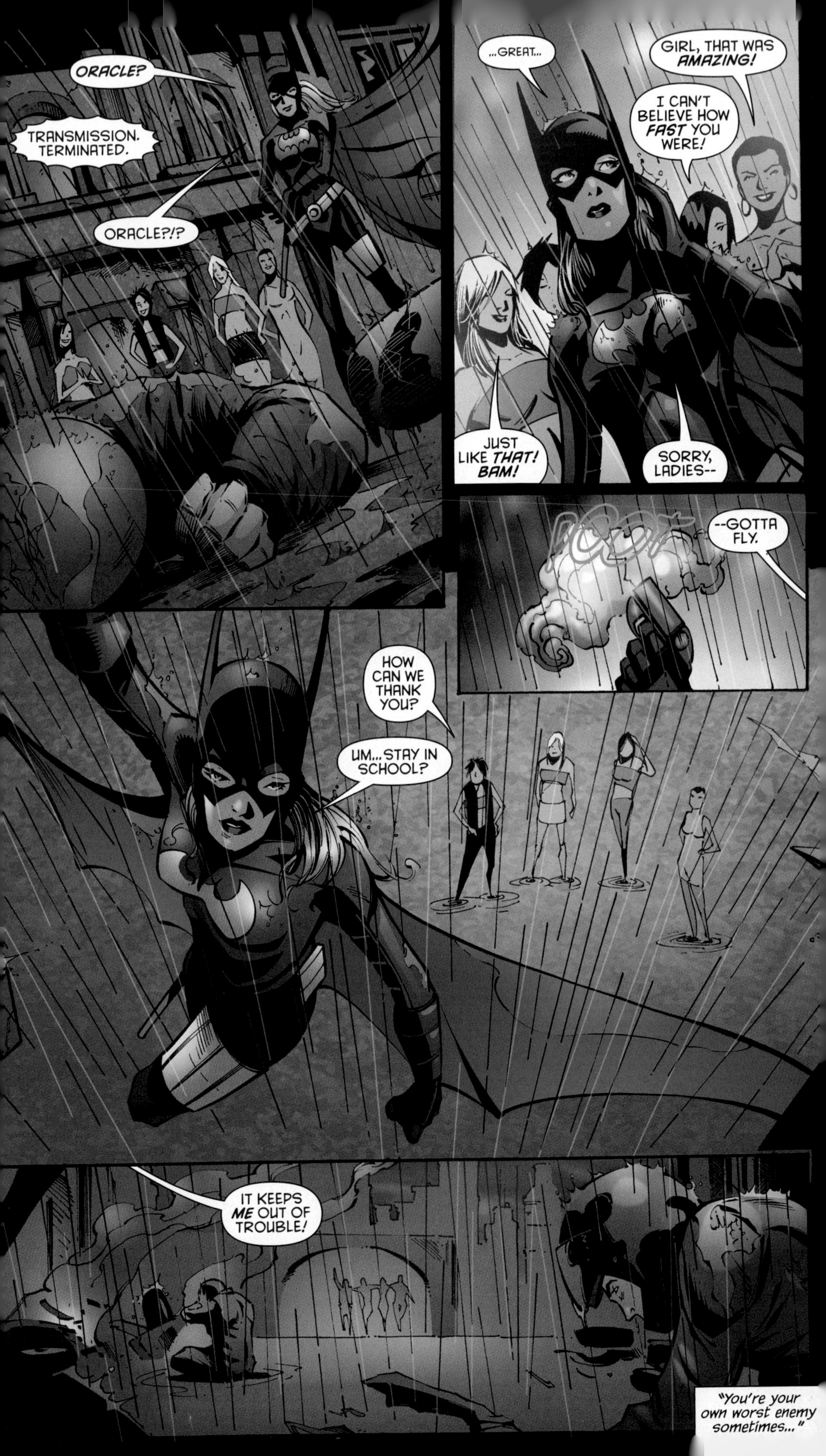
ORACLE?
TRANSMISSION. TERMINATED.
ORACLE?!?
...GREAT...
GIRL, THAT WAS AMAZING!
I CAN'T BELIEVE HOW FAST YOU WERE!
JUST LIKE THAT! BAM!
SORRY, LADIES--
--GOTTA FLY.
HOW CAN WE THANK YOU?
UM...STAY IN SCHOOL?
IT KEEPS ME OUT OF TROUBLE!
"You're your own worst enemy sometimes..."

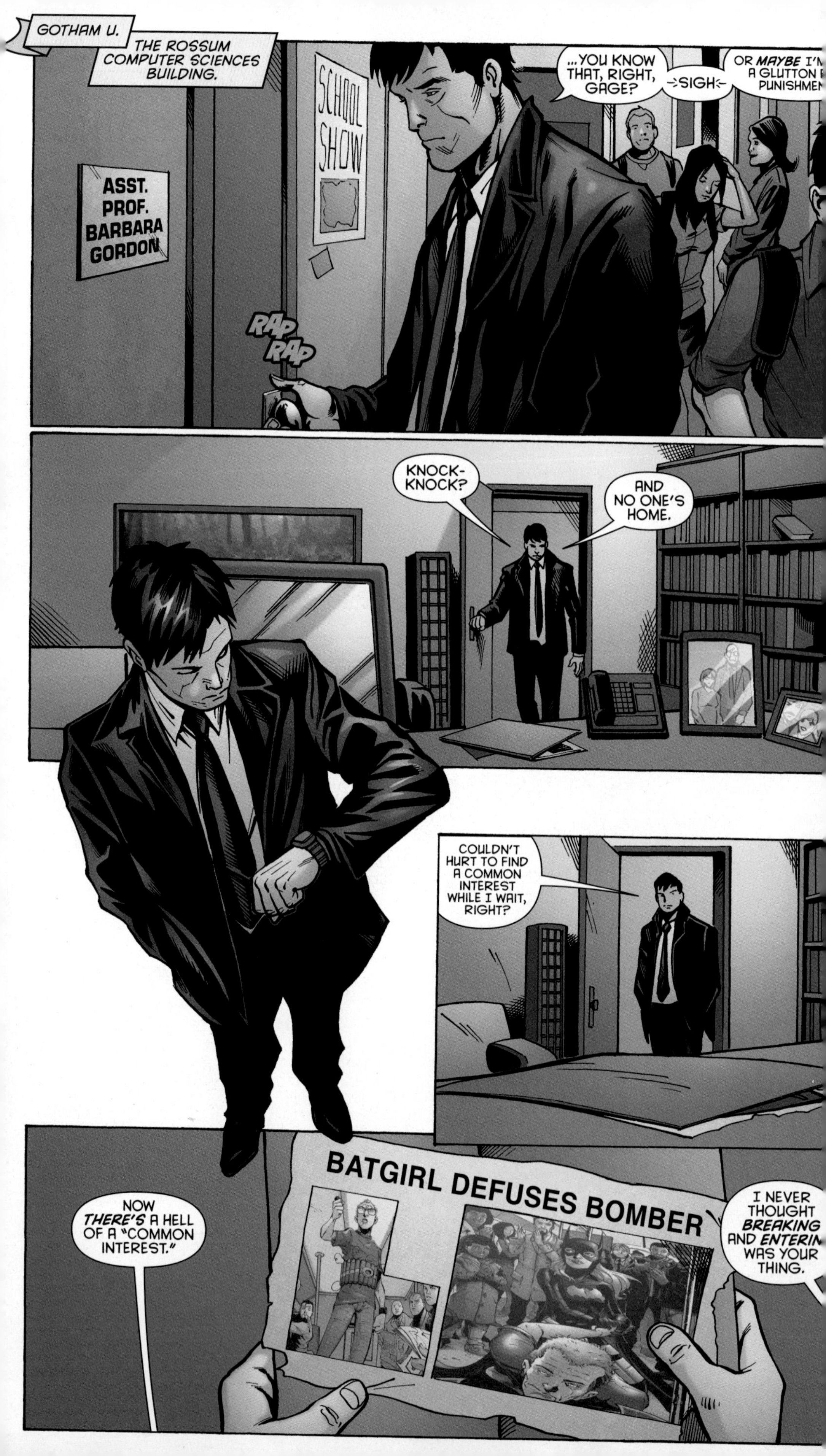
GOTHAM U.
THE ROSSUM COMPUTER SCIENCES BUILDING.
SCHOOL SHOW
ASST. PROF. BARBARA GORDON
RAP RAP
...YOU KNOW THAT, RIGHT, GAGE?
SIGH
OR MAYBE I'M A GLUTTON F PUNISHMEN
KNOCK-KNOCK?
AND NO ONE'S HOME.
COULDN'T HURT TO FIND A COMMON INTEREST WHILE I WAIT, RIGHT?
BATGIRL DEFUSES BOMBER
NOW THERE'S A HELL OF A "COMMON INTEREST."
I NEVER THOUGHT BREAKING AND ENTERIN WAS YOUR THING.

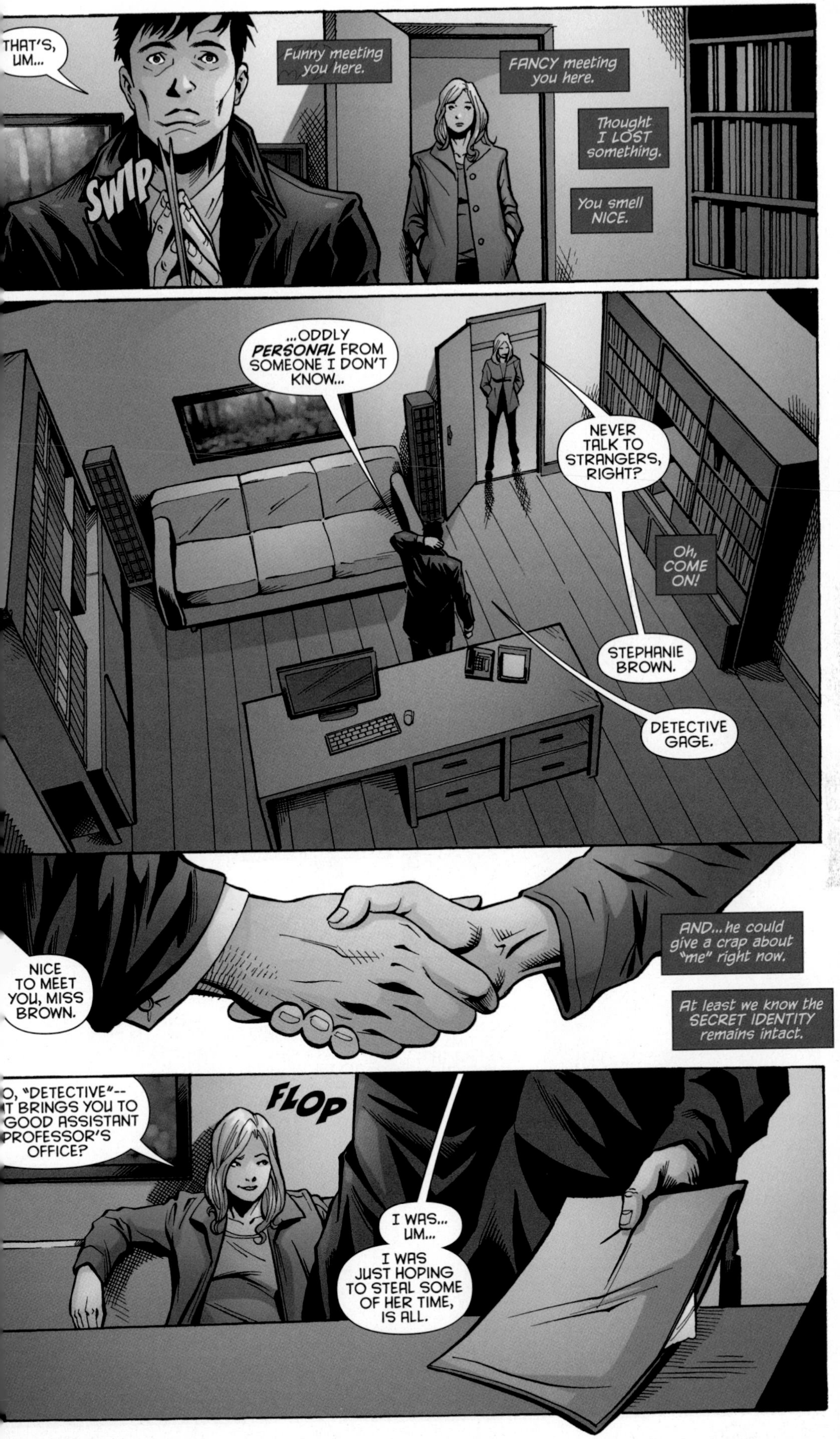
THAT'S, UM...
SWIP
Funny meeting you here.
FANCY meeting you here.
Thought I LOST something.
You smell NICE.
...ODDLY PERSONAL FROM SOMEONE I DON'T KNOW...
NEVER TALK TO STRANGERS, RIGHT?
Oh, COME ON!
STEPHANIE BROWN.
DETECTIVE GAGE.
NICE TO MEET YOU, MISS BROWN.
AND...he could give a crap about "me" right now.
At least we know the SECRET IDENTITY remains intact.
O, "DETECTIVE"-- T BRINGS YOU TO GOOD ASSISTANT PROFESSOR'S OFFICE?
FLOP
I WAS... UM...
I WAS JUST HOPING TO STEAL SOME OF HER TIME, IS ALL.

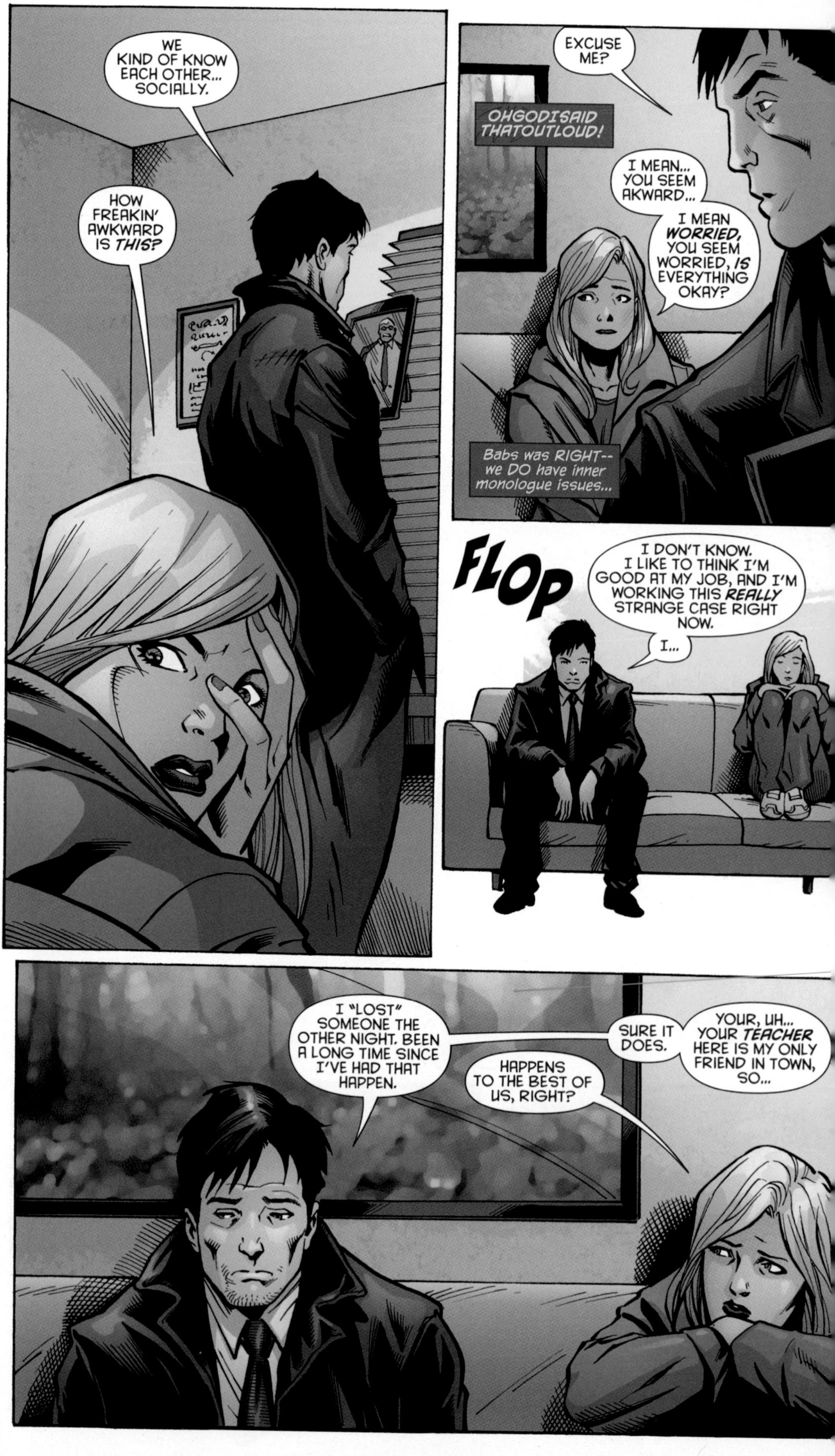
WE KIND OF KNOW EACH OTHER... SOCIALLY.
HOW FREAKIN' AWKWARD IS *THIS?*
EXCUSE ME?
OHGODISAID THATOUTLOUD!
I MEAN... YOU SEEM AKWARD...
I MEAN *WORRIED,* YOU SEEM WORRIED, *IS* EVERYTHING OKAY?
Babs was RIGHT-- we DO have inner monologue issues...
FLOP
I DON'T KNOW. I LIKE TO THINK I'M GOOD AT MY JOB, AND I'M WORKING THIS *REALLY* STRANGE CASE RIGHT NOW.
I...
I "LOST" SOMEONE THE OTHER NIGHT. BEEN A LONG TIME SINCE I'VE HAD THAT HAPPEN.
SURE IT DOES.
HAPPENS TO THE BEST OF US, RIGHT?
YOUR, UH... YOUR *TEACHER* HERE IS MY ONLY FRIEND IN TOWN, SO...

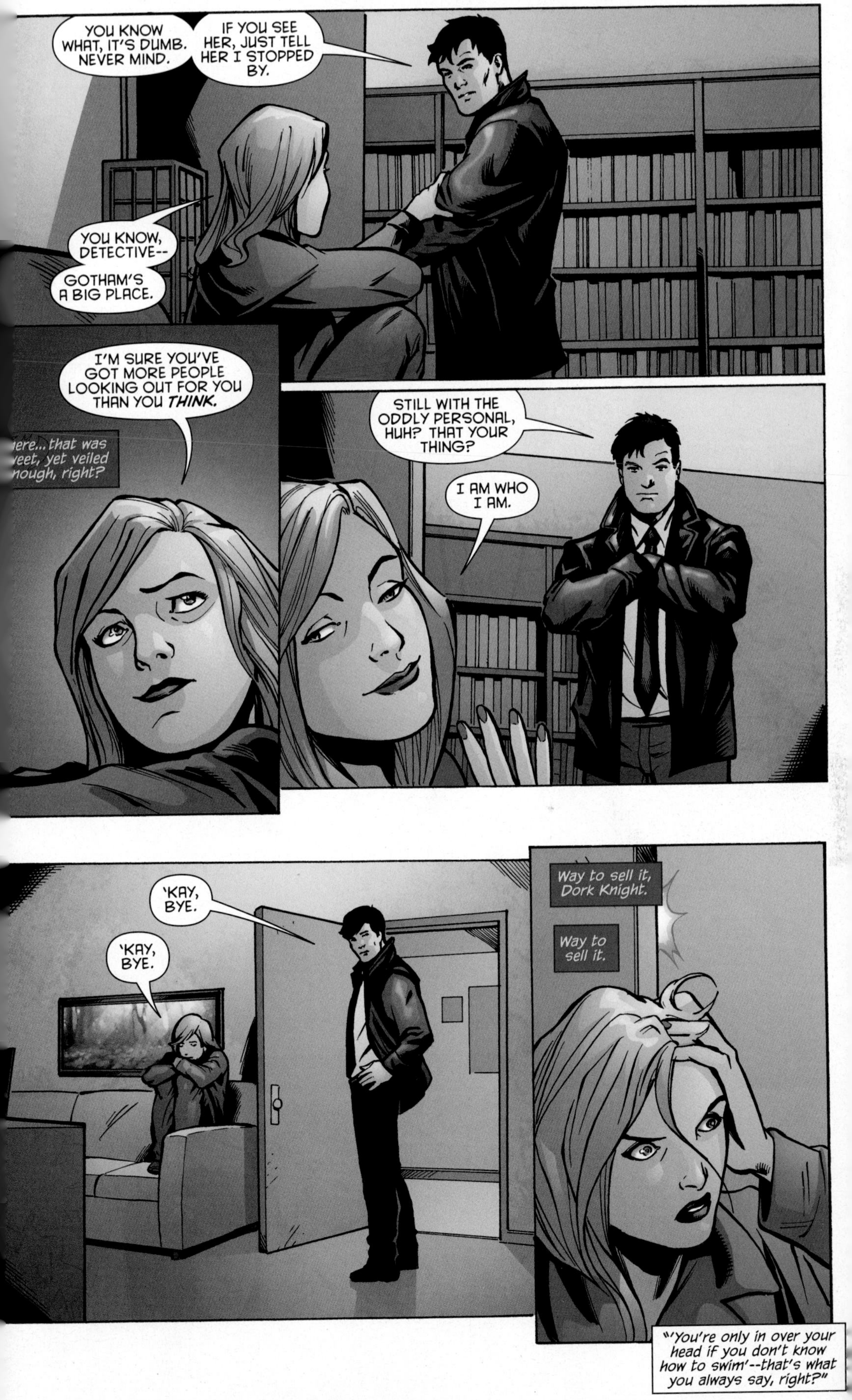
YOU KNOW WHAT, IT'S DUMB. NEVER MIND.
IF YOU SEE HER, JUST TELL HER I STOPPED BY.
YOU KNOW, DETECTIVE--
GOTHAM'S A BIG PLACE.
I'M SURE YOU'VE GOT MORE PEOPLE LOOKING OUT FOR YOU THAN YOU *THINK.*
...that was ...eet, yet veiled ...nough, right?
STILL WITH THE ODDLY PERSONAL, HUH? THAT YOUR THING?
I AM WHO I AM.
'KAY, BYE.
'KAY, BYE.
Way to sell it, Dork Knight.
Way to sell it.
"'You're only in over your head if you don't know how to swim'--that's what you always say, right?"

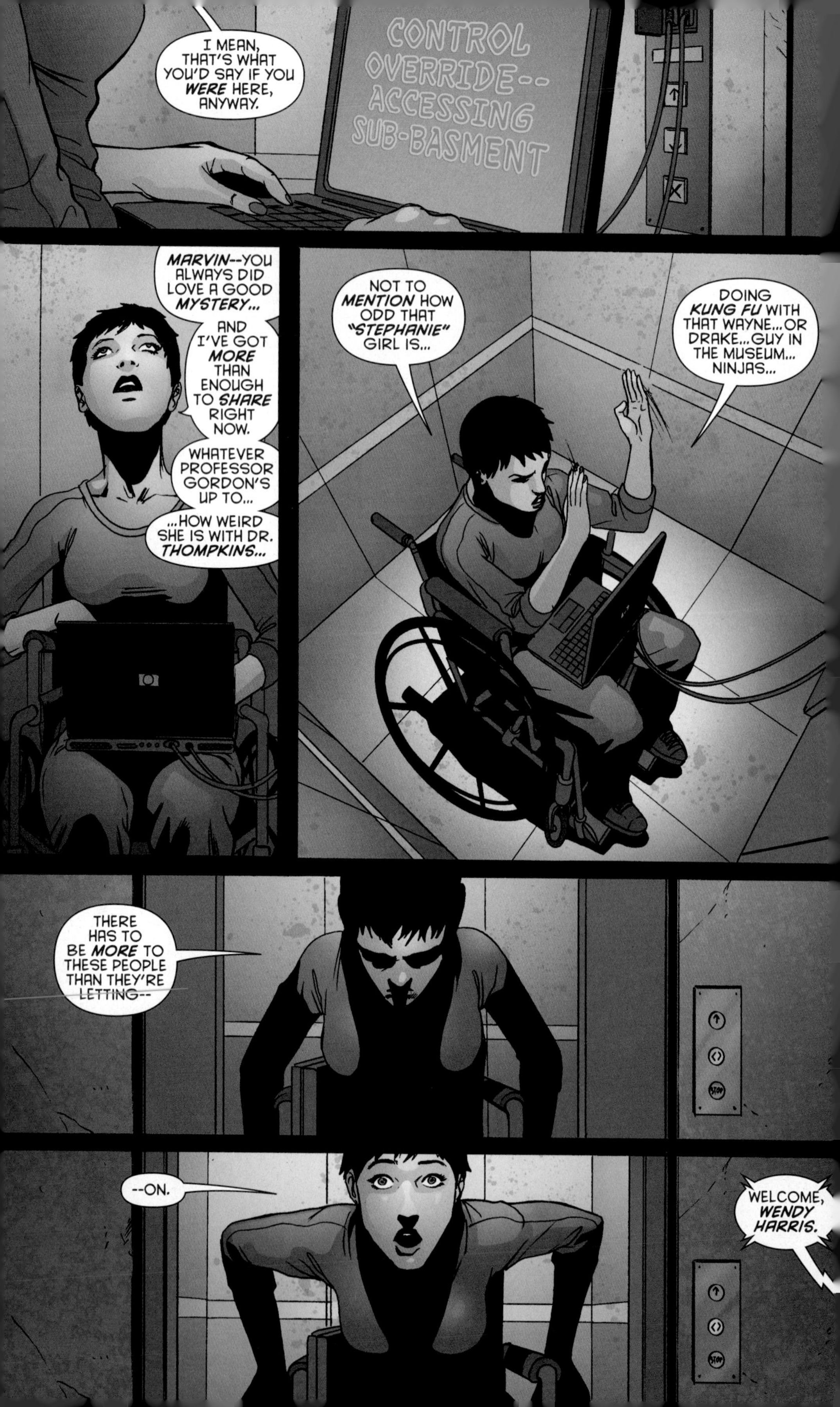

I MEAN, THAT'S WHAT YOU'D SAY IF YOU *WERE* HERE, ANYWAY.
CONTROL OVERRIDE-- ACCESSING SUB-BASMENT
MARVIN--YOU ALWAYS DID LOVE A GOOD *MYSTERY*...
AND I'VE GOT *MORE* THAN ENOUGH TO *SHARE* RIGHT NOW.
WHATEVER PROFESSOR GORDON'S UP TO...
...HOW WEIRD SHE IS WITH DR. *THOMPKINS*...
NOT TO *MENTION* HOW ODD THAT *"STEPHANIE"* GIRL IS...
DOING *KUNG FU* WITH THAT WAYNE...OR DRAKE...GUY IN THE MUSEUM... NINJAS...
THERE HAS TO BE *MORE* TO THESE PEOPLE THAN THEY'RE LETTING--
--ON.
WELCOME, *WENDY HARRIS.*

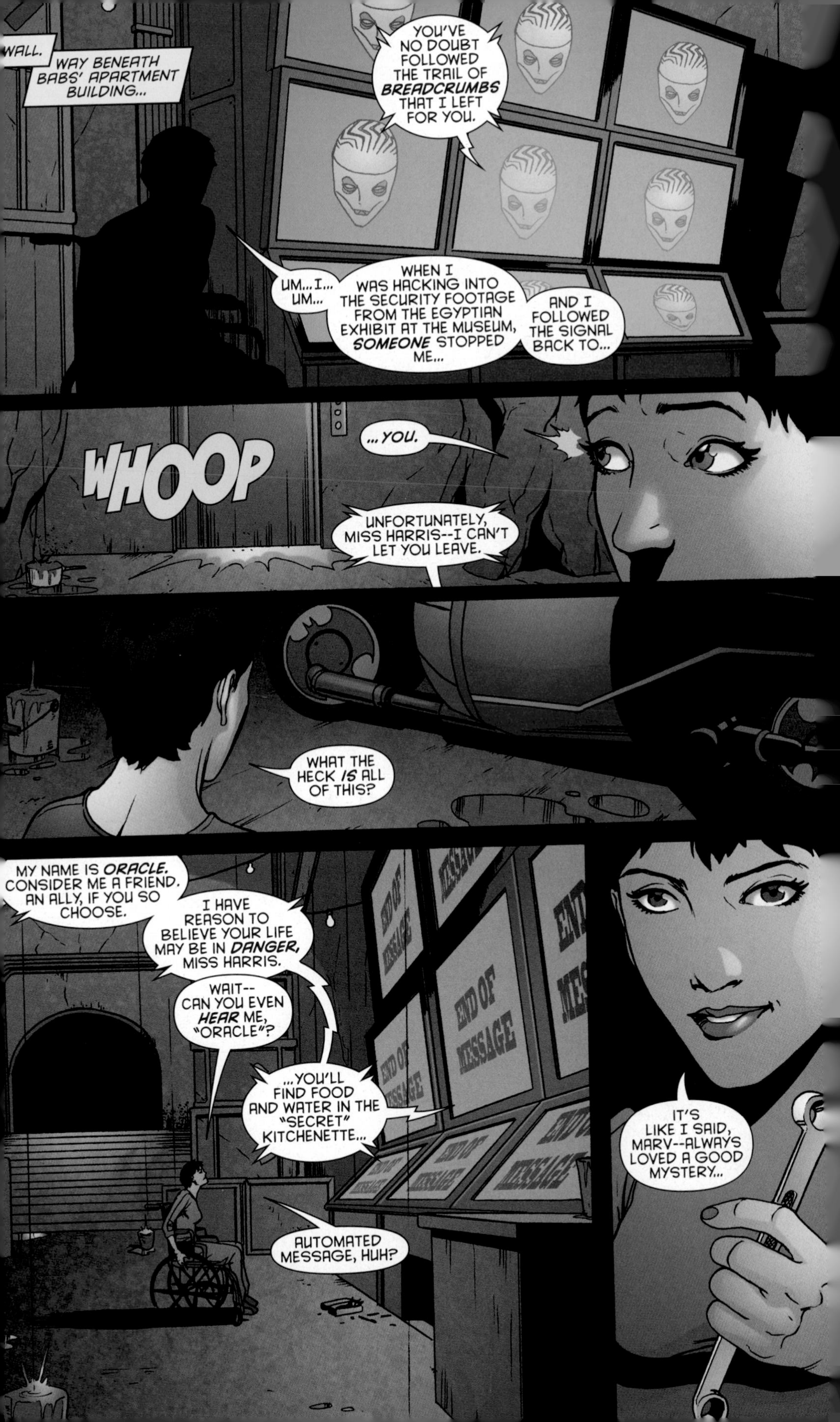
WALL.
WAY BENEATH BABS' APARTMENT BUILDING...
YOU'VE NO DOUBT FOLLOWED THE TRAIL OF BREADCRUMBS THAT I LEFT FOR YOU.
UM... I... UM...
WHEN I WAS HACKING INTO THE SECURITY FOOTAGE FROM THE EGYPTIAN EXHIBIT AT THE MUSEUM, SOMEONE STOPPED ME...
AND I FOLLOWED THE SIGNAL BACK TO...
WHOOP
...YOU.
UNFORTUNATELY, MISS HARRIS--I CAN'T LET YOU LEAVE.
WHAT THE HECK IS ALL OF THIS?
MY NAME IS ORACLE. CONSIDER ME A FRIEND. AN ALLY, IF YOU SO CHOOSE.
I HAVE REASON TO BELIEVE YOUR LIFE MAY BE IN DANGER, MISS HARRIS.
WAIT-- CAN YOU EVEN HEAR ME, "ORACLE"?
...YOU'LL FIND FOOD AND WATER IN THE "SECRET" KITCHENETTE...
AUTOMATED MESSAGE, HUH?
IT'S LIKE I SAID, MARV--ALWAYS LOVED A GOOD MYSTERY...
END OF MESSAGE

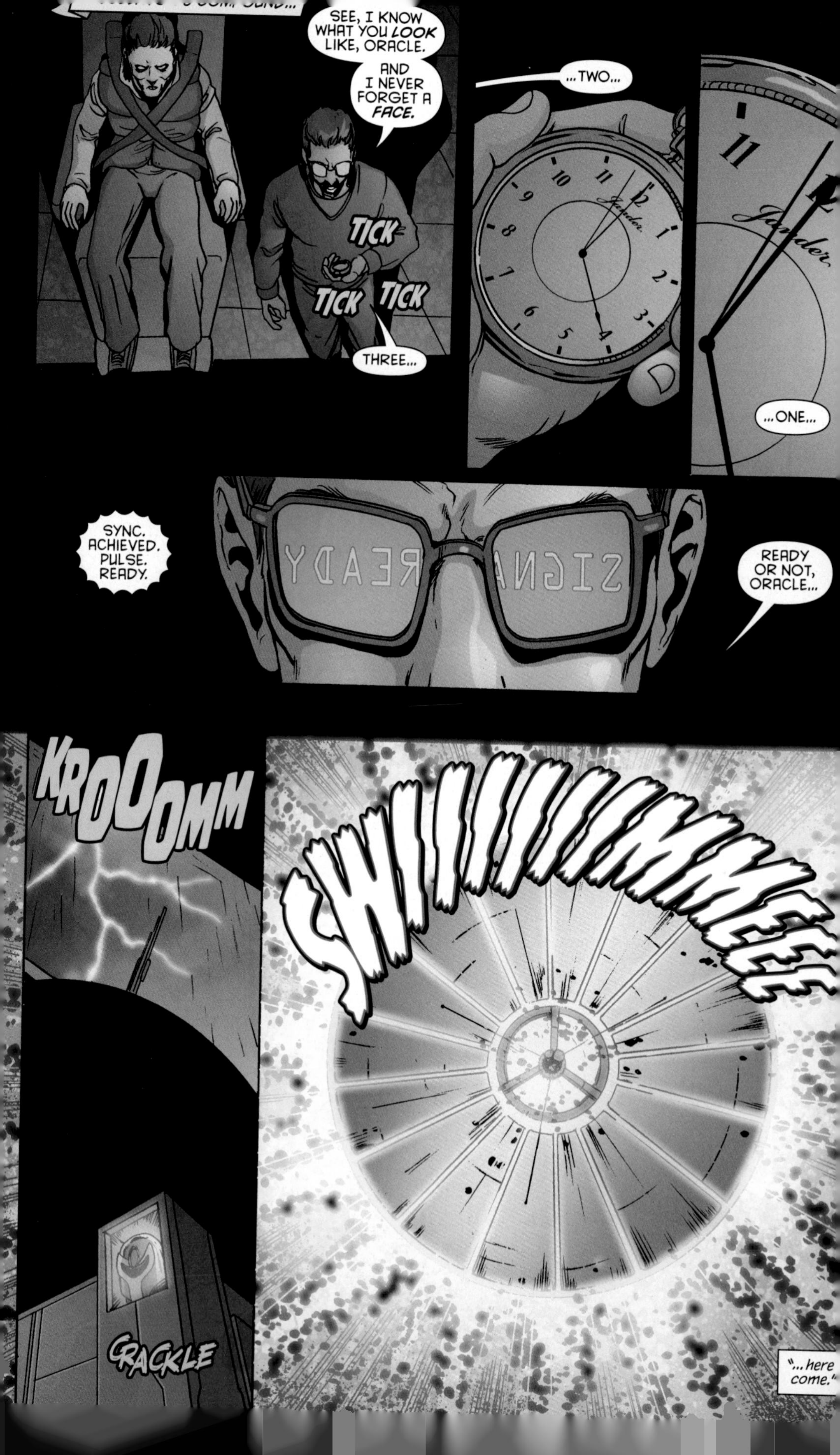
SEE, I KNOW WHAT YOU LOOK LIKE, ORACLE.
AND I NEVER FORGET A FACE.
TICK
TICK
TICK
THREE...
...TWO...
...ONE...
SYNC. ACHIEVED. PULSE. READY.
READY OR NOT, ORACLE...
KROOOMM
CRACKLE
SHIIIIIIMMEEE
"...here come."

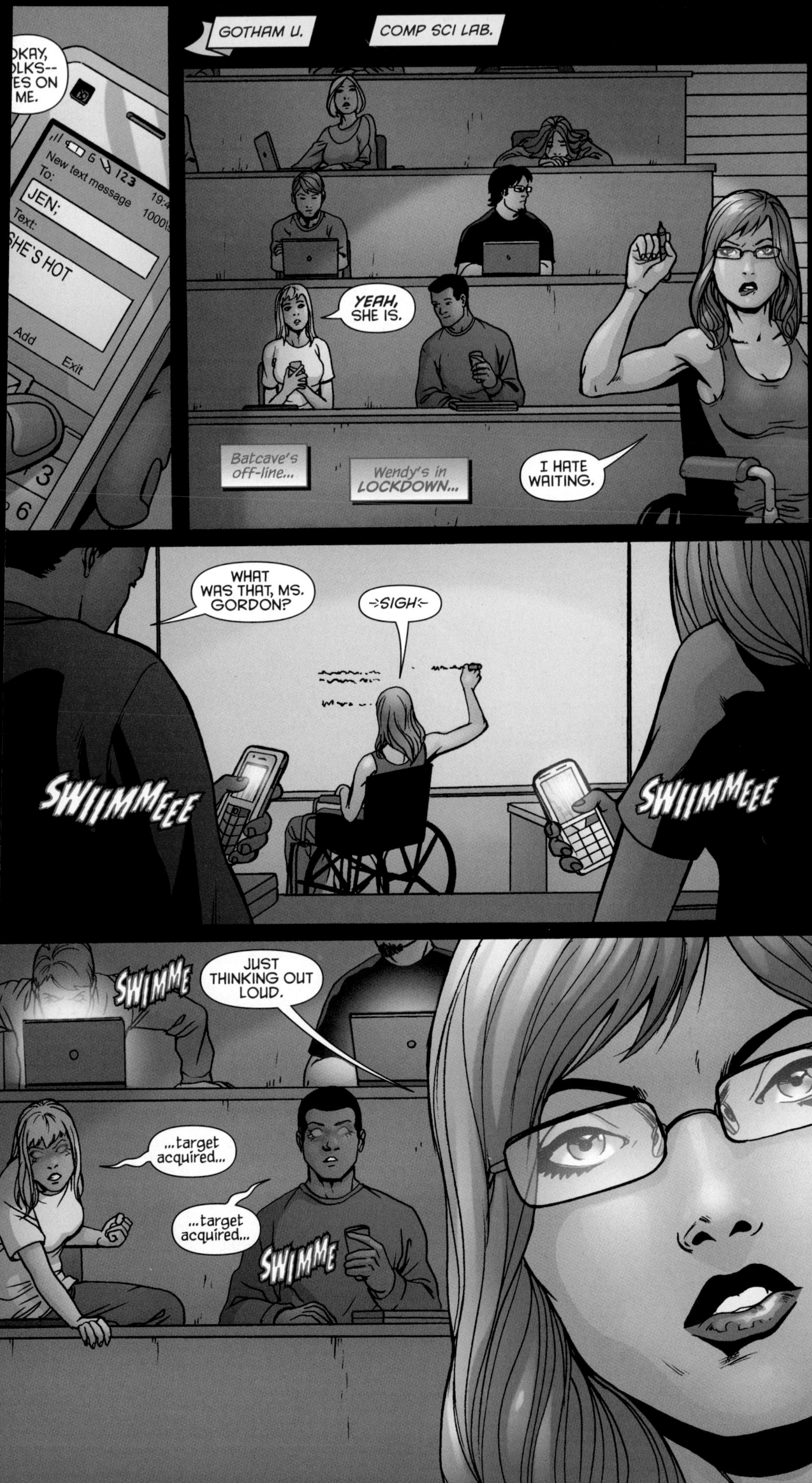

OKAY, FOLKS-- EYES ON ME.
New text message
To:
JEN;
Text:
SHE'S HOT
Add
Exit
GOTHAM U.
COMP SCI LAB.
YEAH, SHE IS.
Batcave's off-line...
Wendy's in LOCKDOWN...
I HATE WAITING.
WHAT WAS THAT, MS. GORDON?
SIGH
SWIIMMEEE
SWIIMMEEE
SWIMME
JUST THINKING OUT LOUD.
...target acquired...
...target acquired...
SWIMME

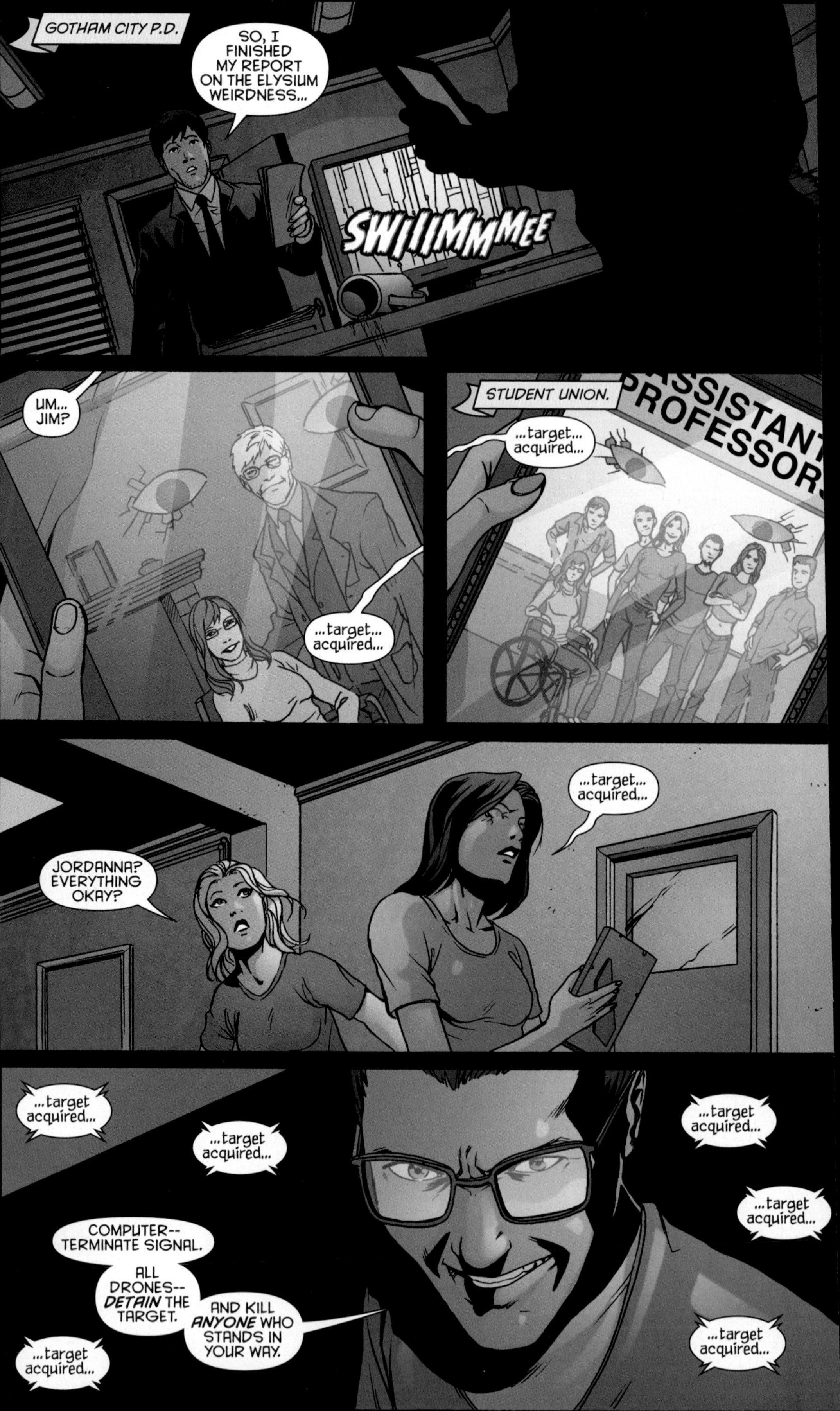
GOTHAM CITY P.D.
SO, I FINISHED MY REPORT ON THE ELYSIUM WEIRDNESS...
SWIIIMMMEE
UM... JIM?
...target... acquired...
STUDENT UNION.
ASSISTANT PROFESSOR
...target... acquired...
...target... acquired...
JORDANNA? EVERYTHING OKAY?
...target acquired...
...target acquired...
...target acquired...
...target acquired...
COMPUTER-- TERMINATE SIGNAL.
ALL DRONES-- DETAIN THE TARGET.
AND KILL ANYONE WHO STANDS IN YOUR WAY.
...target acquired...
...target acquired...

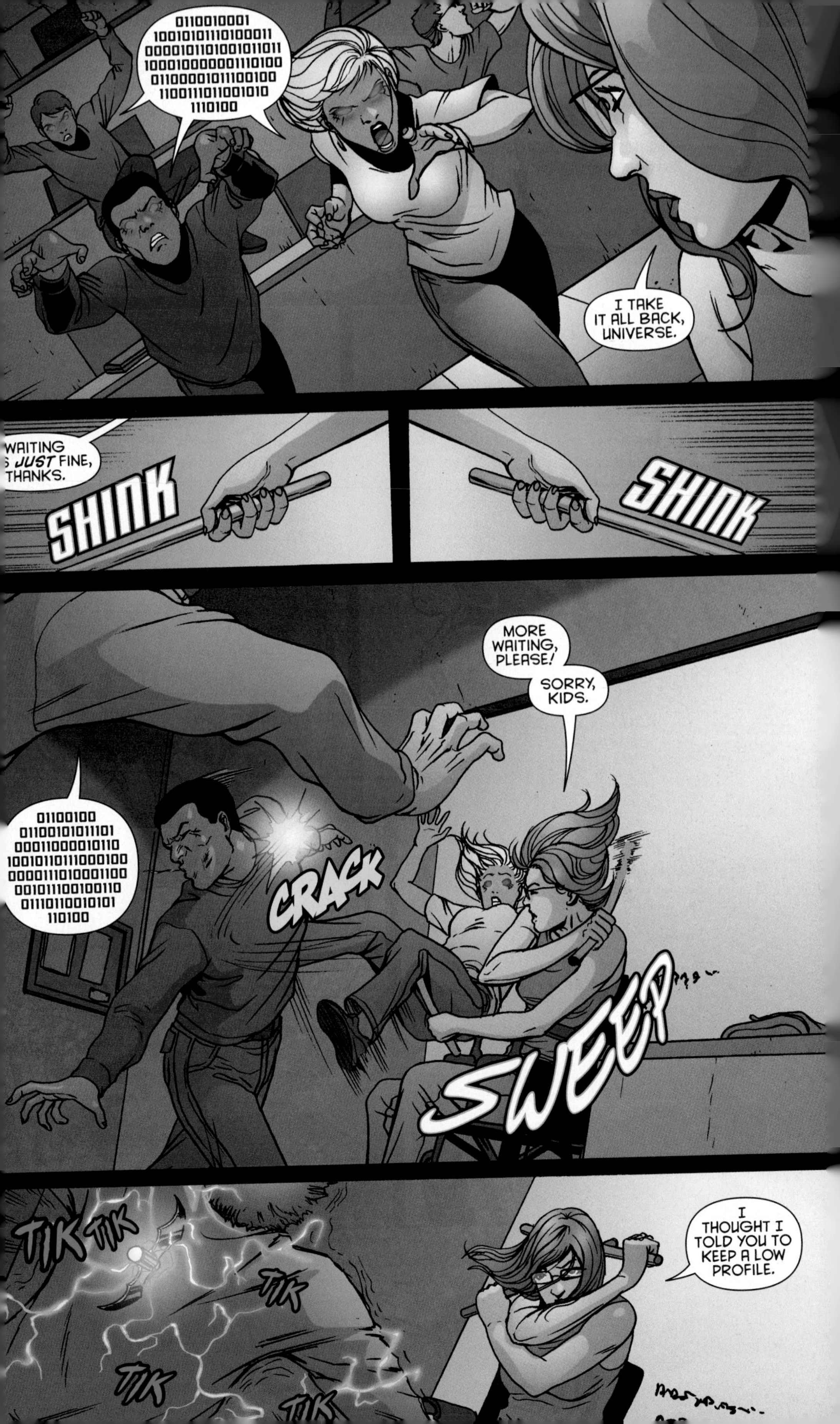
0110010001 10010101110100011 0000101101001011011 1000100000001110100 01100001011100100 1100111011001010 1110100
I TAKE IT ALL BACK, UNIVERSE.
WAITING IS JUST FINE, THANKS.
SHINK
SHINK
MORE WAITING, PLEASE!
SORRY, KIDS.
01100100 01100101011101 00011000010110 1001011011100100 0000111010001100 001011100100110 01110110010101 110100
CRACK
SWEEP
TIK TIK
TIK
TIK
TIK
I THOUGHT I TOLD YOU TO KEEP A LOW PROFILE.

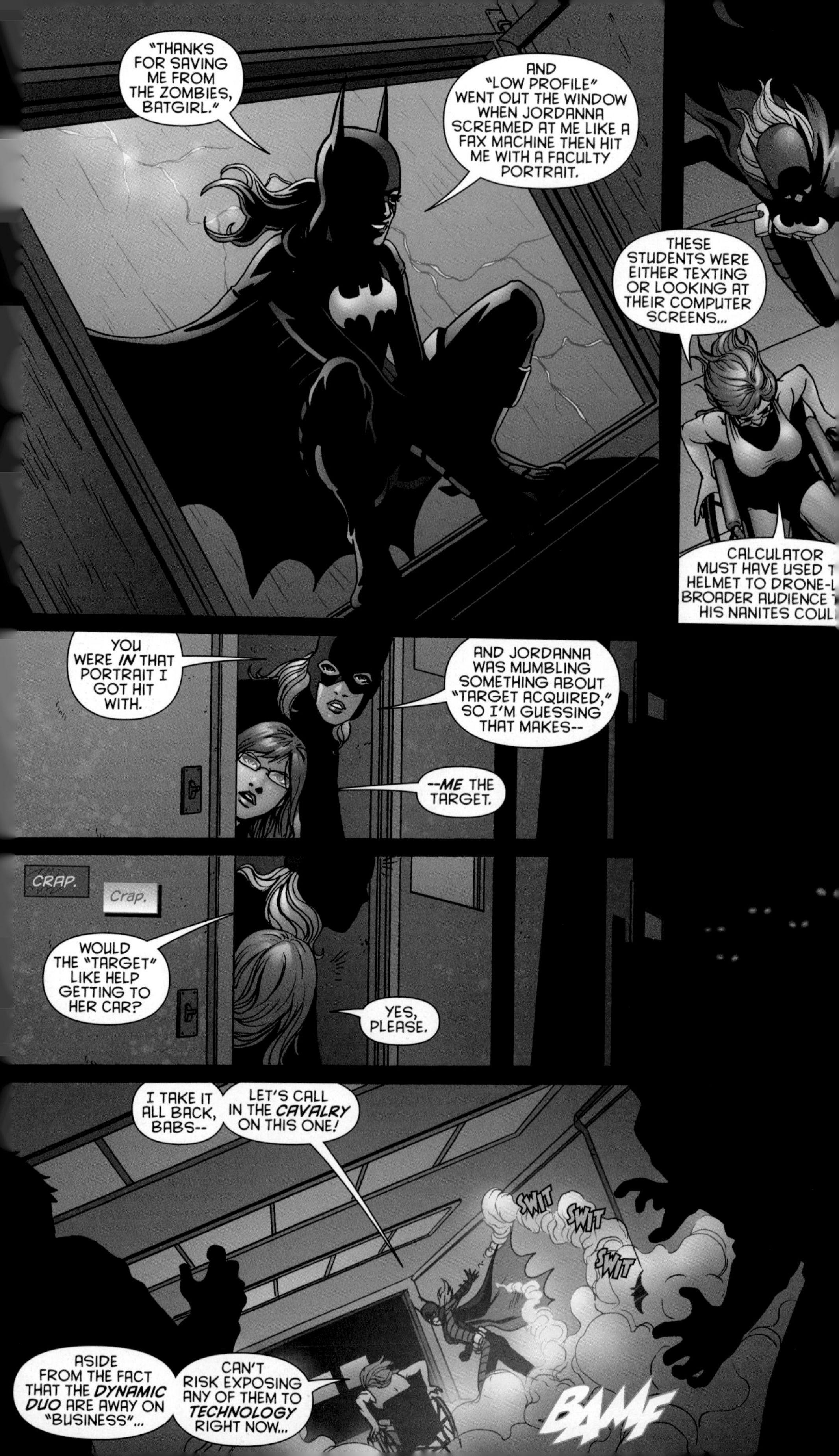

"THANKS FOR SAVING ME FROM THE ZOMBIES, BATGIRL."
AND "LOW PROFILE" WENT OUT THE WINDOW WHEN JORDANNA SCREAMED AT ME LIKE A FAX MACHINE THEN HIT ME WITH A FACULTY PORTRAIT.
THESE STUDENTS WERE EITHER TEXTING OR LOOKING AT THEIR COMPUTER SCREENS...
CALCULATOR MUST HAVE USED T HELMET TO DRONE-L BROADER AUDIENCE T HIS NANITES COUL
YOU WERE *IN* THAT PORTRAIT I GOT HIT WITH.
AND JORDANNA WAS MUMBLING SOMETHING ABOUT "TARGET ACQUIRED," SO I'M GUESSING THAT MAKES--
--*ME* THE TARGET.
CRAP.
Crap.
WOULD THE "TARGET" LIKE HELP GETTING TO HER CAR?
YES, PLEASE.
I TAKE IT ALL BACK, BABS--
LET'S CALL IN THE *CAVALRY* ON THIS ONE!
SWIT
SWIT
SWIT
ASIDE FROM THE FACT THAT THE *DYNAMIC DUO* ARE AWAY ON "BUSINESS"...
CAN'T RISK EXPOSING ANY OF THEM TO *TECHNOLOGY* RIGHT NOW...
BAMF

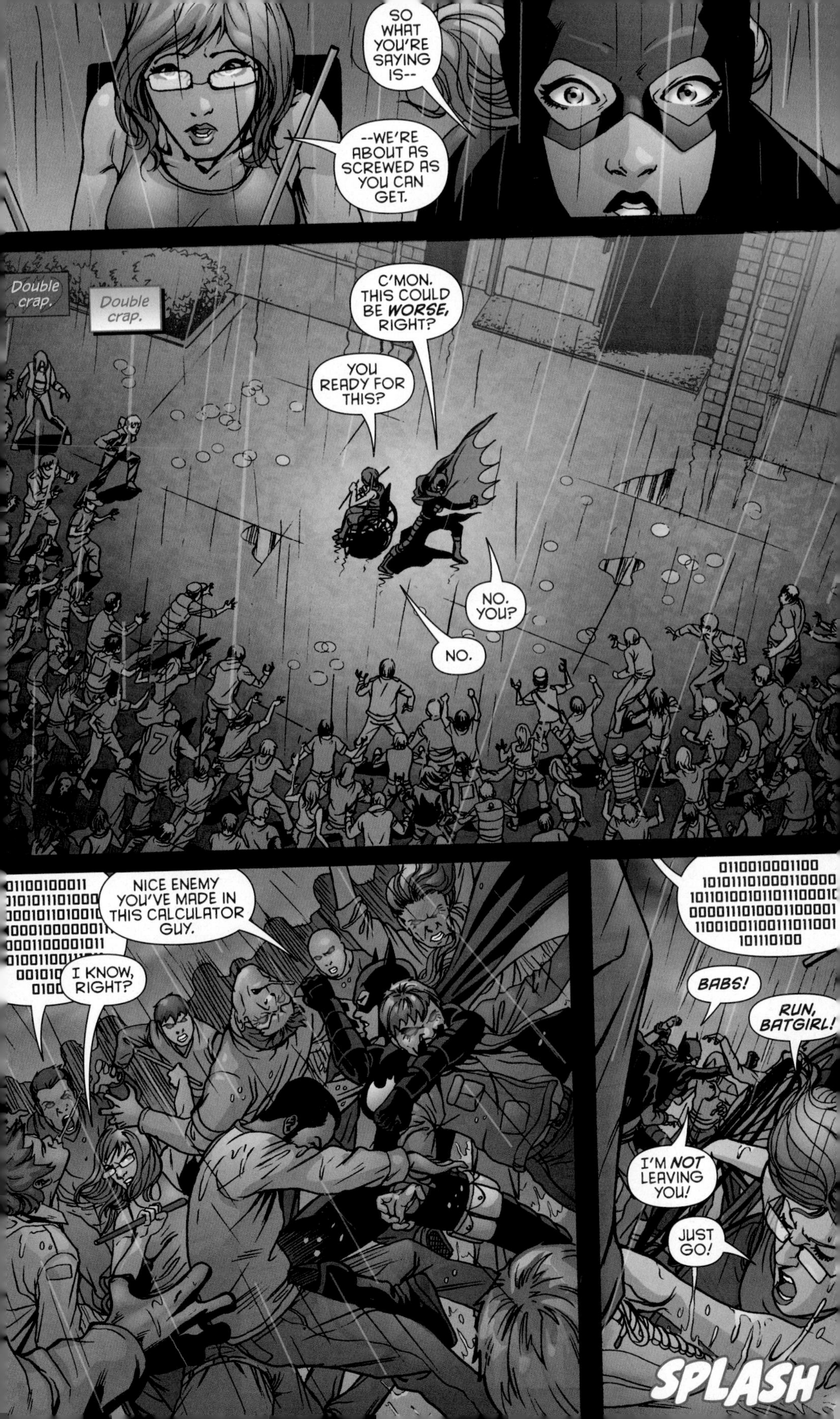
SO WHAT YOU'RE SAYING IS--
--WE'RE ABOUT AS SCREWED AS YOU CAN GET.
Double crap.
Double crap.
C'MON. THIS COULD BE *WORSE,* RIGHT?
YOU READY FOR THIS?
NO. YOU?
NO.
01100100011
0101011101000
000101101001
1000100000011
0001100001011
0100110001
001010
0100
NICE ENEMY YOU'VE MADE IN THIS CALCULATOR GUY.
I KNOW, RIGHT?
0110010001100
101011101000110000
101101001011011100010
000011101000110000 1
1100100110011101 1001
101110100
BABS!
RUN, BATGIRL!
I'M *NOT* LEAVING YOU!
JUST GO!
SPLASH

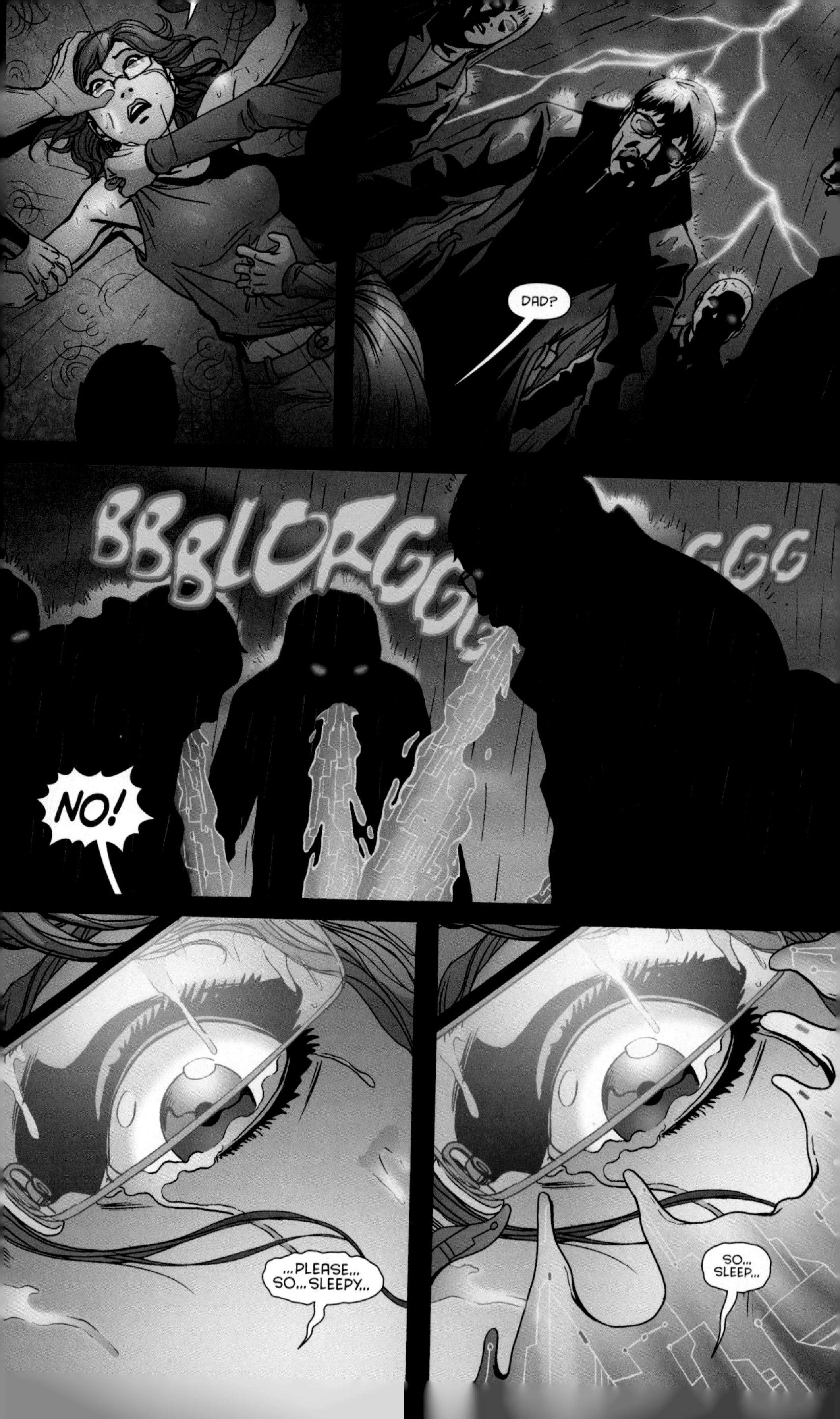
DAD?
BBBLORGGGGGGGG
NO!
...PLEASE... SO... SLEEPY...
SO... SLEEP...

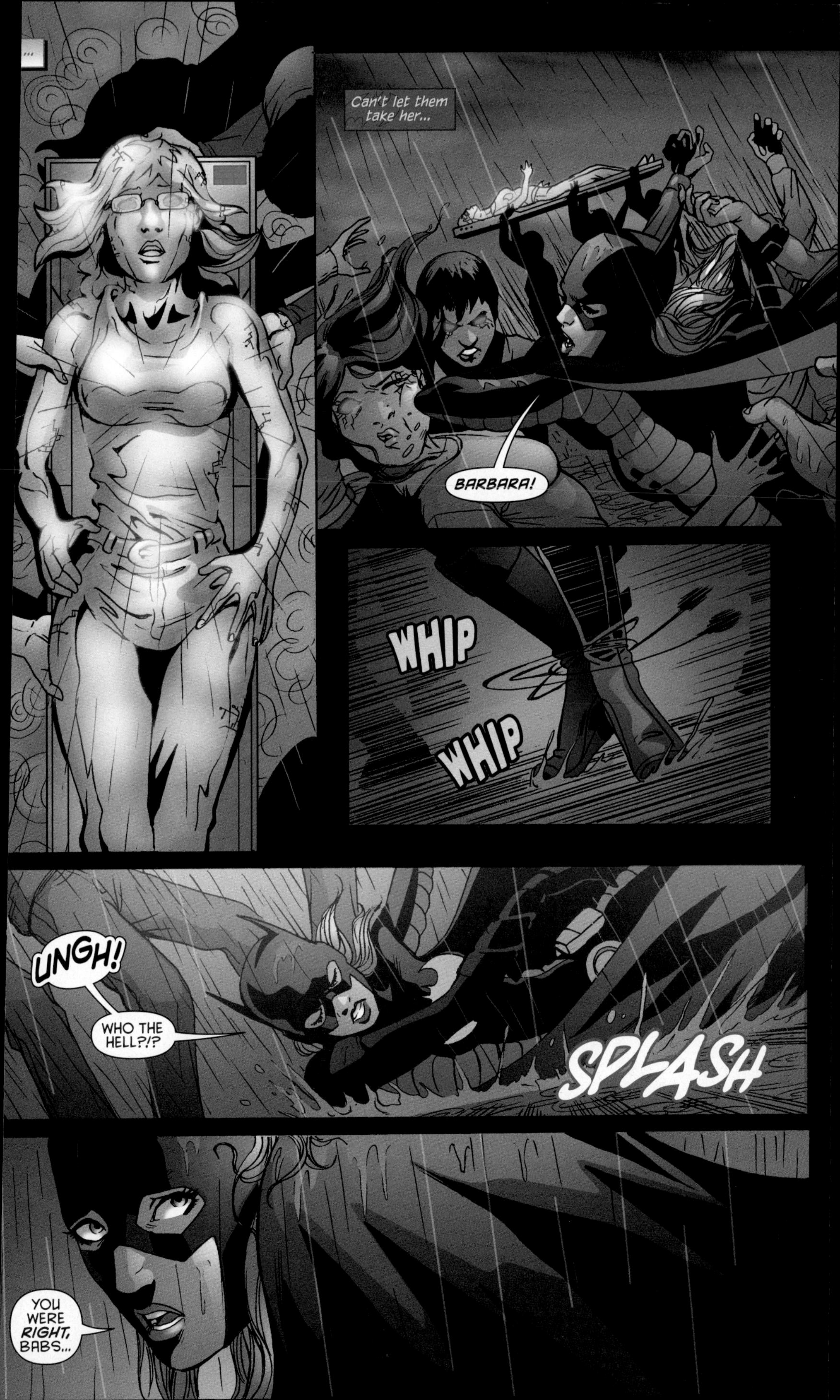
...
Can't let them take her...
BARBARA!
WHIP
WHIP
UNGH!
WHO THE HELL?!?
SPLASH
YOU WERE RIGHT, BABS...

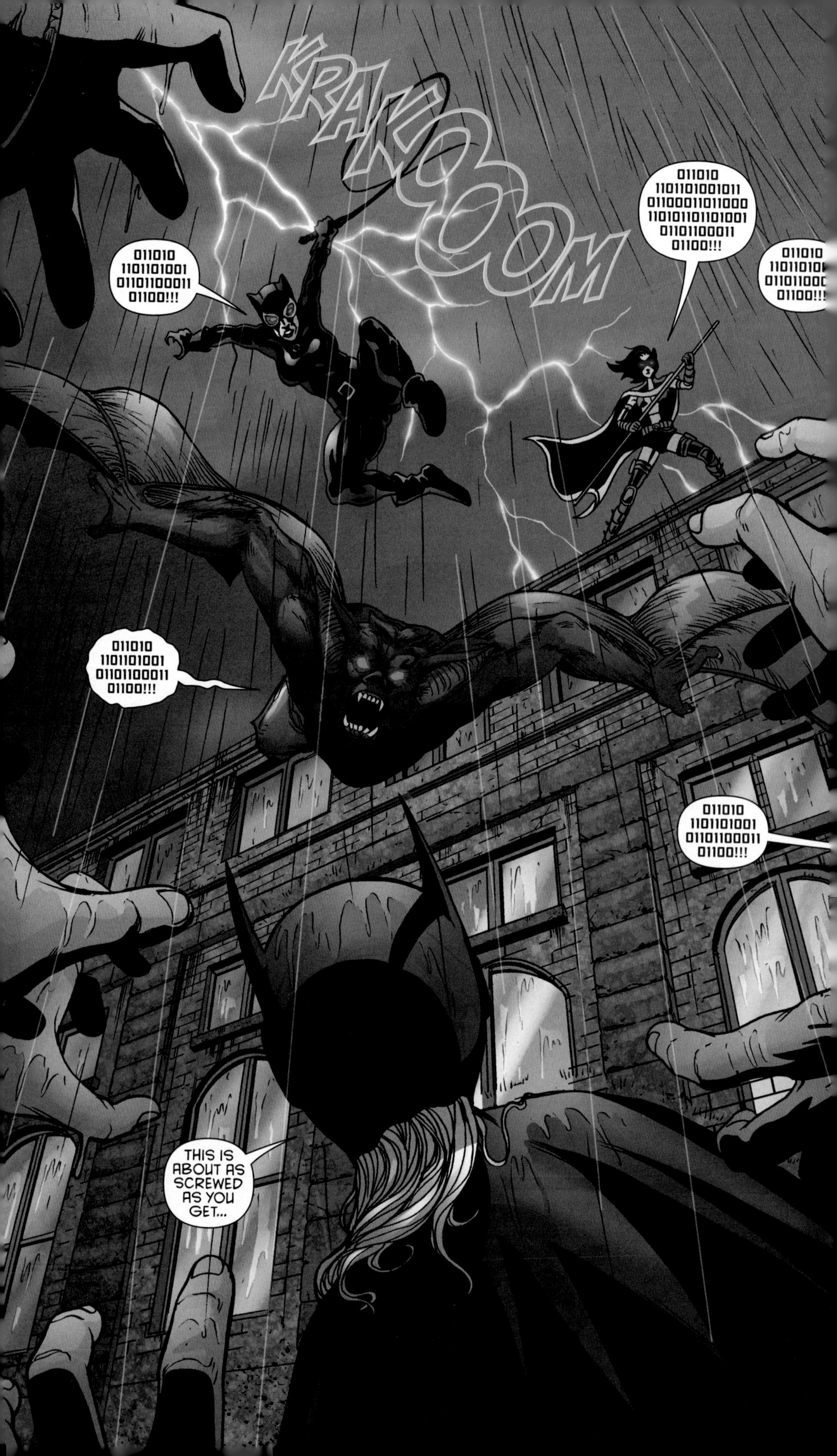
KRAKOOOOM
011010 1101101001 01101100011 01100!!!
011010 1101101001011 01100011011000 11010110110100 01101100011 01100!!!
011010 11011010 01101100 01100!!!
011010 1101101001 01101100011 01100!!!
011010 1101101001 01101100011 01100!!!
THIS IS ABOUT AS SCREWED AS YOU GET...

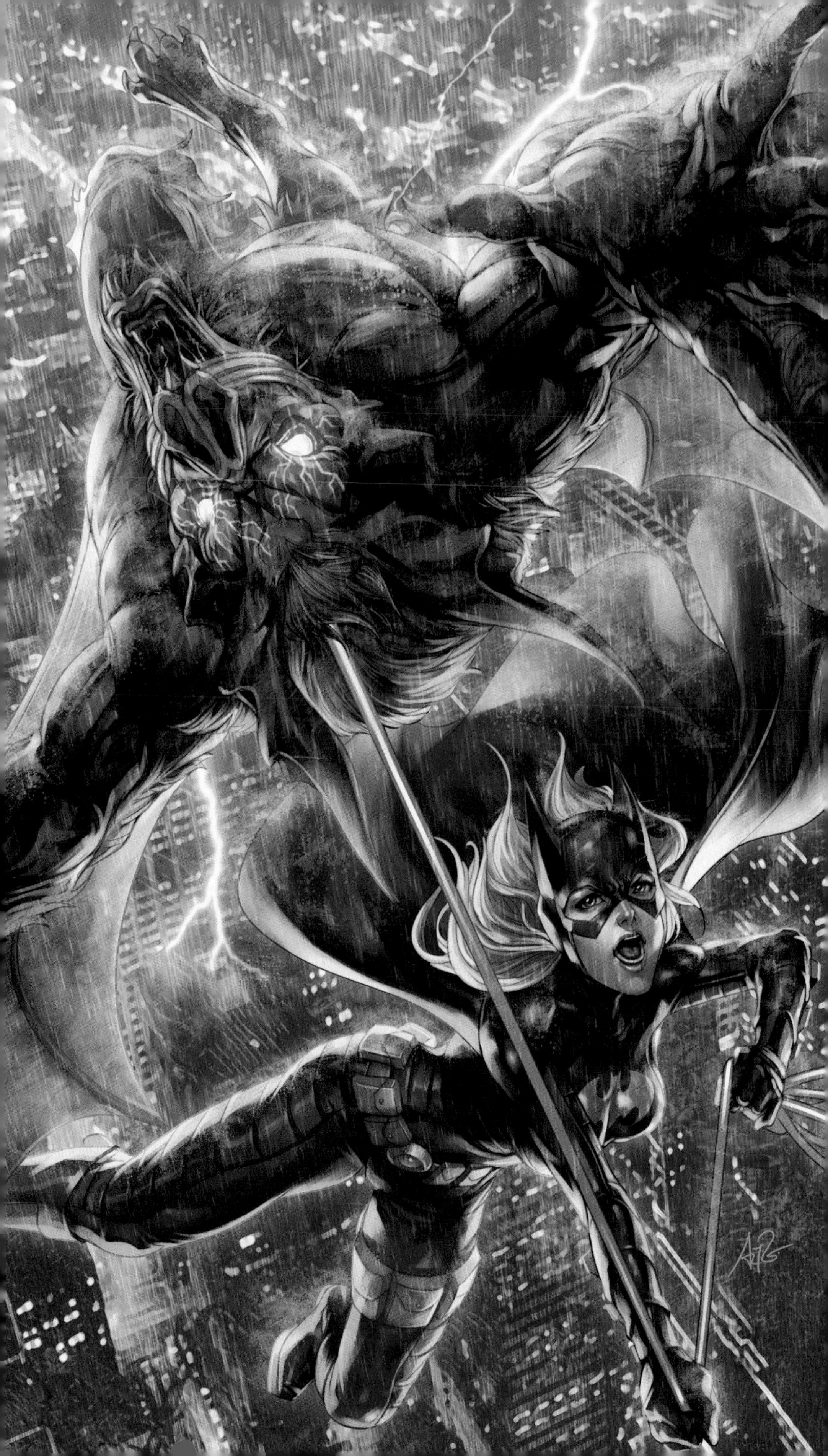

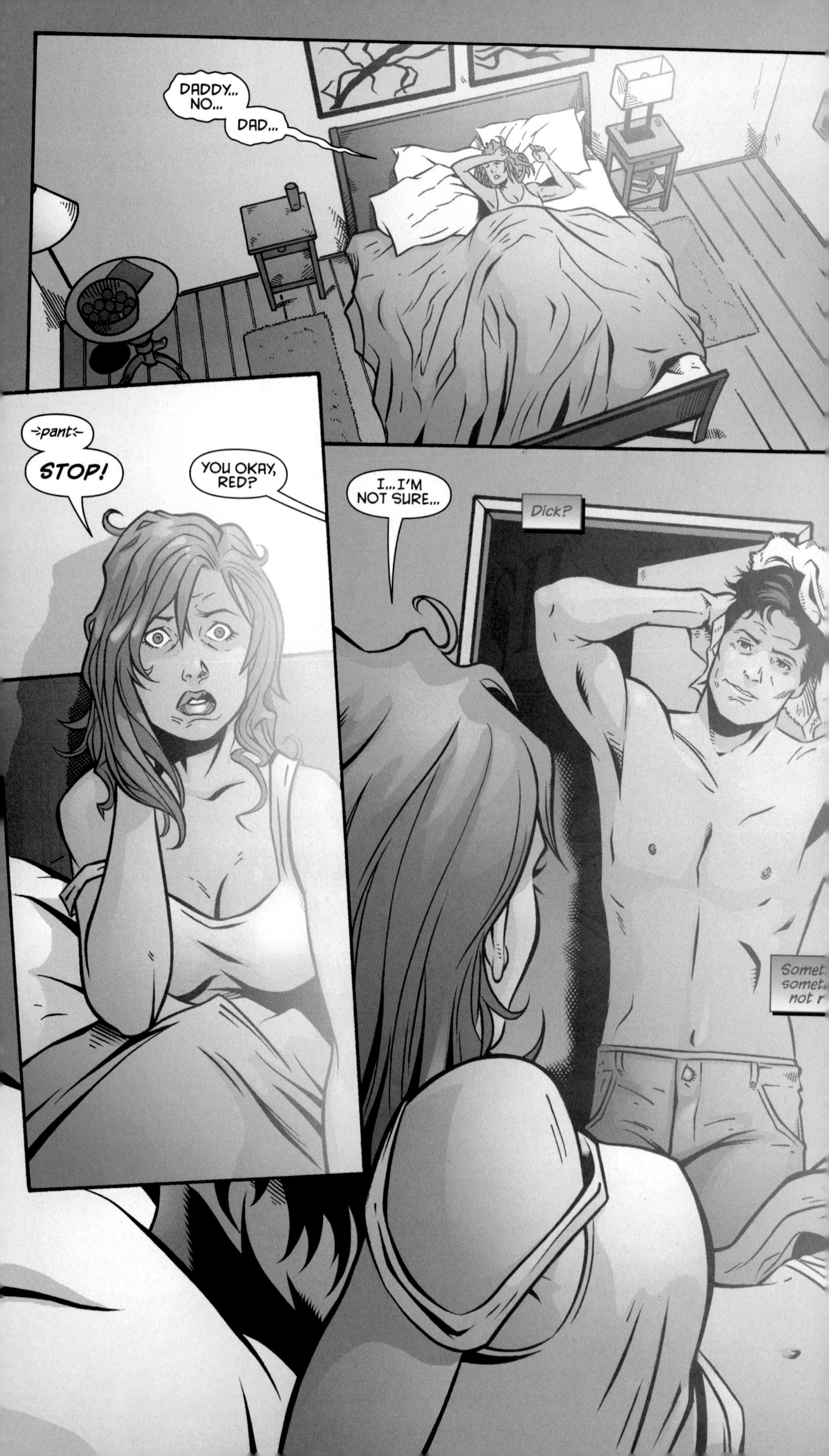

DADDY... NO... DAD...
pant
STOP!
YOU OKAY, RED?
I... I'M NOT SURE...
Dick?

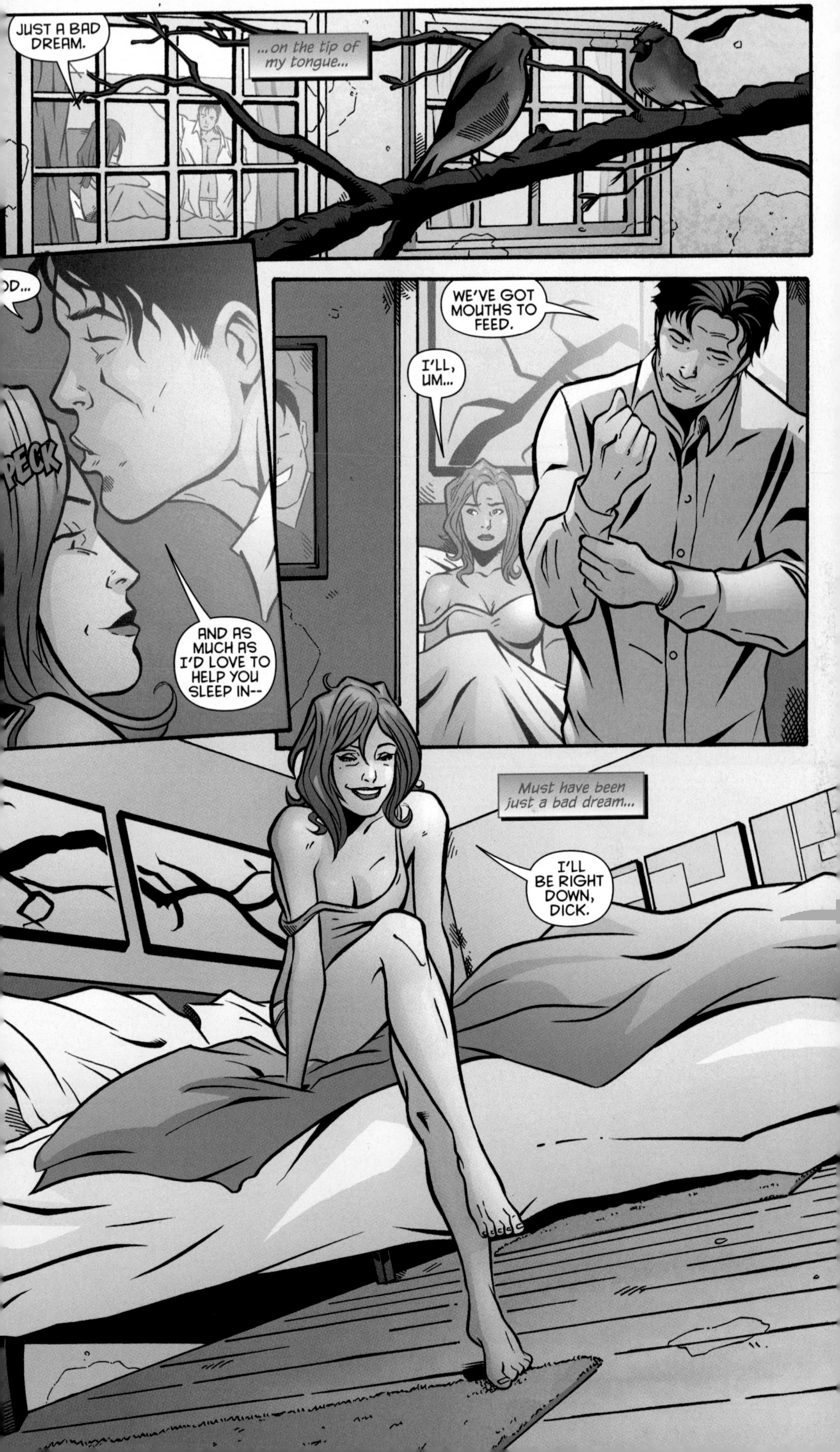
JUST A BAD DREAM.
...on the tip of my tongue...
OD...
PECK
AND AS MUCH AS I'D LOVE TO HELP YOU SLEEP IN--
WE'VE GOT MOUTHS TO FEED.
I'LL, UM...
Must have been just a bad dream...
I'LL BE RIGHT DOWN, DICK.

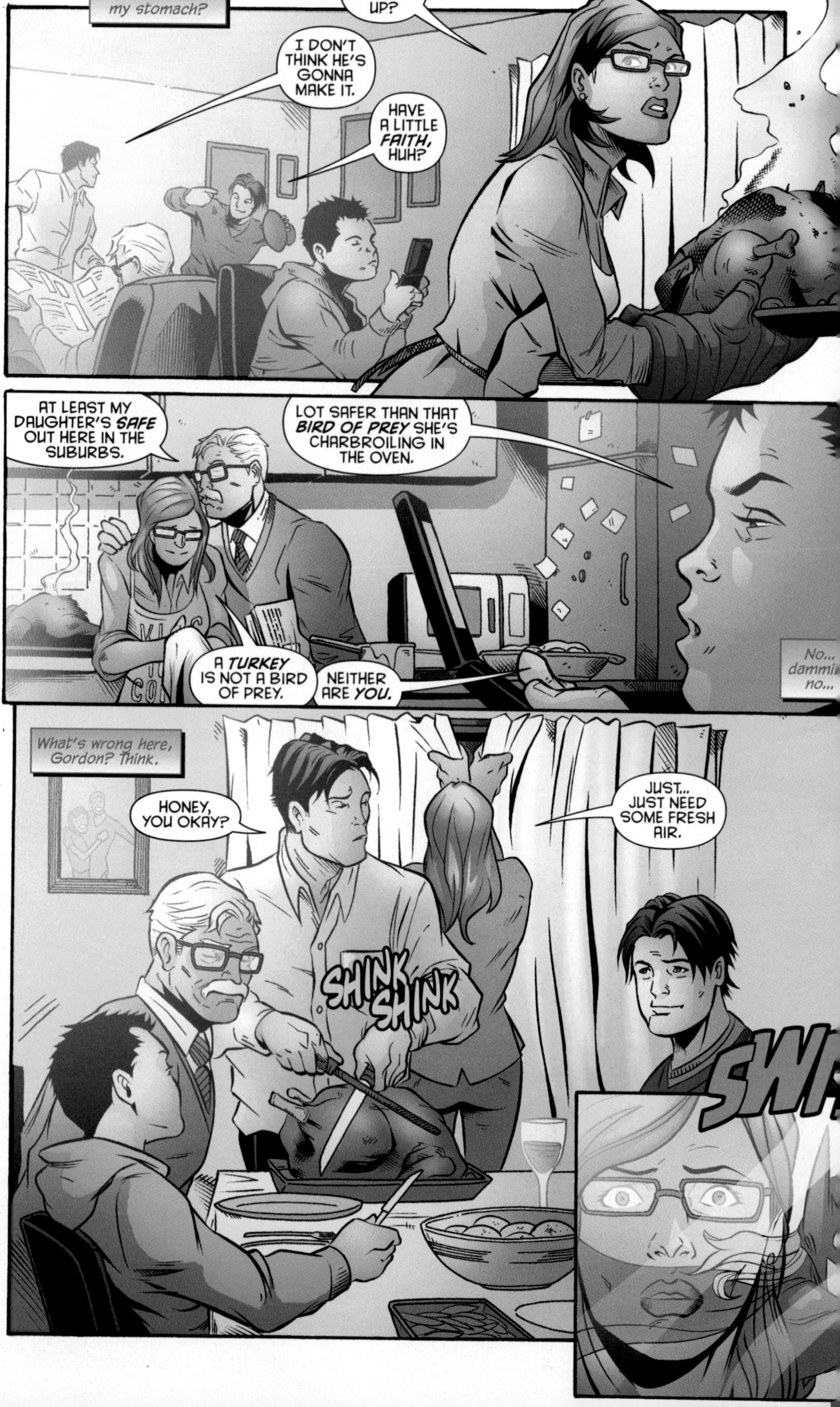

It's all... perfect.
So why do I have this knot in my stomach?
WHEN'S BRUCE SHOWING UP?
I DON'T THINK HE'S GONNA MAKE IT.
HAVE A LITTLE FAITH, HUH?
AT LEAST MY DAUGHTER'S SAFE OUT HERE IN THE SUBURBS.
LOT SAFER THAN THAT BIRD OF PREY SHE'S CHARBROILING IN THE OVEN.
A TURKEY IS NOT A BIRD OF PREY.
NEITHER ARE YOU.
What's wrong here, Gordon? Think.
HONEY, YOU OKAY?
JUST... JUST NEED SOME FRESH AIR.
SHINK SHINK

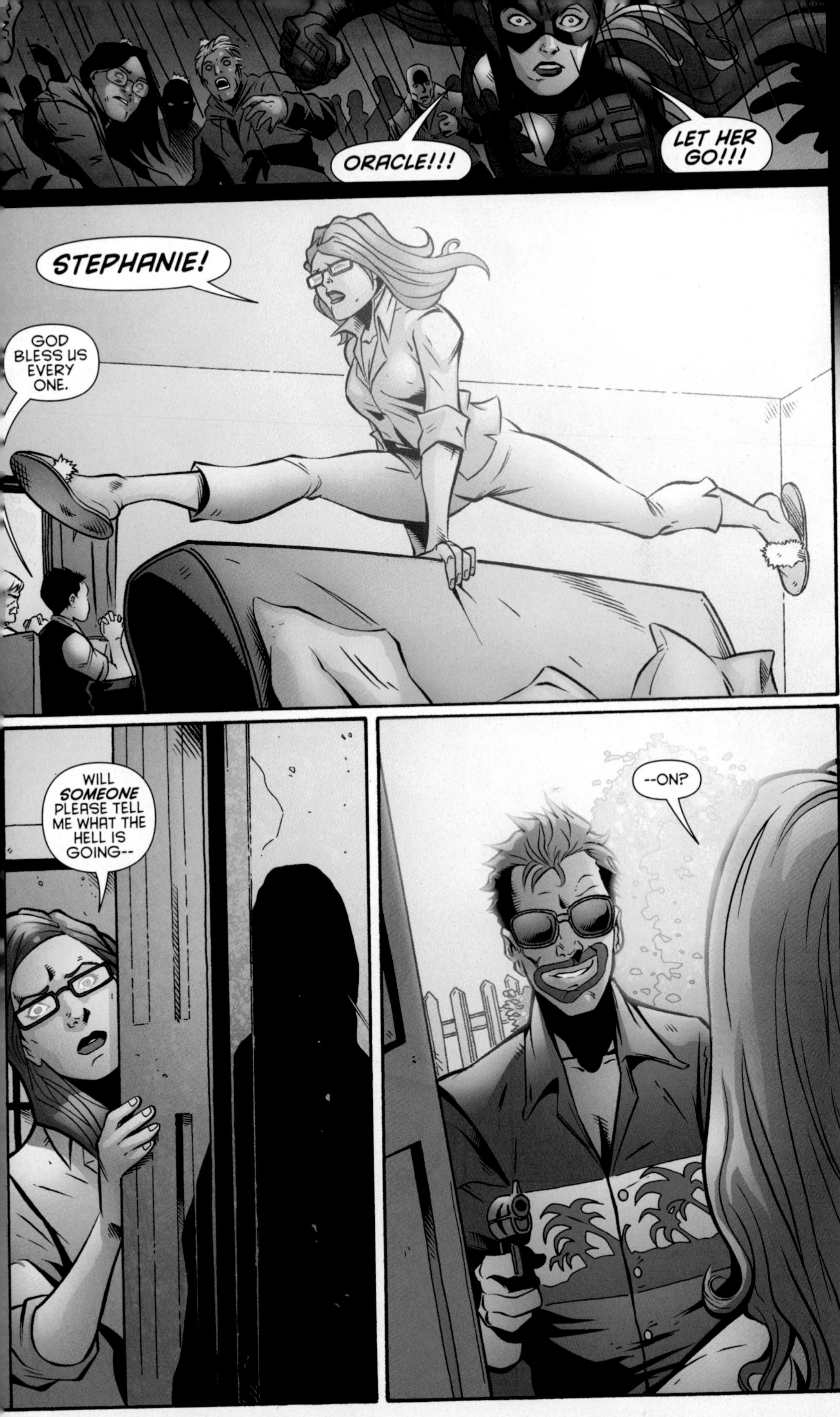
ORACLE!!!
LET HER GO!!!
STEPHANIE!
GOD BLESS US EVERY ONE.
WILL *SOMEONE* PLEASE TELL ME WHAT THE HELL IS GOING--
--ON?

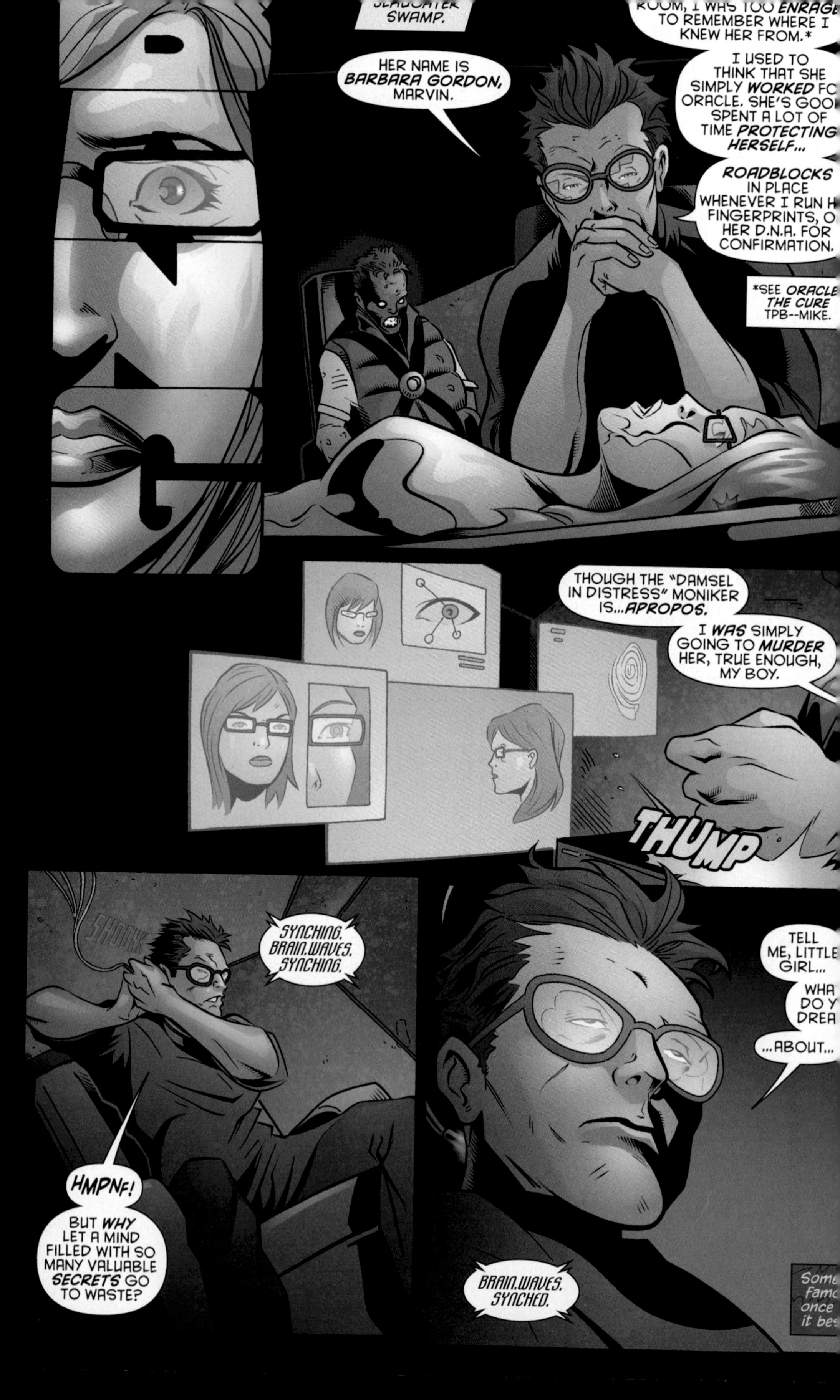
SWAMP.
ROOM, I WAS TOO ENRAGE TO REMEMBER WHERE I KNEW HER FROM.*
HER NAME IS BARBARA GORDON, MARVIN.
I USED TO THINK THAT SHE SIMPLY WORKED FO ORACLE. SHE'S GOO SPENT A LOT OF TIME PROTECTING HERSELF...
ROADBLOCKS IN PLACE WHENEVER I RUN H FINGERPRINTS, O HER D.N.A. FOR CONFIRMATION.
*SEE ORACLE THE CURE TPB--MIKE.
THOUGH THE "DAMSEL IN DISTRESS" MONIKER IS...APROPOS.
I WAS SIMPLY GOING TO MURDER HER, TRUE ENOUGH, MY BOY.
THUMP
SHOOK
SYNCHING. BRAIN.WAVES. SYNCHING.
HMPNF!
BUT WHY LET A MIND FILLED WITH SO MANY VALUABLE SECRETS GO TO WASTE?
TELL ME, LITTLE GIRL...
WHA DO Y DREA
...ABOUT...
BRAIN.WAVES. SYNCHED.
Som fam once it be

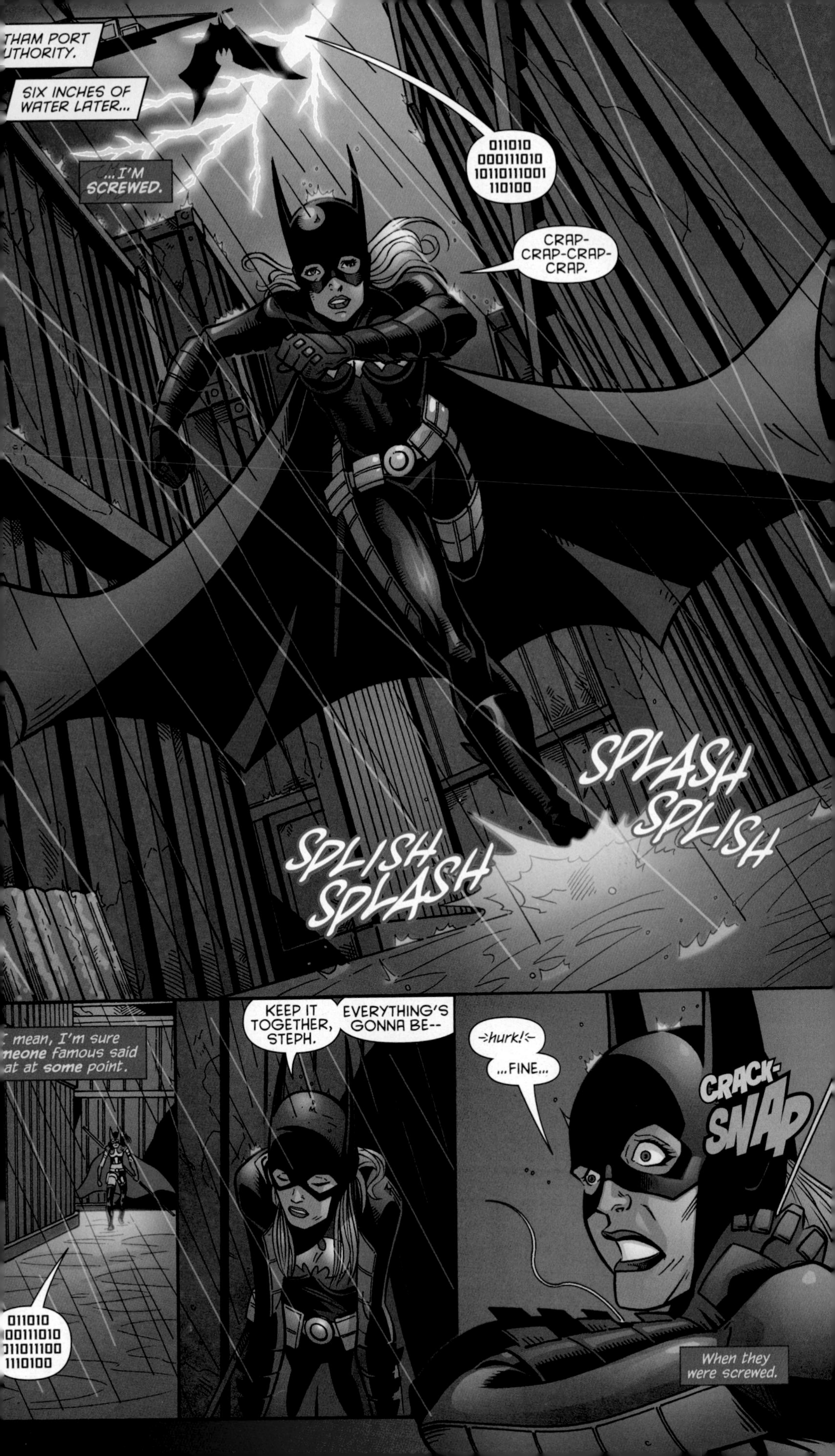

THAM PORT
UTHORITY.
SIX INCHES OF WATER LATER...
...I'M SCREWED.
011010 000111010 10110111001 110100
CRAP-CRAP-CRAP-CRAP.
SPLISH SPLASH
SPLASH SPLISH
I mean, I'm sure
meone famous said
at at some point.
011010 00111010 011011100 1110100
KEEP IT TOGETHER, STEPH.
EVERYTHING'S GONNA BE--
hurk!
...FINE...
CRACK-SNAP
When they were screwed.

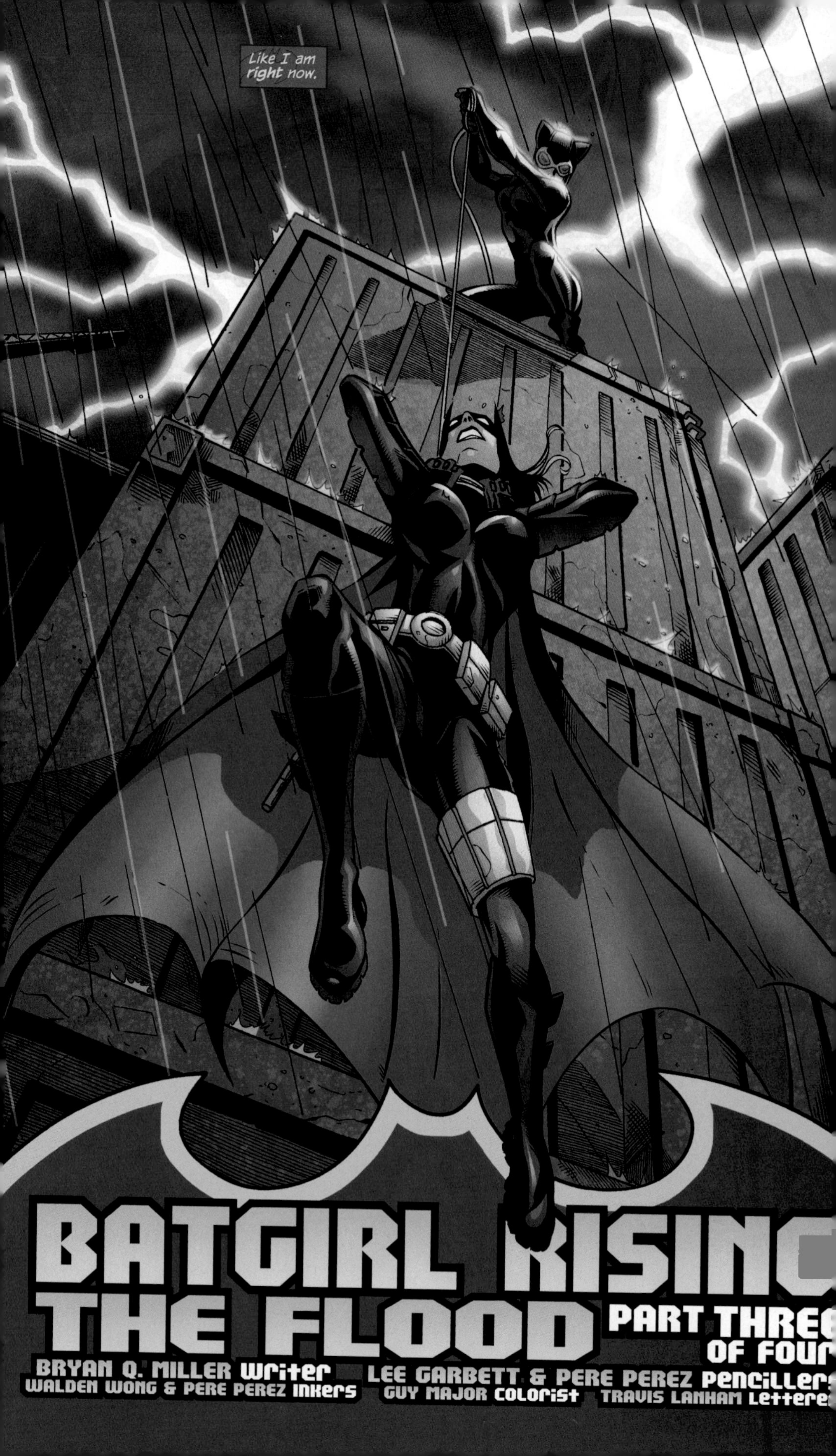
Like I am right now.
BATGIRL RISING
THE FLOOD
PART THREE OF FOUR
BRYAN Q. MILLER Writer
LEE GARBETT & PERE PEREZ Pencillers
WALDEN WONG & PERE PEREZ Inkers
GUY MAJOR Colorist
TRAVIS LANHAM Letterer

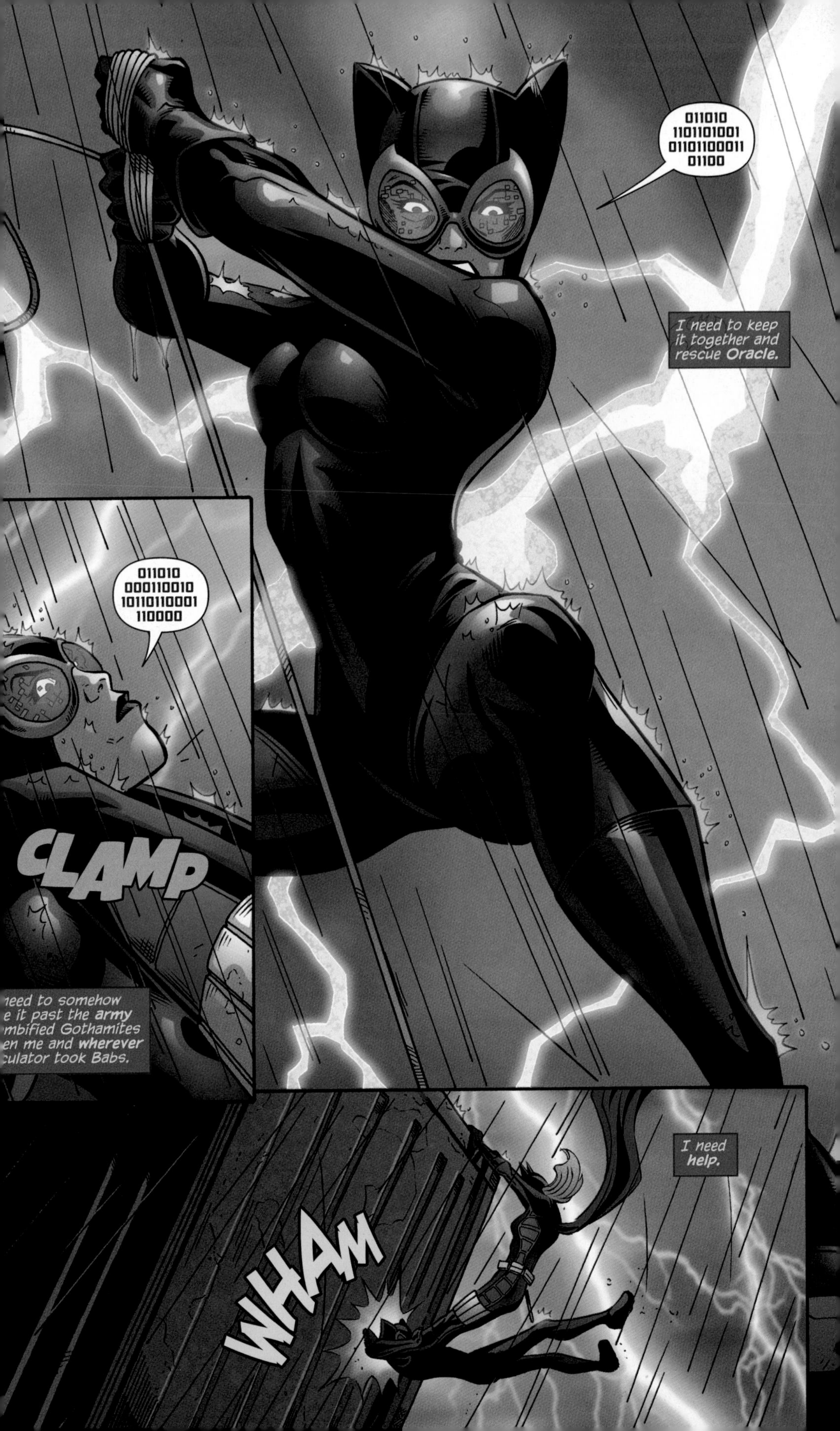

011010 1101101001 01101100011 01100
I need to keep it together and rescue Oracle.
011010 000110010 10110110001 110000
CLAMP
need to somehow e it past the army mbified Gothamites en me and wherever culator took Babs.
I need help.
WHAM

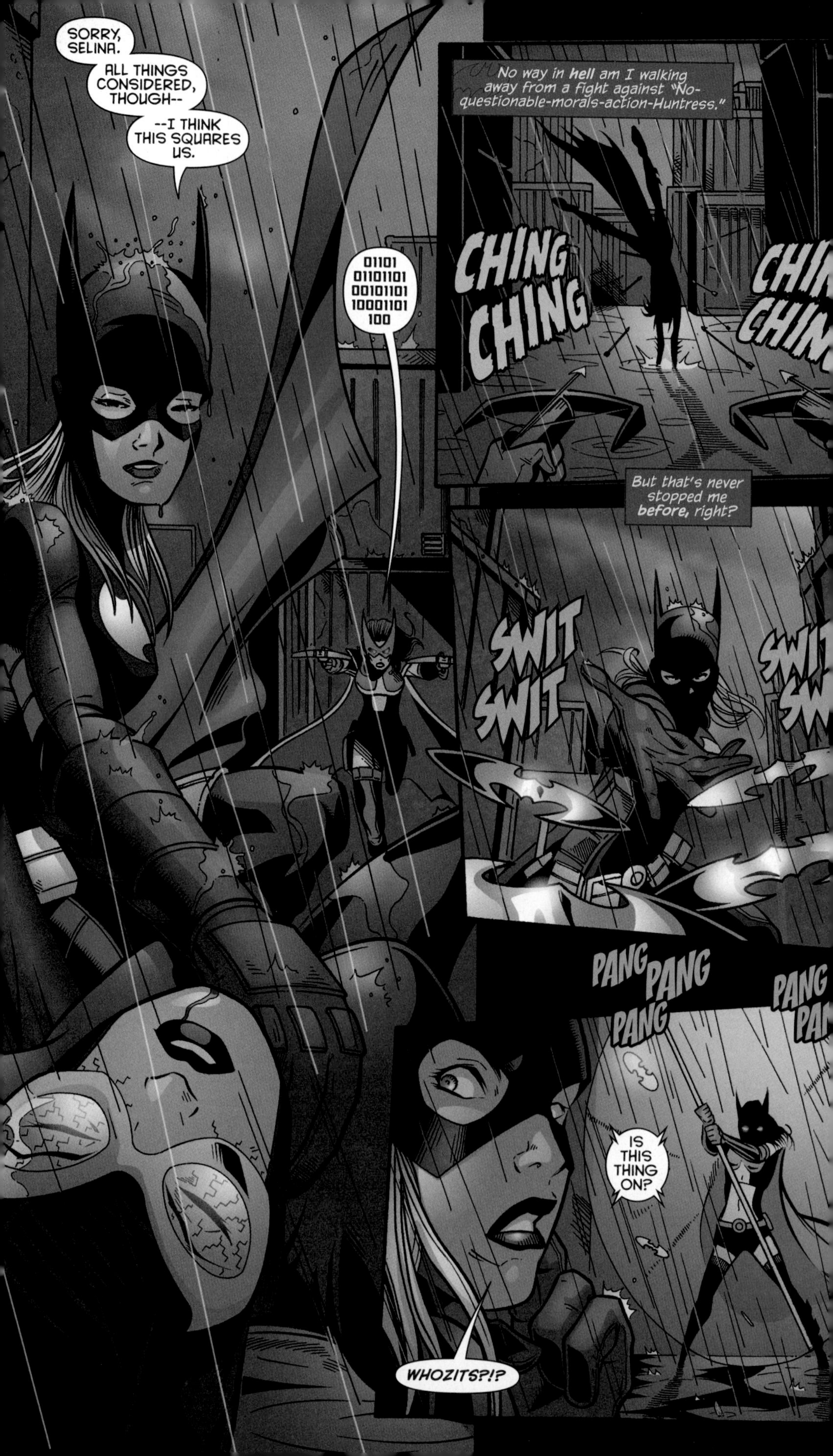

SORRY, SELINA.
ALL THINGS CONSIDERED, THOUGH--
--I THINK THIS SQUARES US.
01101 01101101 00101101 10001101 100
No way in **hell** am I walking away from a fight against "No-questionable-morals-action-Huntress."
CHING CHING
But that's never stopped me **before,** right?
SWIT SWIT
PANG PANG PANG
IS THIS THING ON?
WHOZITS?!?

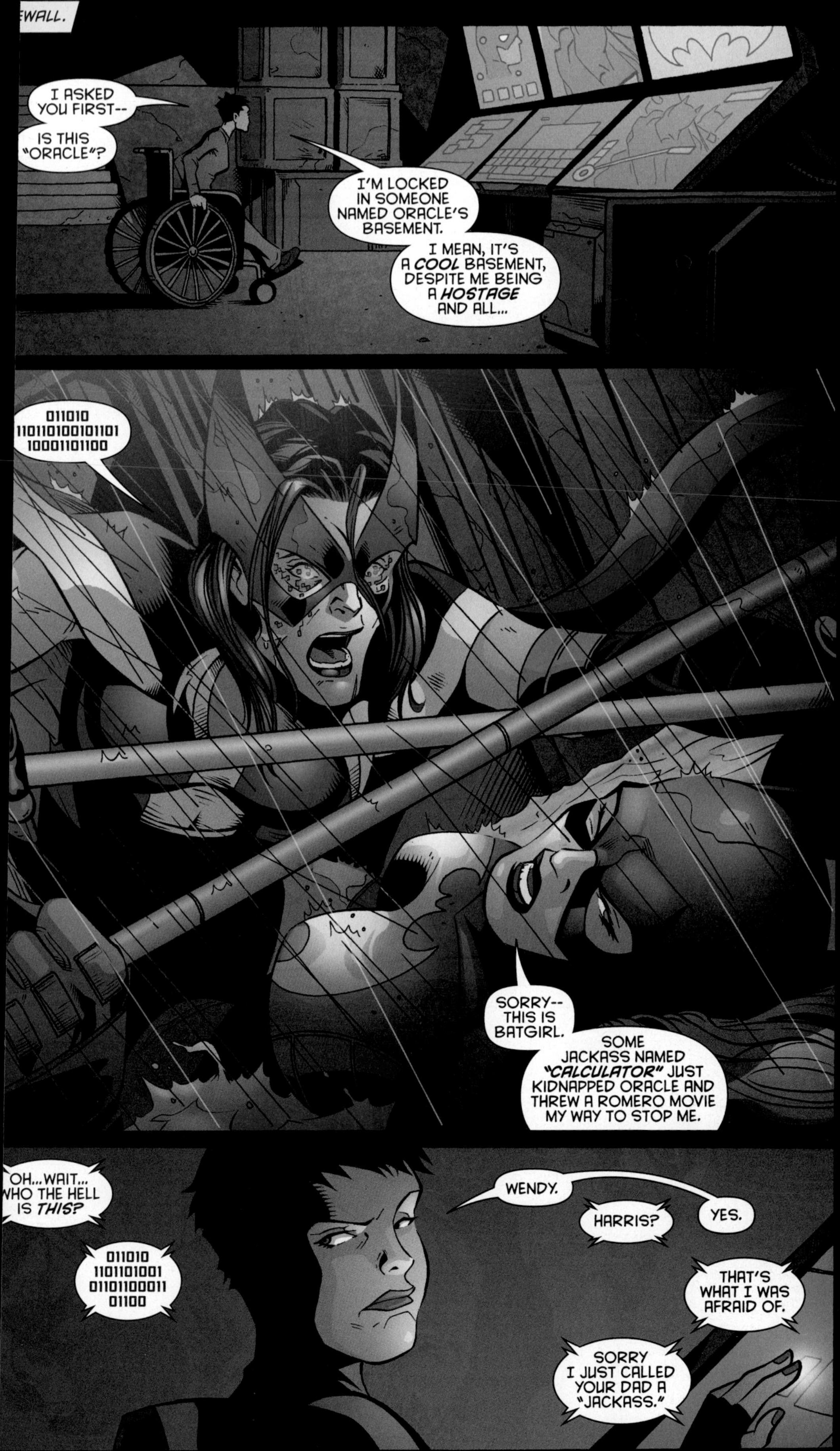
EWALL.
I ASKED YOU FIRST--
IS THIS "ORACLE"?
I'M LOCKED IN SOMEONE NAMED ORACLE'S BASEMENT.
I MEAN, IT'S A COOL BASEMENT, DESPITE ME BEING A HOSTAGE AND ALL...
011010 11011010010110 110001101100
SORRY-- THIS IS BATGIRL.
SOME JACKASS NAMED "CALCULATOR" JUST KIDNAPPED ORACLE AND THREW A ROMERO MOVIE MY WAY TO STOP ME.
OH...WAIT... WHO THE HELL IS THIS?
011010 1101101001 01101100011 01100
WENDY.
HARRIS?
YES.
THAT'S WHAT I WAS AFRAID OF.
SORRY I JUST CALLED YOUR DAD A "JACKASS."

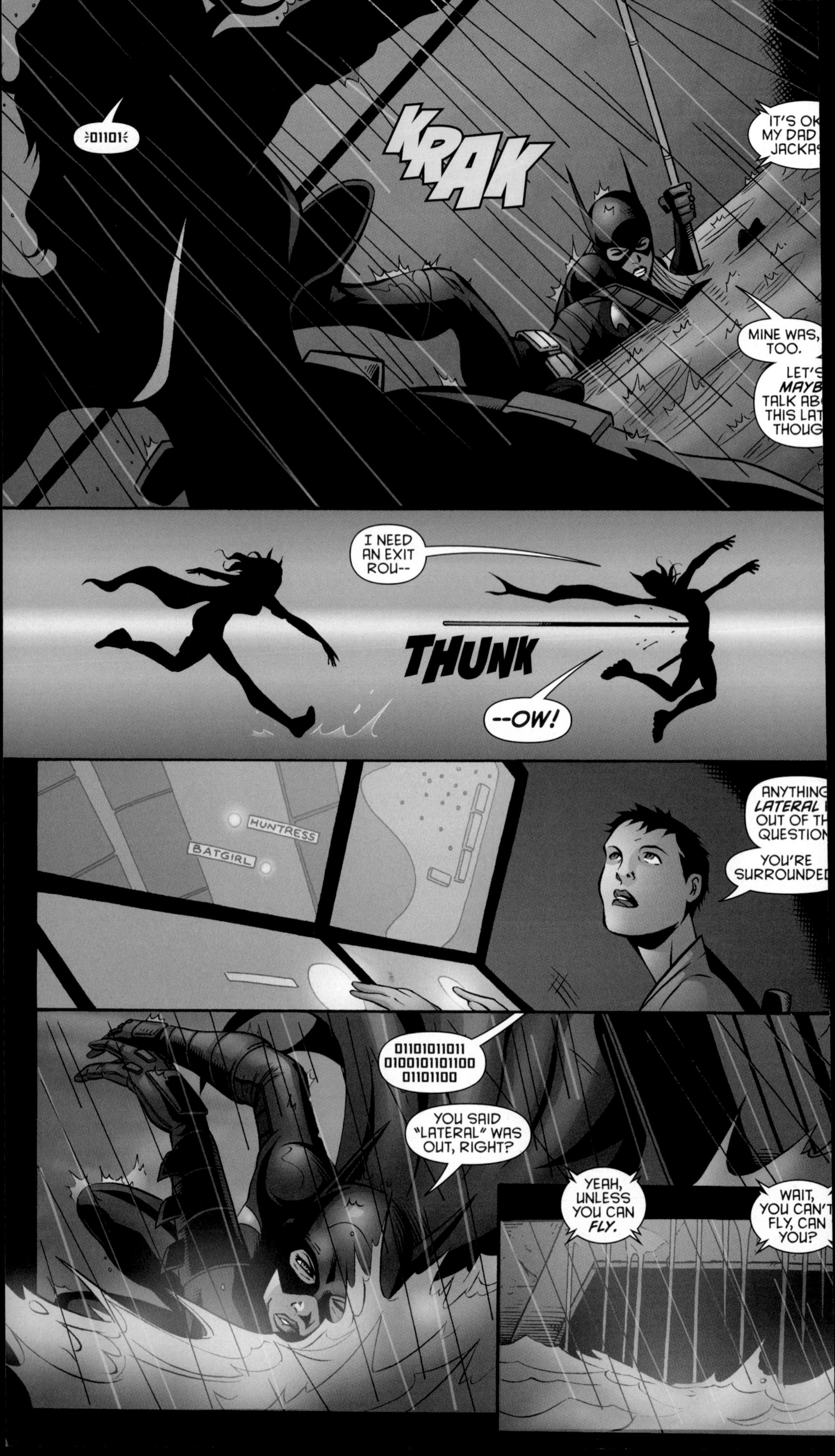
01101
KRAK
IT'S OK MY DAD JACKA
MINE WAS, TOO.
LET'S MAYB TALK AB THIS LAT THOUG
I NEED AN EXIT ROU--
THUNK
--OW!
HUNTRESS
BATGIRL
ANYTHING LATERAL OUT OF TH QUESTION
YOU'RE SURROUNDED
01101011011 0100101101100 01101100
YOU SAID "LATERAL" WAS OUT, RIGHT?
YEAH, UNLESS YOU CAN FLY.
WAIT, YOU CAN'T FLY, CAN YOU?

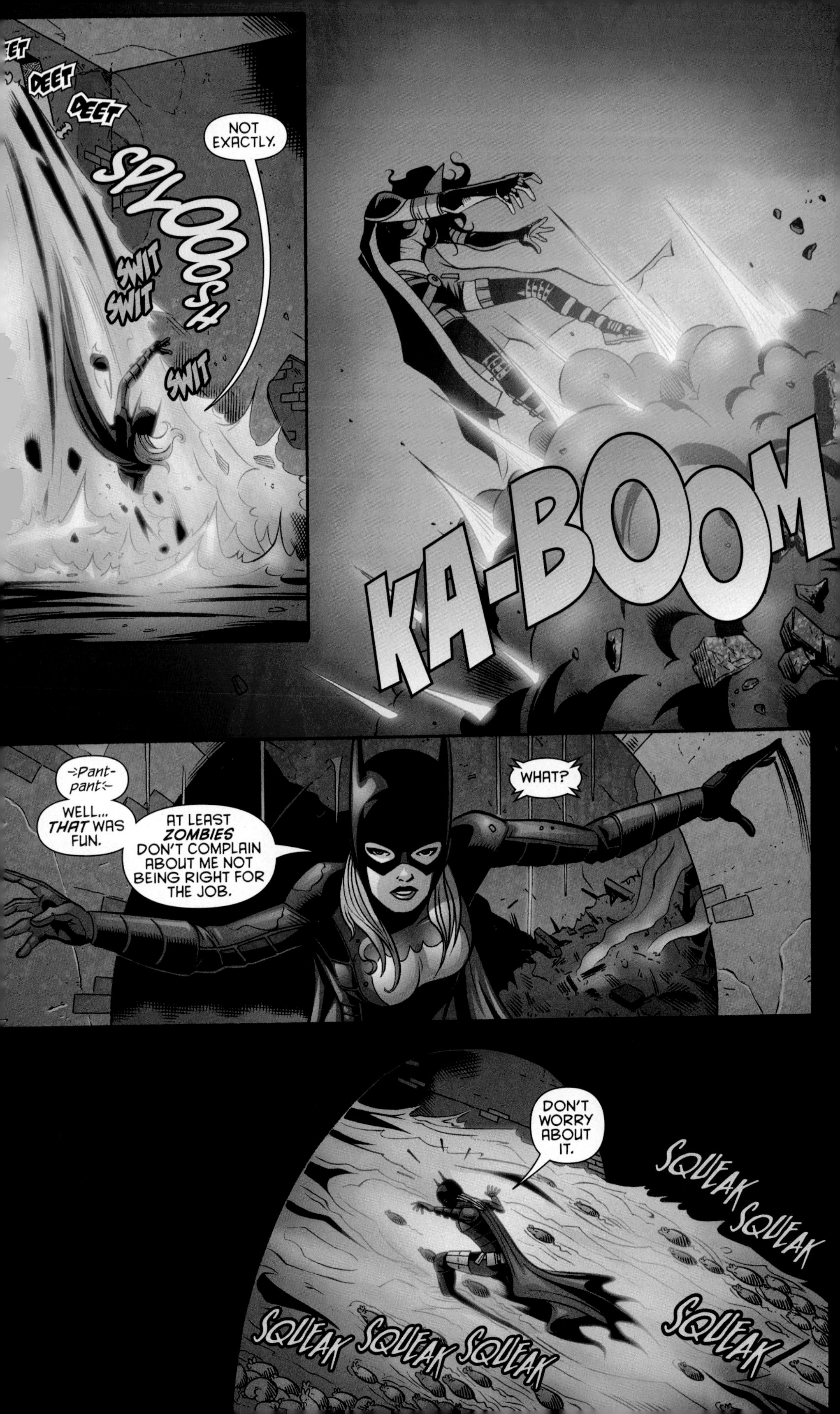

EET
DEET
DEET
NOT EXACTLY.
SPLOOOSH
SWIT SWIT
SWIT
KA-BOOM
>Pant-pant<
WELL... THAT WAS FUN.
AT LEAST ZOMBIES DON'T COMPLAIN ABOUT ME NOT BEING RIGHT FOR THE JOB.
WHAT?
DON'T WORRY ABOUT IT.
SQUEAK SQUEAK
SQUEAK SQUEAK SQUEAK
SQUEAK

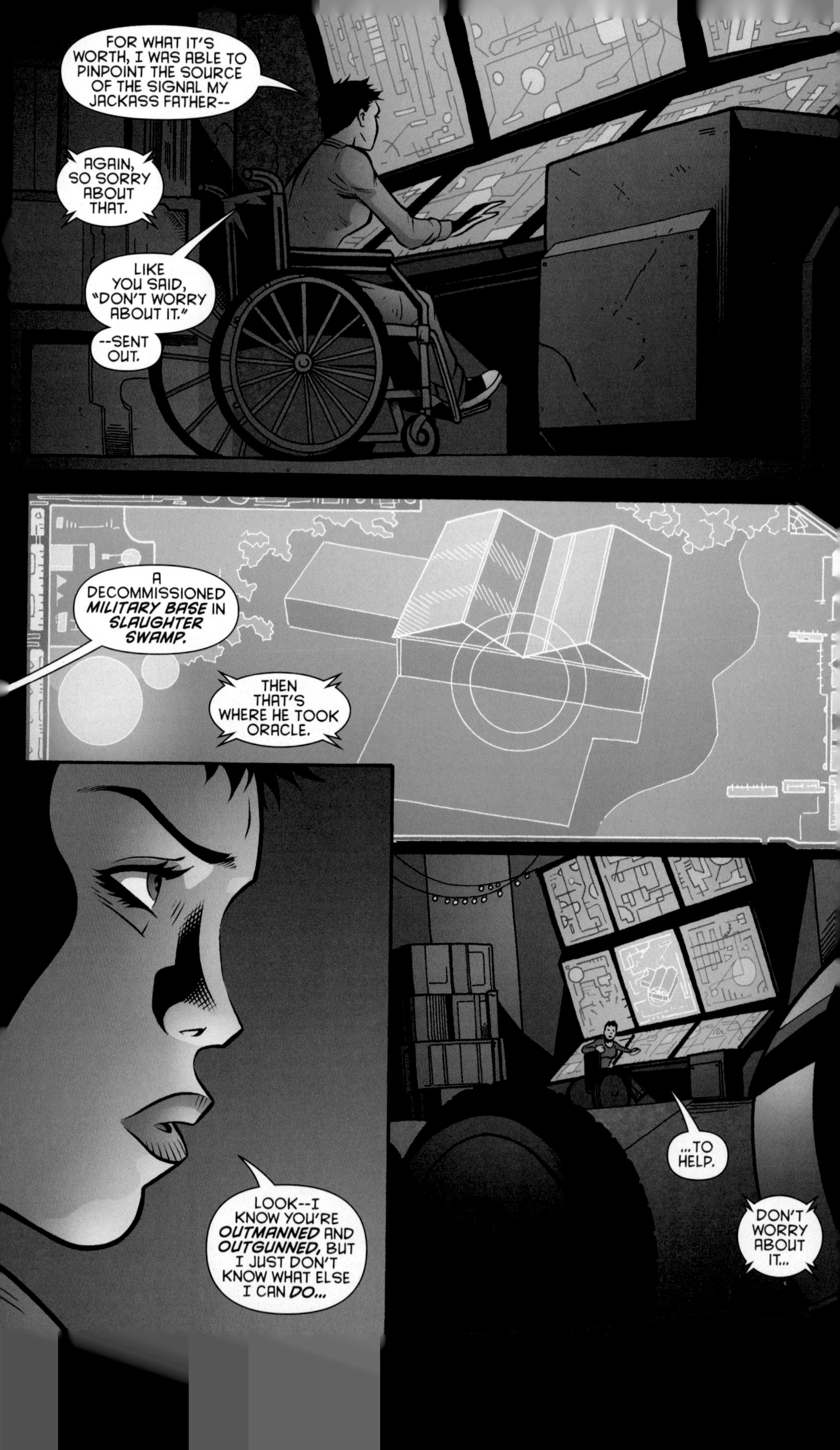
FOR WHAT IT'S WORTH, I WAS ABLE TO PINPOINT THE SOURCE OF THE SIGNAL MY JACKASS FATHER--
AGAIN, SO SORRY ABOUT THAT.
LIKE YOU SAID, "DON'T WORRY ABOUT IT."
--SENT OUT.
A DECOMMISSIONED *MILITARY BASE* IN *SLAUGHTER SWAMP.*
THEN THAT'S WHERE HE TOOK ORACLE.
LOOK--I KNOW YOU'RE *OUTMANNED* AND *OUTGUNNED,* BUT I JUST DON'T KNOW WHAT ELSE I CAN *DO*...
...TO HELP.
DON'T WORRY ABOUT IT...

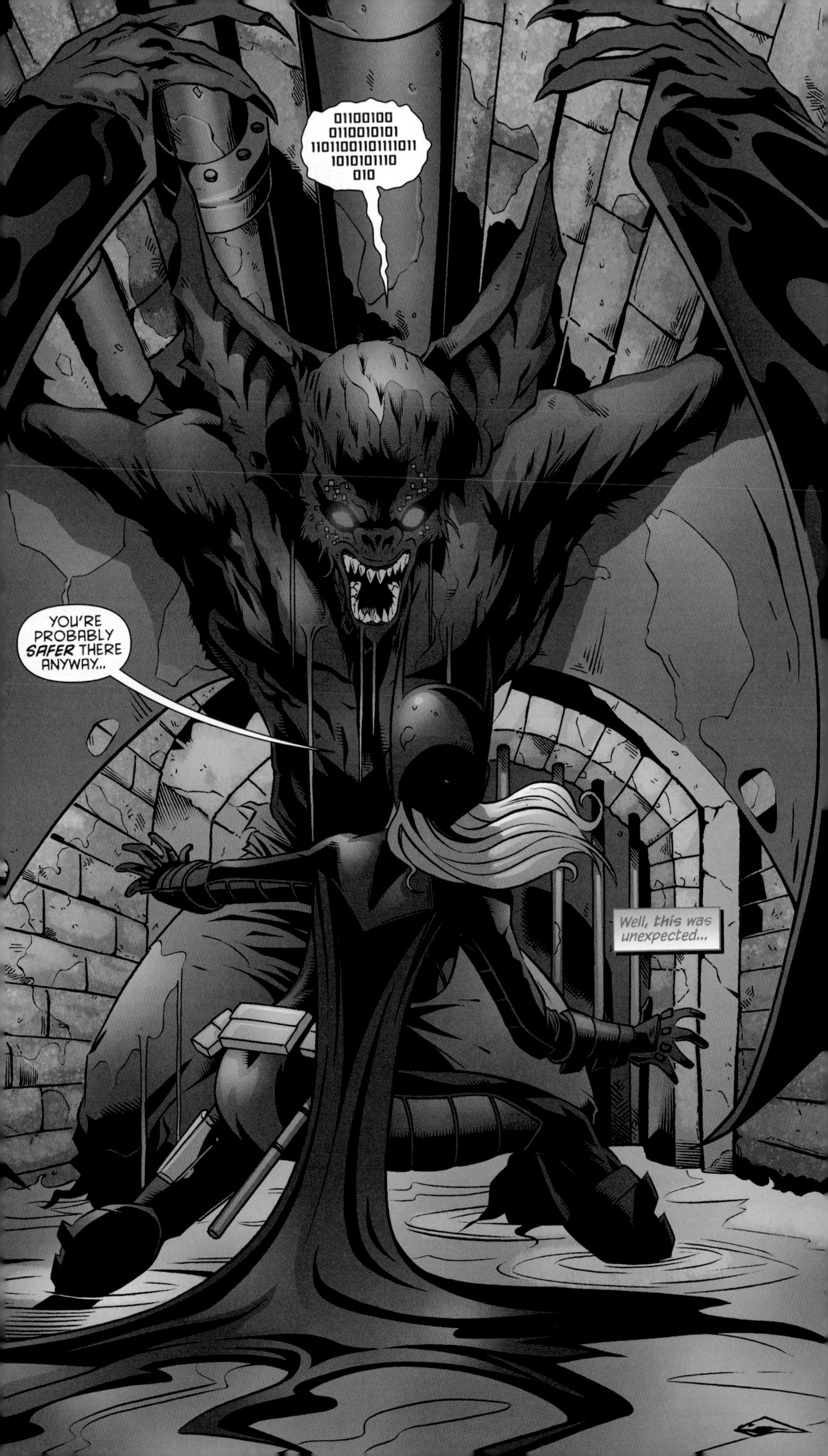

01100100 0110010101 11011001101111011 1010101110 010
YOU'RE PROBABLY SAFER THERE ANYWAY...
Well, this was unexpected...

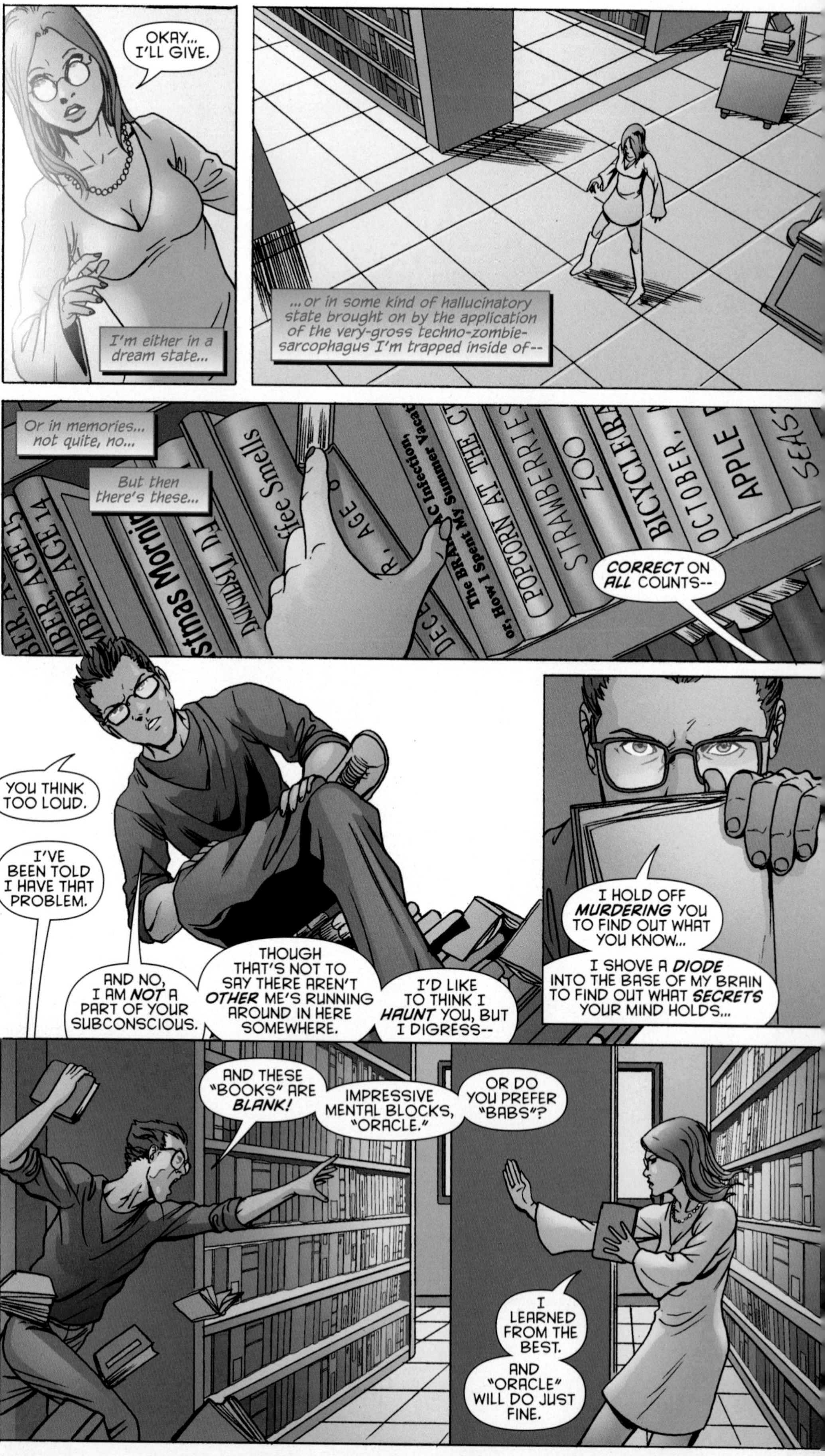

OKAY... I'LL GIVE.
I'm either in a dream state...
...or in some kind of hallucinatory state brought on by the application of the very-gross techno-zombie-sarcophagus I'm trapped inside of--
Or in memories... not quite, no...
But then there's these...
ZOO
OCTOBER
APPLE
CORRECT ON ALL COUNTS--
YOU THINK TOO LOUD.
I'VE BEEN TOLD I HAVE THAT PROBLEM.
AND NO, I AM NOT A PART OF YOUR SUBCONSCIOUS.
THOUGH THAT'S NOT TO SAY THERE AREN'T OTHER ME'S RUNNING AROUND IN HERE SOMEWHERE.
I'D LIKE TO THINK I HAUNT YOU, BUT I DIGRESS--
I HOLD OFF MURDERING YOU TO FIND OUT WHAT YOU KNOW...
I SHOVE A DIODE INTO THE BASE OF MY BRAIN TO FIND OUT WHAT SECRETS YOUR MIND HOLDS...
AND THESE "BOOKS" ARE BLANK!
IMPRESSIVE MENTAL BLOCKS, "ORACLE."
OR DO YOU PREFER "BABS"?
I LEARNED FROM THE BEST.
AND "ORACLE" WILL DO JUST FINE.

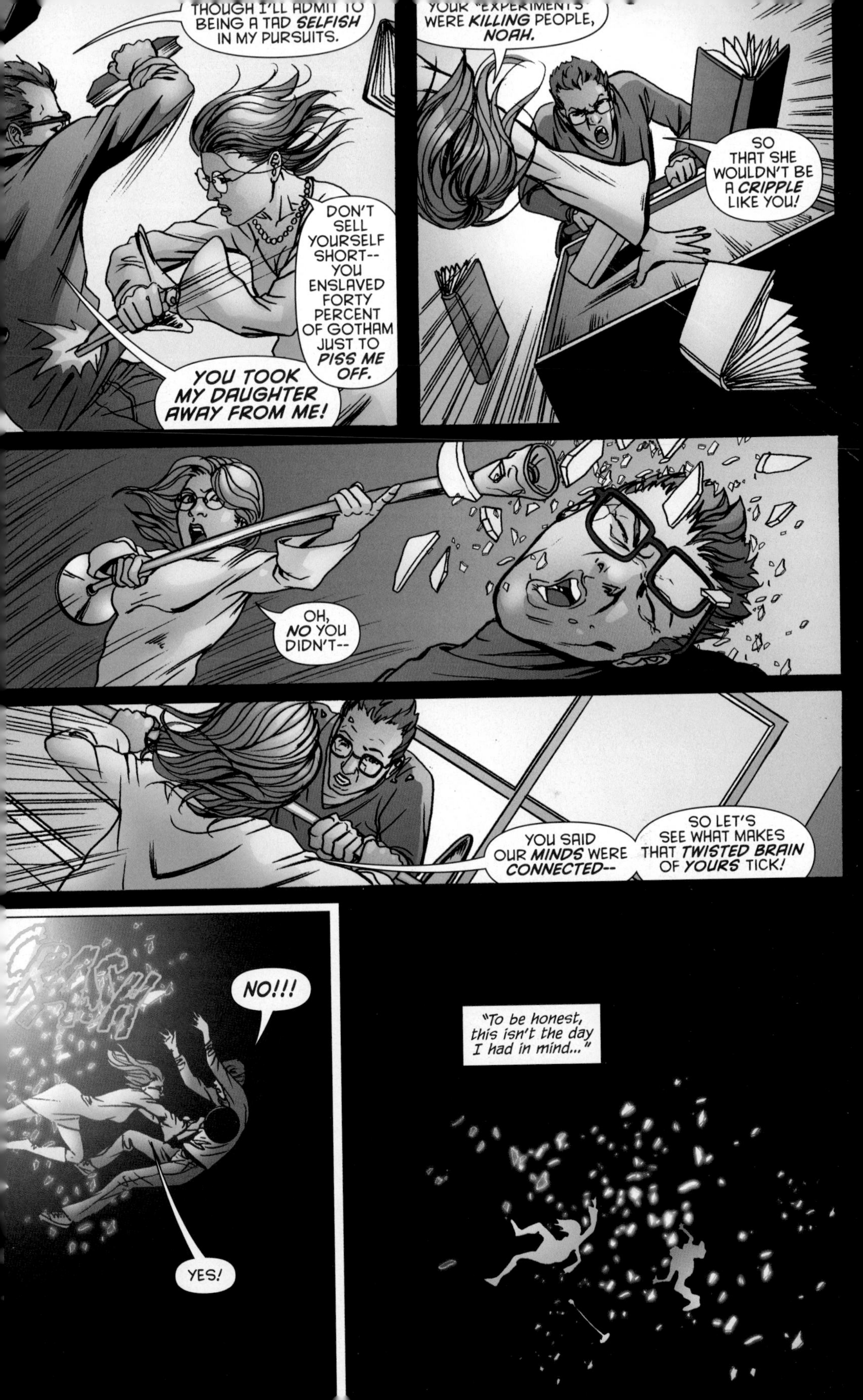
THOUGH I'LL ADMIT TO BEING A TAD *SELFISH* IN MY PURSUITS.
DON'T SELL YOURSELF SHORT-- YOU ENSLAVED FORTY PERCENT OF GOTHAM JUST TO *PISS ME OFF.*
YOU TOOK MY DAUGHTER AWAY FROM ME!
YOUR "EXPERIMENTS" WERE *KILLING* PEOPLE, *NOAH.*
SO THAT SHE WOULDN'T BE A *CRIPPLE* LIKE YOU!
OH, *NO* YOU DIDN'T--
YOU SAID OUR *MINDS* WERE *CONNECTED--*
SO LET'S SEE WHAT MAKES THAT *TWISTED BRAIN* OF *YOURS* TICK!
NO!!!
YES!
"To be honest, this isn't the day I had in mind..."

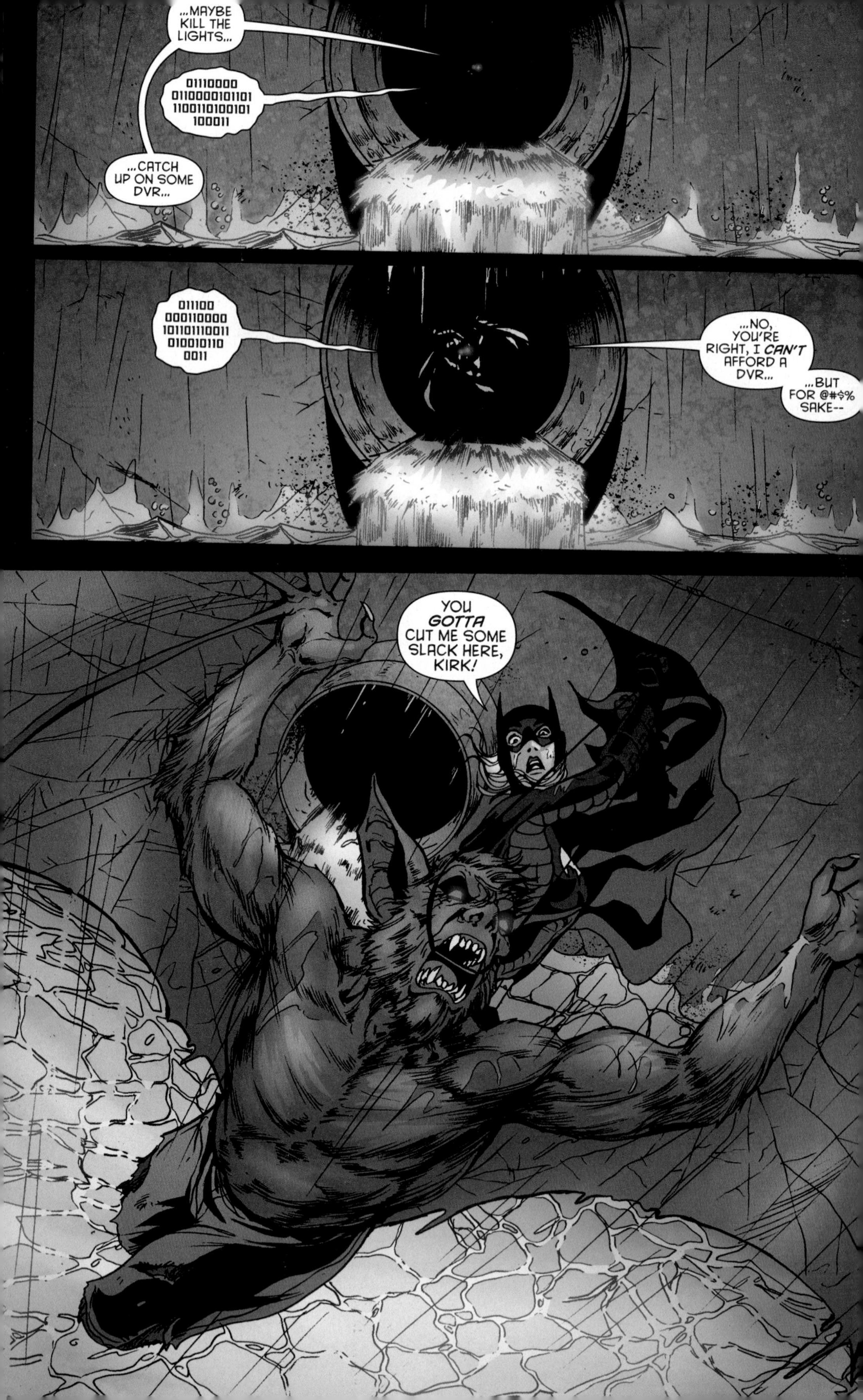
...MAYBE KILL THE LIGHTS...
01110000 0110000101101 1100110100101 100011
...CATCH UP ON SOME DVR...
011100 000110000 101101110011 010010110 0011
...NO, YOU'RE RIGHT, I *CAN'T* AFFORD A DVR...
...BUT FOR @#$% SAKE--
YOU *GOTTA* CUT ME SOME SLACK HERE, KIRK!

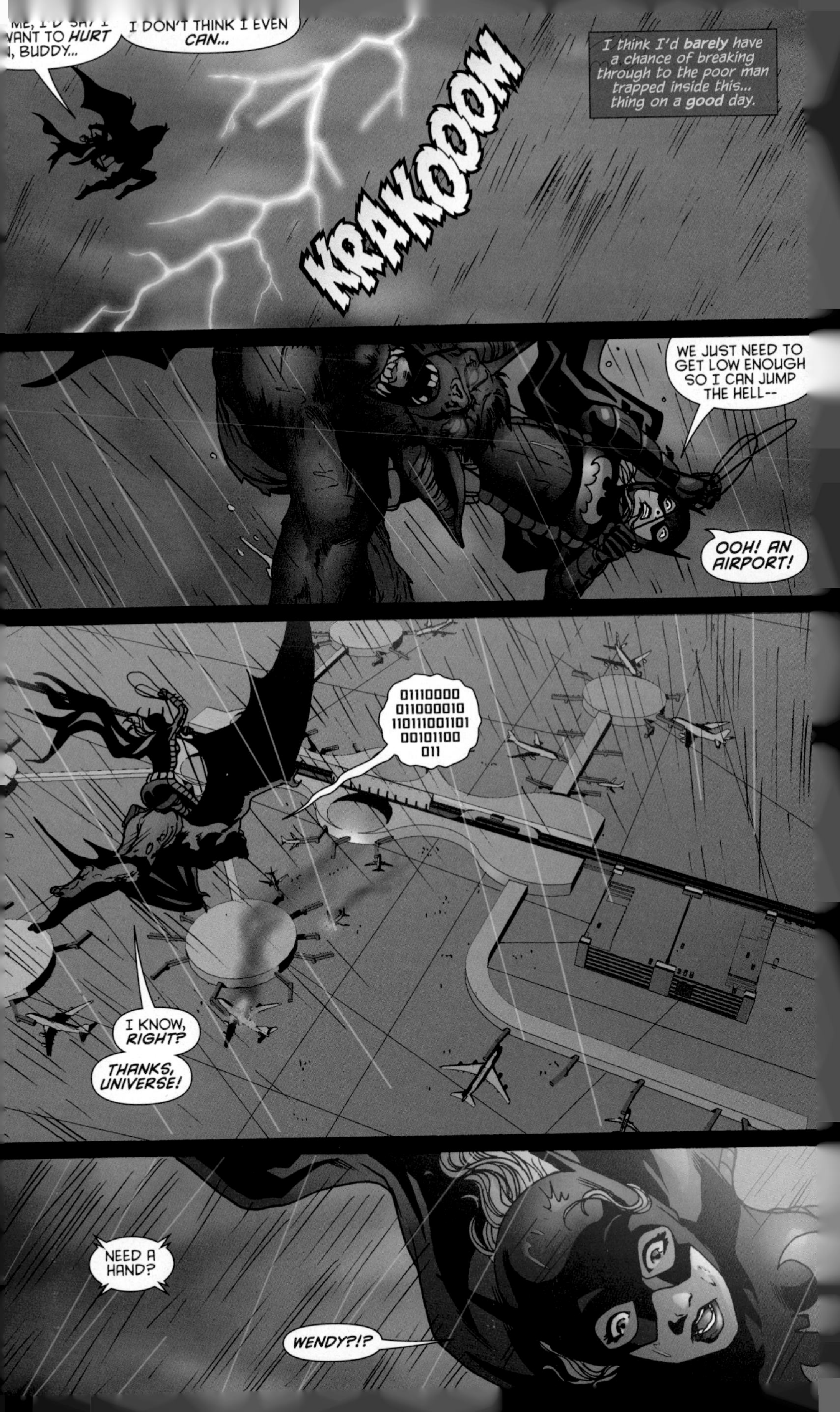
TO *HURT* BUDDY...
I DON'T THINK I EVEN *CAN*...
I think I'd **barely** have a chance of breaking through to the poor man trapped inside this... thing on a **good** day.
KRAKOOOM
WE JUST NEED TO GET LOW ENOUGH SO I CAN JUMP THE HELL--
OOH! AN AIRPORT!
01110000 011000010 110111001101 00101100 011
I KNOW, *RIGHT?*
THANKS, UNIVERSE!
NEED A HAND?
WENDY?!?

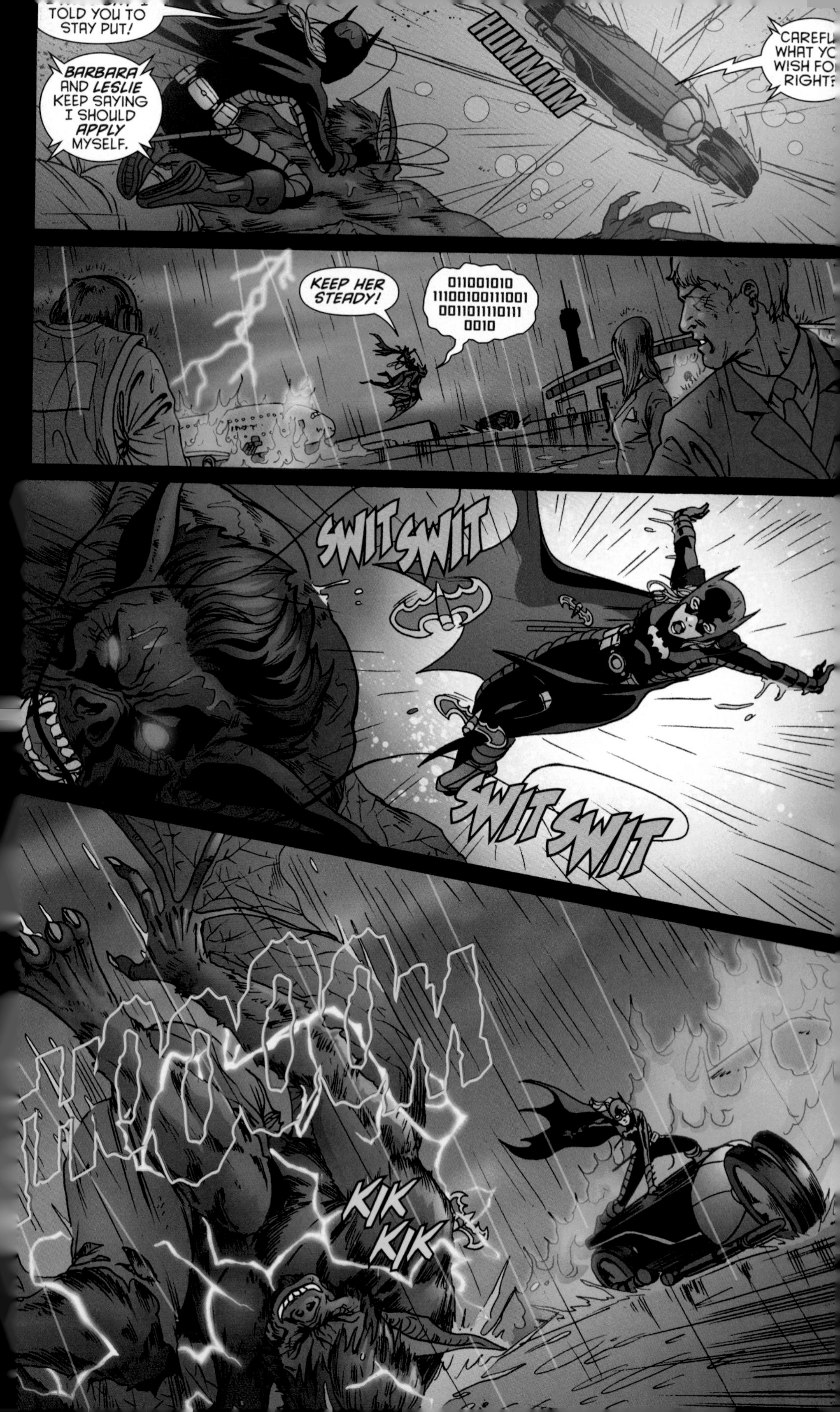
TOLD YOU TO STAY PUT!
BARBARA AND LESLIE KEEP SAYING I SHOULD APPLY MYSELF.
HUMMMMM
CAREFU WHAT YO WISH FO RIGHT?
KEEP HER STEADY!
011001010 11100100111001 0011011110111 0010
SWIT SWIT
SWIT SWIT
KKOOOOM
KIK KIK

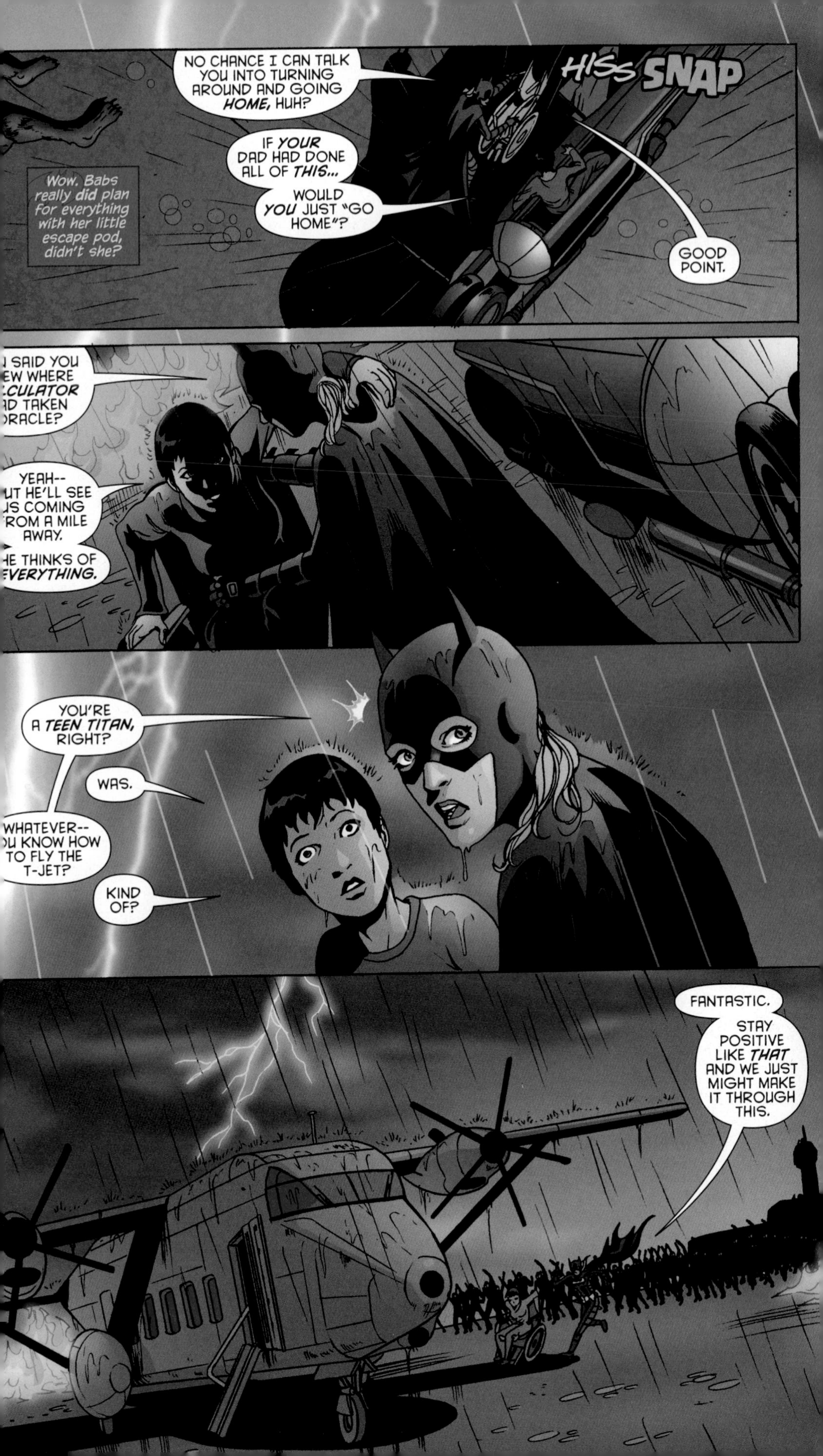

NO CHANCE I CAN TALK YOU INTO TURNING AROUND AND GOING *HOME*, HUH?
HISS SNAP
IF *YOUR* DAD HAD DONE ALL OF *THIS*...
WOULD *YOU* JUST "GO HOME"?
*Wow. Babs really **did** plan for everything with her little escape pod, didn't she?*
GOOD POINT.
SAID YOU EW WHERE CULATOR AD TAKEN RACLE?
YEAH-- UT HE'LL SEE US COMING ROM A MILE AWAY.
HE THINKS OF *EVERYTHING*.
YOU'RE A *TEEN TITAN*, RIGHT?
WAS.
WHATEVER-- U KNOW HOW TO FLY THE T-JET?
KIND OF?
FANTASTIC.
STAY POSITIVE LIKE *THAT* AND WE JUST MIGHT MAKE IT THROUGH THIS.

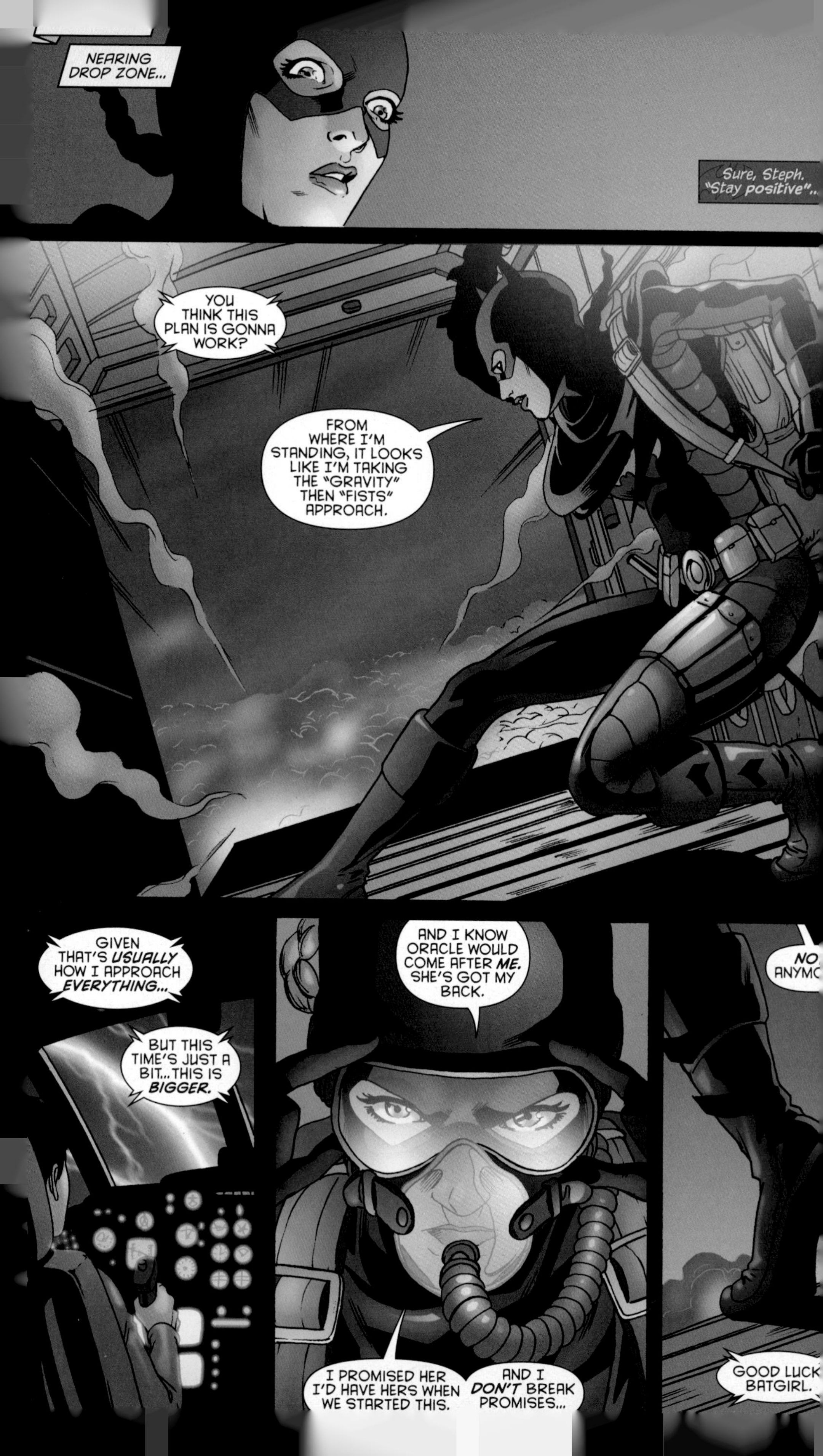
NEARING DROP ZONE...
Sure, Steph. "Stay positive"...
YOU THINK THIS PLAN IS GONNA WORK?
FROM WHERE I'M STANDING, IT LOOKS LIKE I'M TAKING THE "GRAVITY" THEN "FISTS" APPROACH.
GIVEN THAT'S USUALLY HOW I APPROACH EVERYTHING...
BUT THIS TIME'S JUST A BIT...THIS IS BIGGER.
AND I KNOW ORACLE WOULD COME AFTER ME. SHE'S GOT MY BACK.
I PROMISED HER I'D HAVE HERS WHEN WE STARTED THIS.
AND I DON'T BREAK PROMISES...
GOOD LUCK BATGIRL.

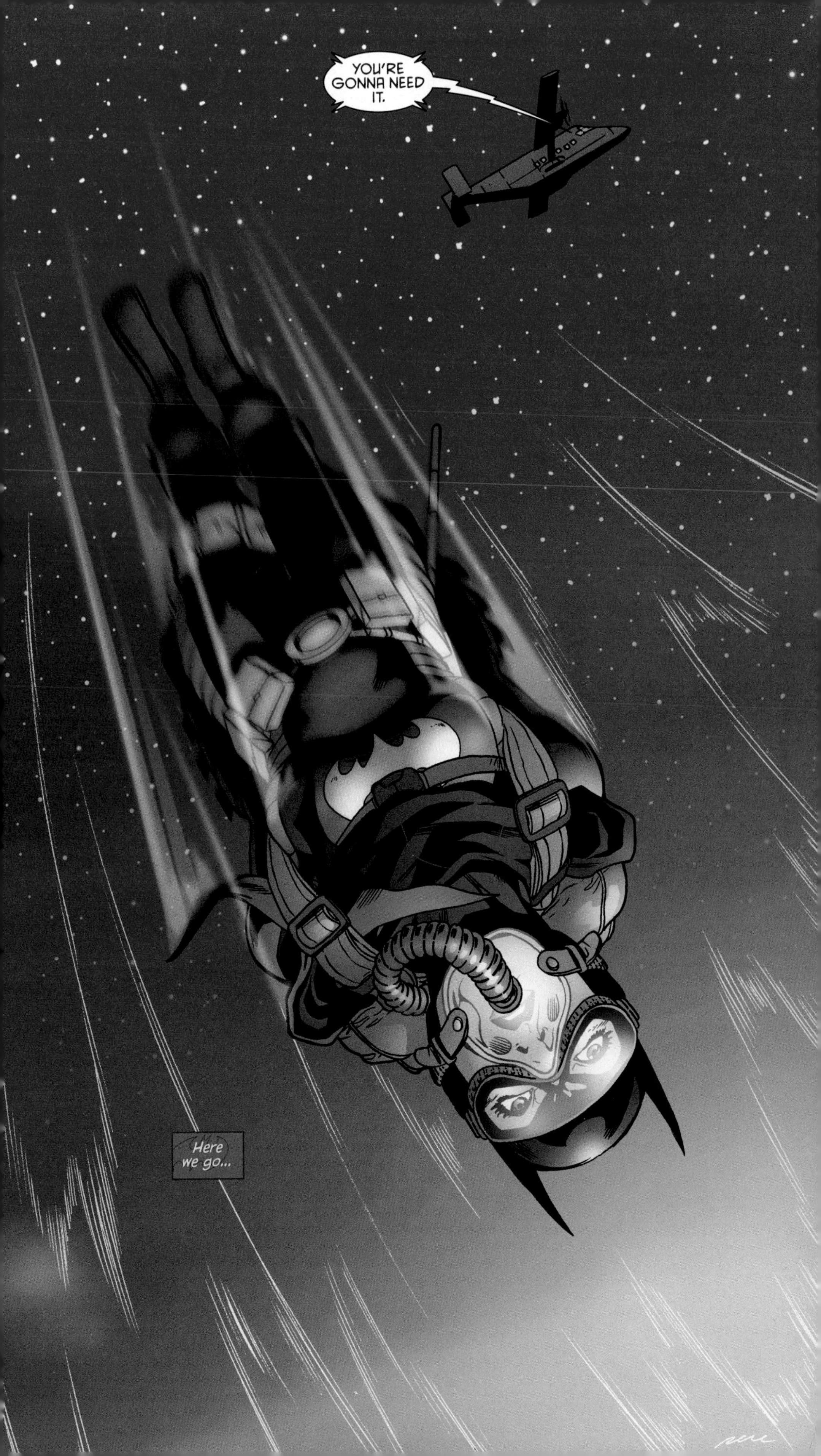
YOU'RE GONNA NEED IT.
Here we go...

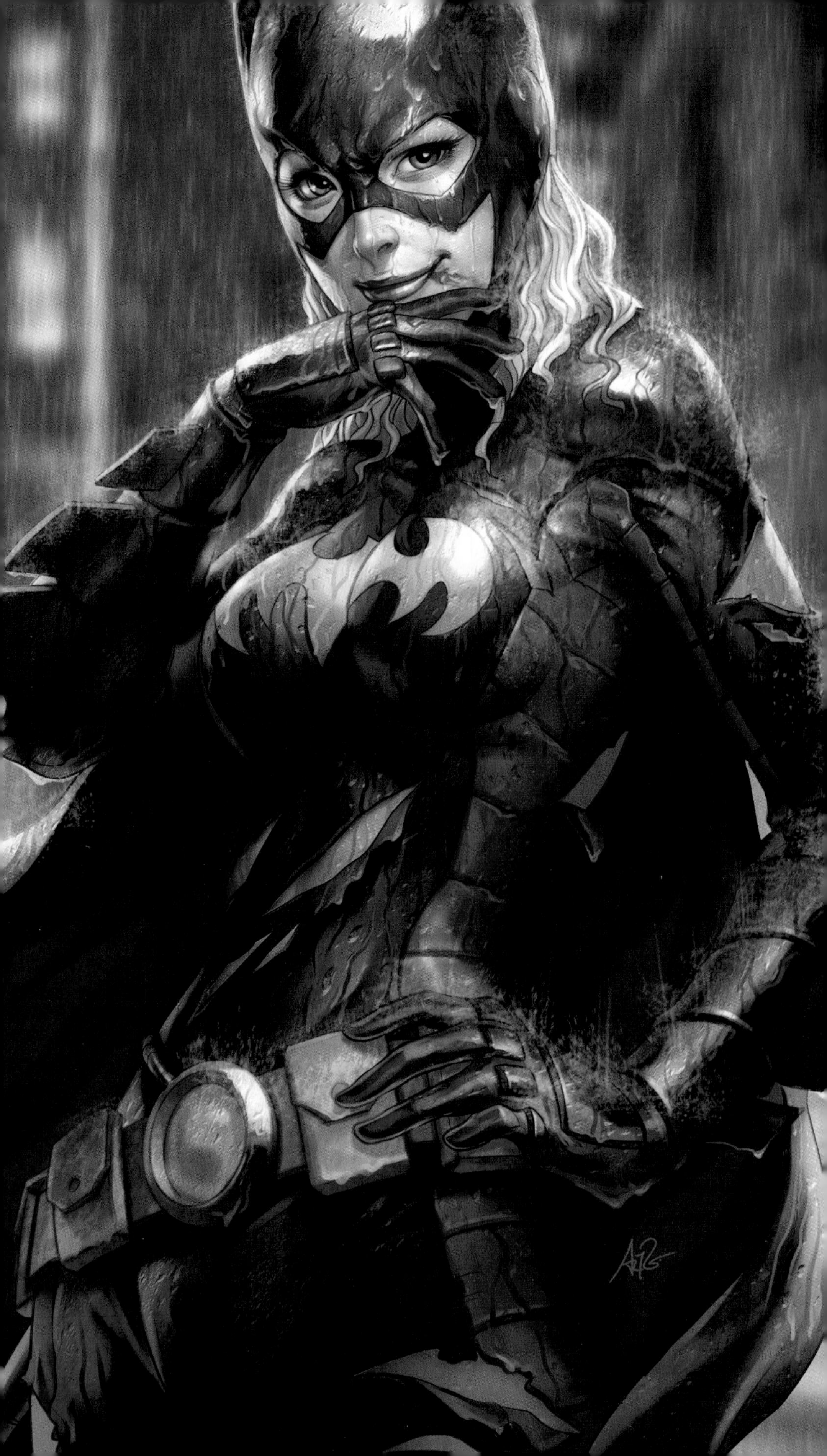

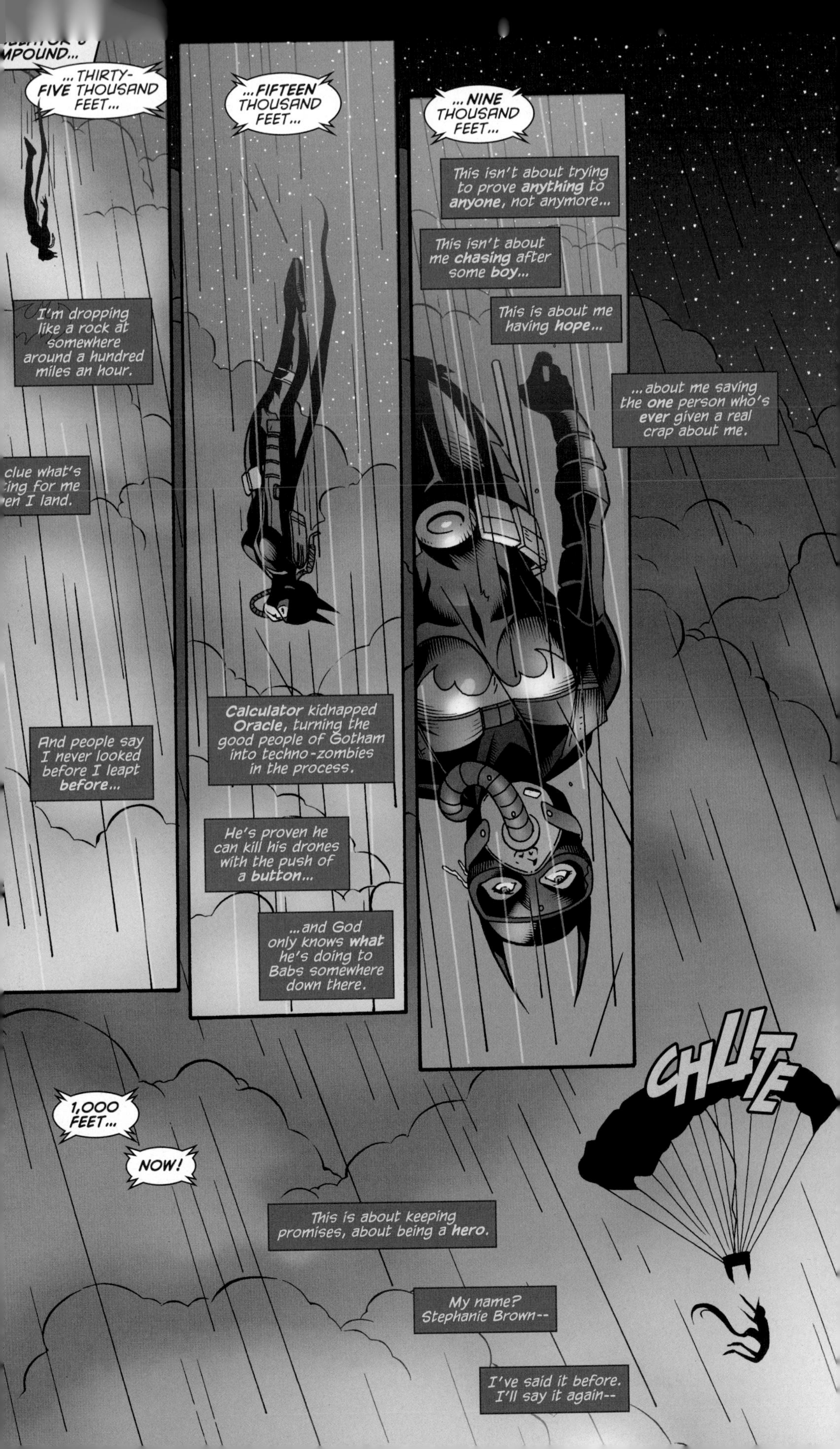

...MPOUND...
...THIRTY-FIVE THOUSAND FEET...
I'm dropping like a rock at somewhere around a hundred miles an hour.
clue what's ...ting for me ...en I land.
And people say I never looked before I leapt before...
...FIFTEEN THOUSAND FEET...
Calculator kidnapped Oracle, turning the good people of Gotham into techno-zombies in the process.
He's proven he can kill his drones with the push of a button...
...and God only knows what he's doing to Babs somewhere down there.
...NINE THOUSAND FEET...
This isn't about trying to prove anything to anyone, not anymore...
This isn't about me chasing after some boy...
This is about me having hope...
...about me saving the one person who's ever given a real crap about me.
1,000 FEET...
NOW!
CHUTE
This is about keeping promises, about being a hero.
My name? Stephanie Brown--
I've said it before. I'll say it again--

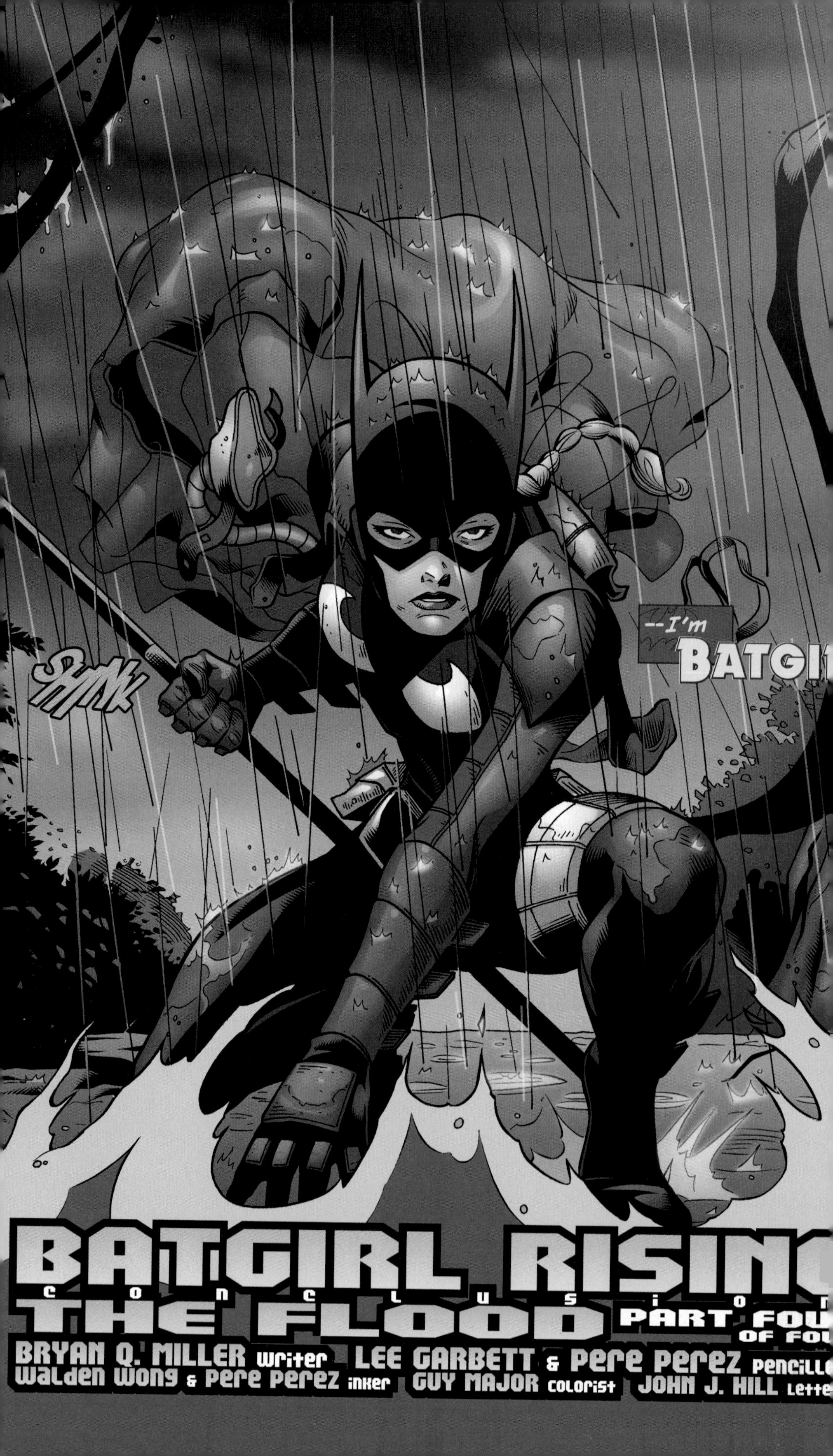

--I'm
BATGI
SHNK
BATGIRL RISING
c o n c l u s i o n
THE FLOOD
PART FOU
OF FO
BRYAN Q. MILLER writer
LEE GARBETT & Pere Perez pencille
Walden Wong & Pere Perez inker
GUY MAJOR colorist
JOHN J. HILL lette

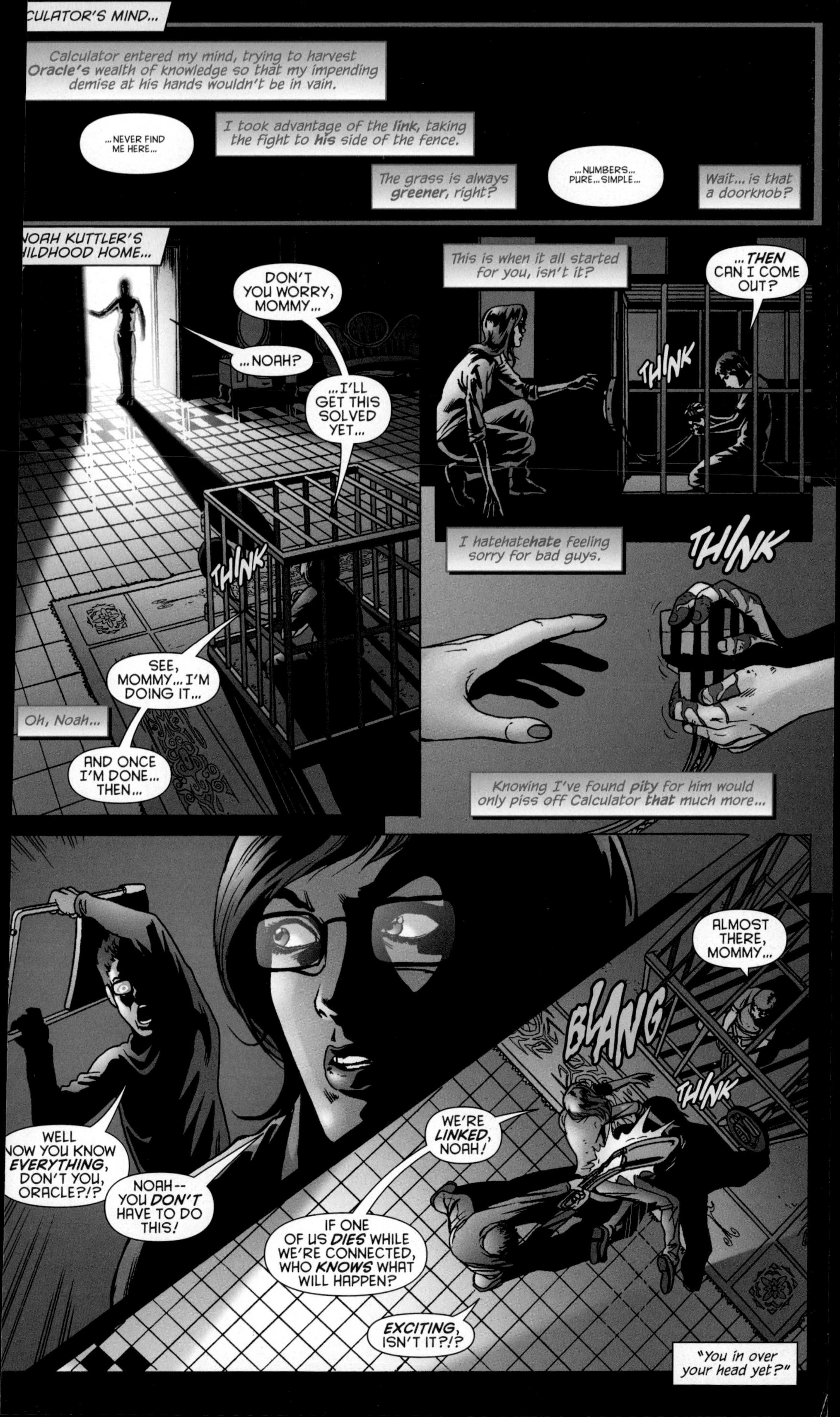
CULATOR'S MIND...
Calculator entered my mind, trying to harvest Oracle's wealth of knowledge so that my impending demise at his hands wouldn't be in vain.
...NEVER FIND ME HERE...
I took advantage of the link, taking the fight to his side of the fence.
The grass is always greener, right?
...NUMBERS... PURE... SIMPLE...
Wait... is that a doorknob?
NOAH KUTTLER'S ILDHOOD HOME...
...NOAH?
DON'T YOU WORRY, MOMMY...
...I'LL GET THIS SOLVED YET...
THINK
SEE, MOMMY... I'M DOING IT...
Oh, Noah...
AND ONCE I'M DONE... THEN...
This is when it all started for you, isn't it?
...THEN CAN I COME OUT?
THINK
I hatehatehate feeling sorry for bad guys.
THINK
Knowing I've found pity for him would only piss off Calculator that much more...
WELL NOW YOU KNOW EVERYTHING, DON'T YOU, ORACLE?!?
NOAH -- YOU DON'T HAVE TO DO THIS!
ALMOST THERE, MOMMY...
BLANG
THINK
WE'RE LINKED, NOAH!
IF ONE OF US DIES WHILE WE'RE CONNECTED, WHO KNOWS WHAT WILL HAPPEN?
EXCITING, ISN'T IT?!?
"You in over your head yet?"

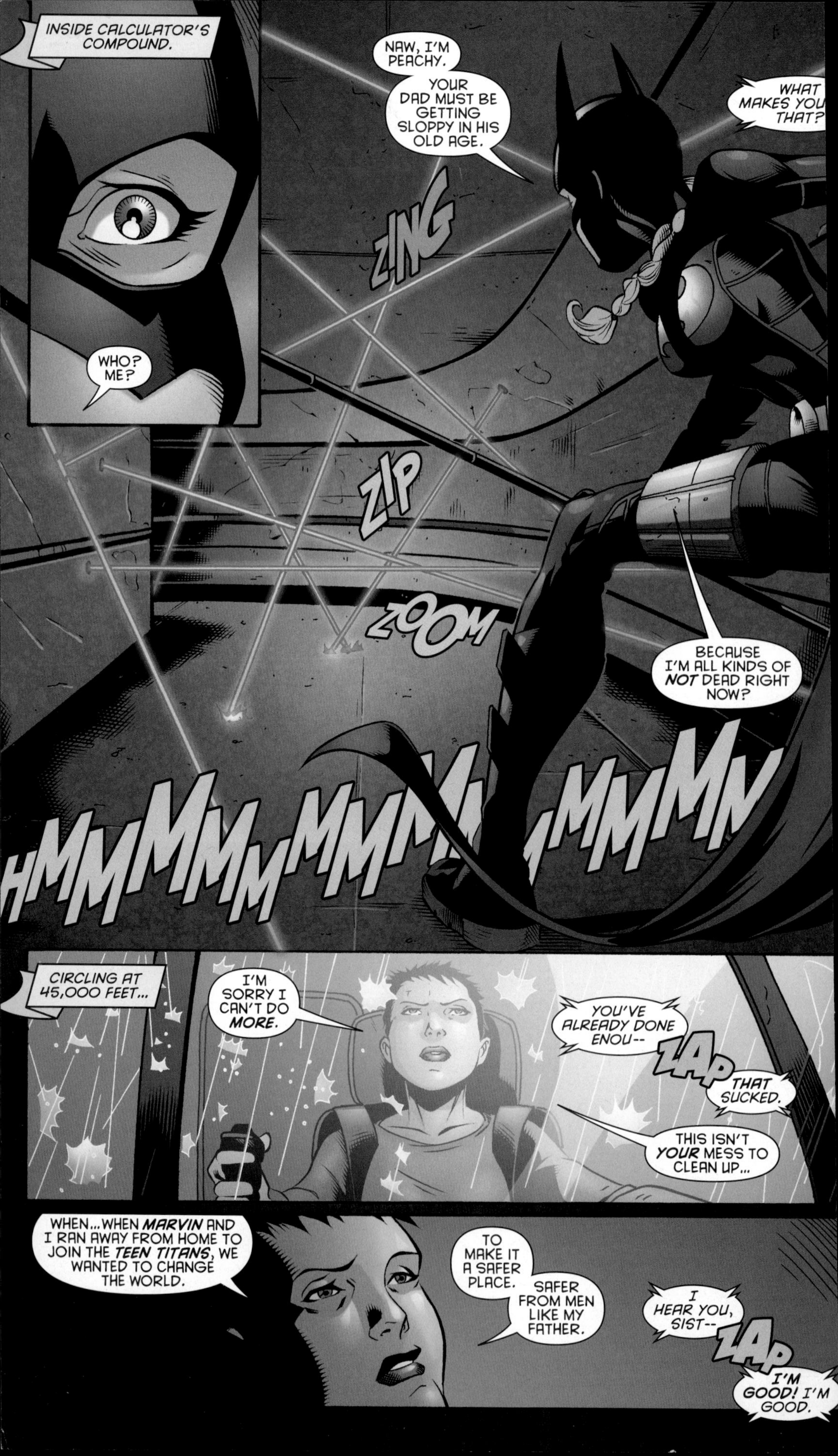
INSIDE CALCULATOR'S COMPOUND.
WHO? ME?
NAW, I'M PEACHY.
YOUR DAD MUST BE GETTING SLOPPY IN HIS OLD AGE.
WHAT MAKES YOU THAT?
ZING
ZIP
ZOOM
BECAUSE I'M ALL KINDS OF NOT DEAD RIGHT NOW?
HMMMMMMMMMMMMMMMMN
CIRCLING AT 45,000 FEET...
I'M SORRY I CAN'T DO MORE.
YOU'VE ALREADY DONE ENOU--
ZAP
THAT SUCKED.
THIS ISN'T YOUR MESS TO CLEAN UP...
WHEN...WHEN MARVIN AND I RAN AWAY FROM HOME TO JOIN THE TEEN TITANS, WE WANTED TO CHANGE THE WORLD.
TO MAKE IT A SAFER PLACE.
SAFER FROM MEN LIKE MY FATHER.
I HEAR YOU, SIST--
ZAP
I'M GOOD! I'M GOOD.

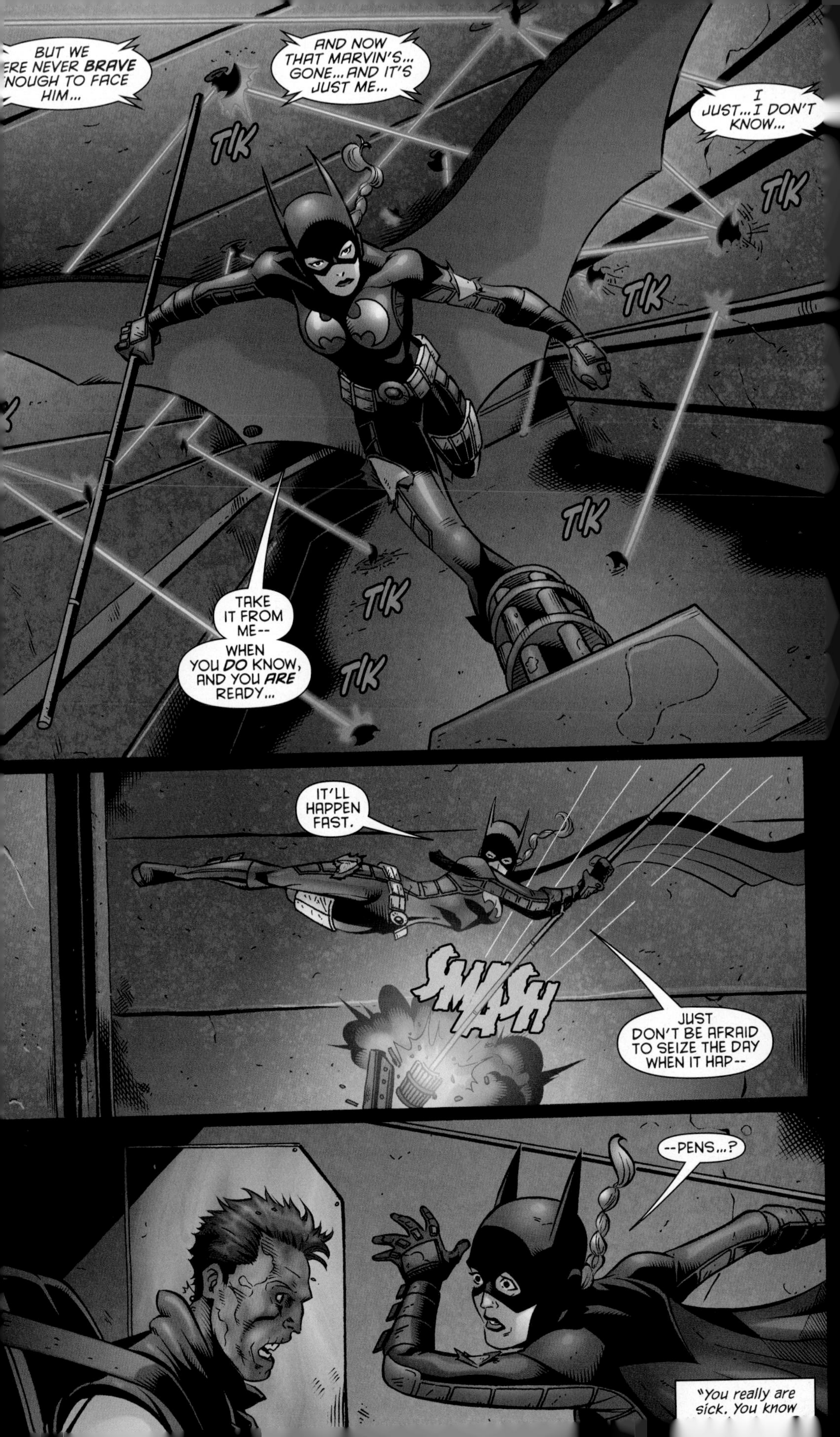

BUT WE ERE NEVER BRAVE NOUGH TO FACE HIM...
AND NOW THAT MARVIN'S... GONE... AND IT'S JUST ME...
I JUST... I DON'T KNOW...
TIK
TIK
TIK
TIK
TIK
TIK
TAKE IT FROM ME-- WHEN YOU DO KNOW, AND YOU ARE READY...
IT'LL HAPPEN FAST.
SMASH
JUST DON'T BE AFRAID TO SEIZE THE DAY WHEN IT HAP--
--PENS...?
"You really are sick. You know

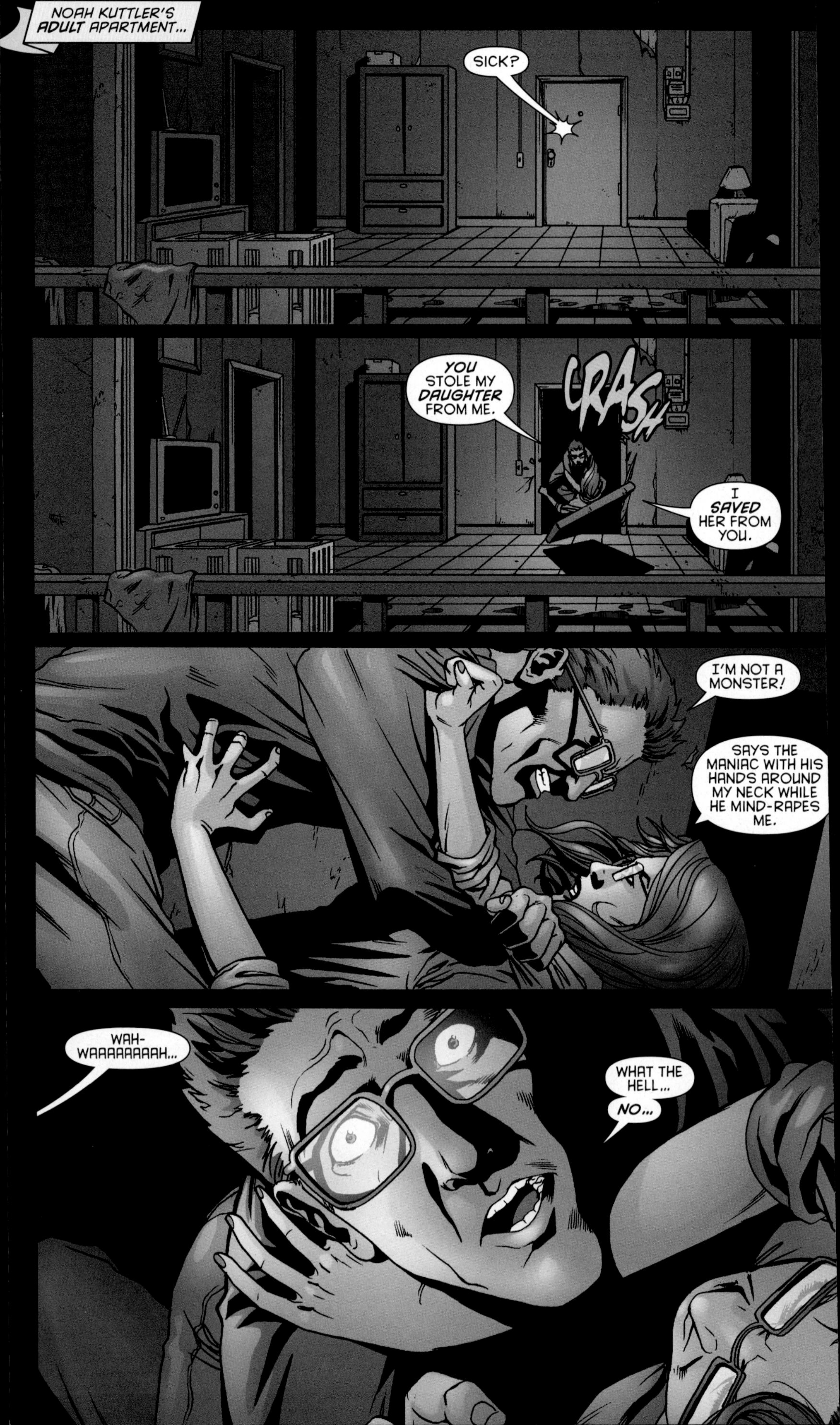
NOAH KUTTLER'S ADULT APARTMENT...
SICK?
CRASH
YOU STOLE MY DAUGHTER FROM ME.
I SAVED HER FROM YOU.
I'M NOT A MONSTER!
SAYS THE MANIAC WITH HIS HANDS AROUND MY NECK WHILE HE MIND-RAPES ME.
WAH-WAAAAAAAAH...
WHAT THE HELL... NO...

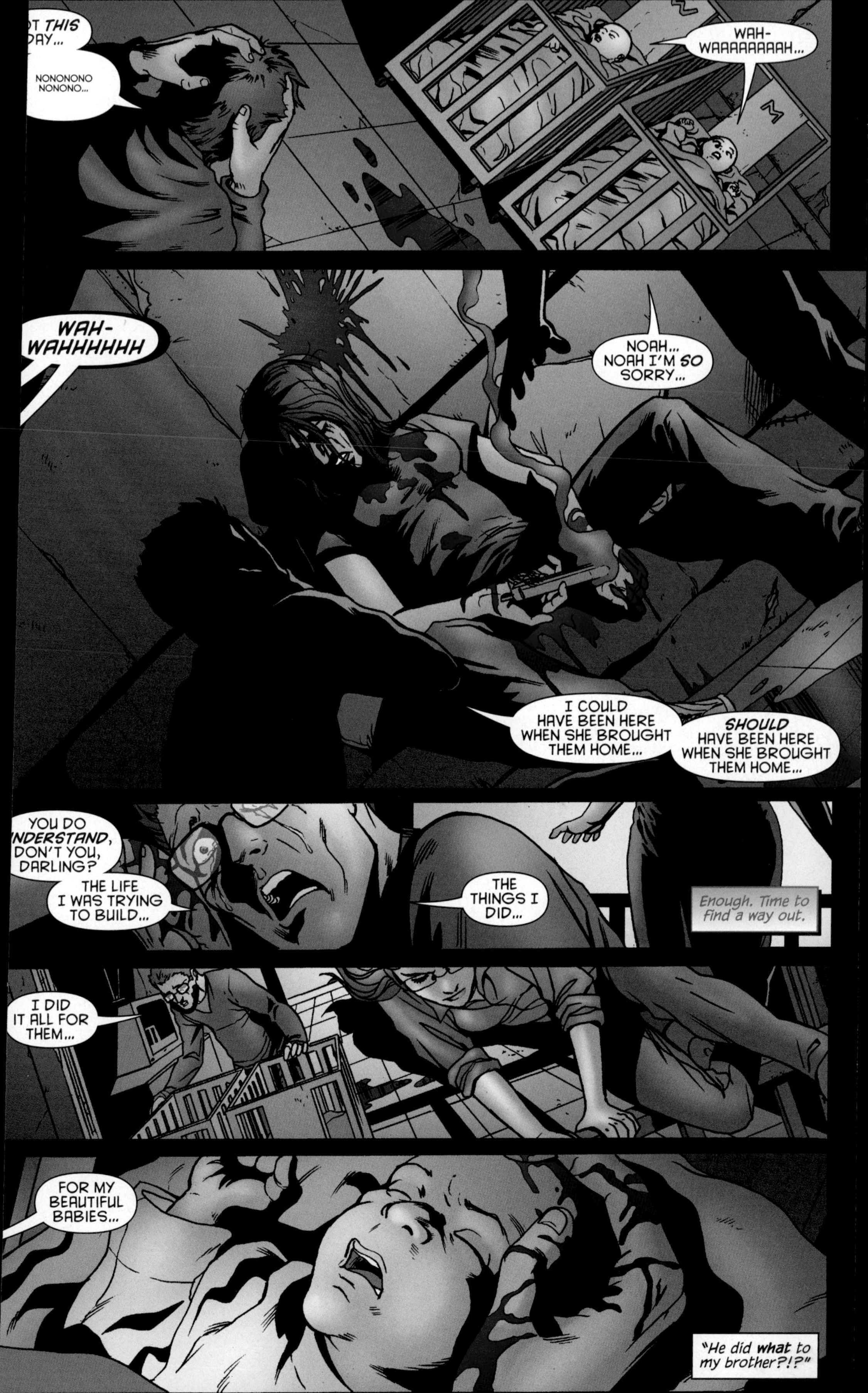

...OT THIS ...DAY...
NONONONO NONONO...
WAH-WAAAAAAAAH...
WAH-WAHHHHHH
NOAH... NOAH I'M SO SORRY...
I COULD HAVE BEEN HERE WHEN SHE BROUGHT THEM HOME...
SHOULD HAVE BEEN HERE WHEN SHE BROUGHT THEM HOME...
YOU DO ...NDERSTAND, DON'T YOU, DARLING?
THE LIFE I WAS TRYING TO BUILD...
THE THINGS I DID...
Enough. Time to find a way out.
I DID IT ALL FOR THEM...
FOR MY BEAUTIFUL BABIES...
"He did what to my brother?!?"

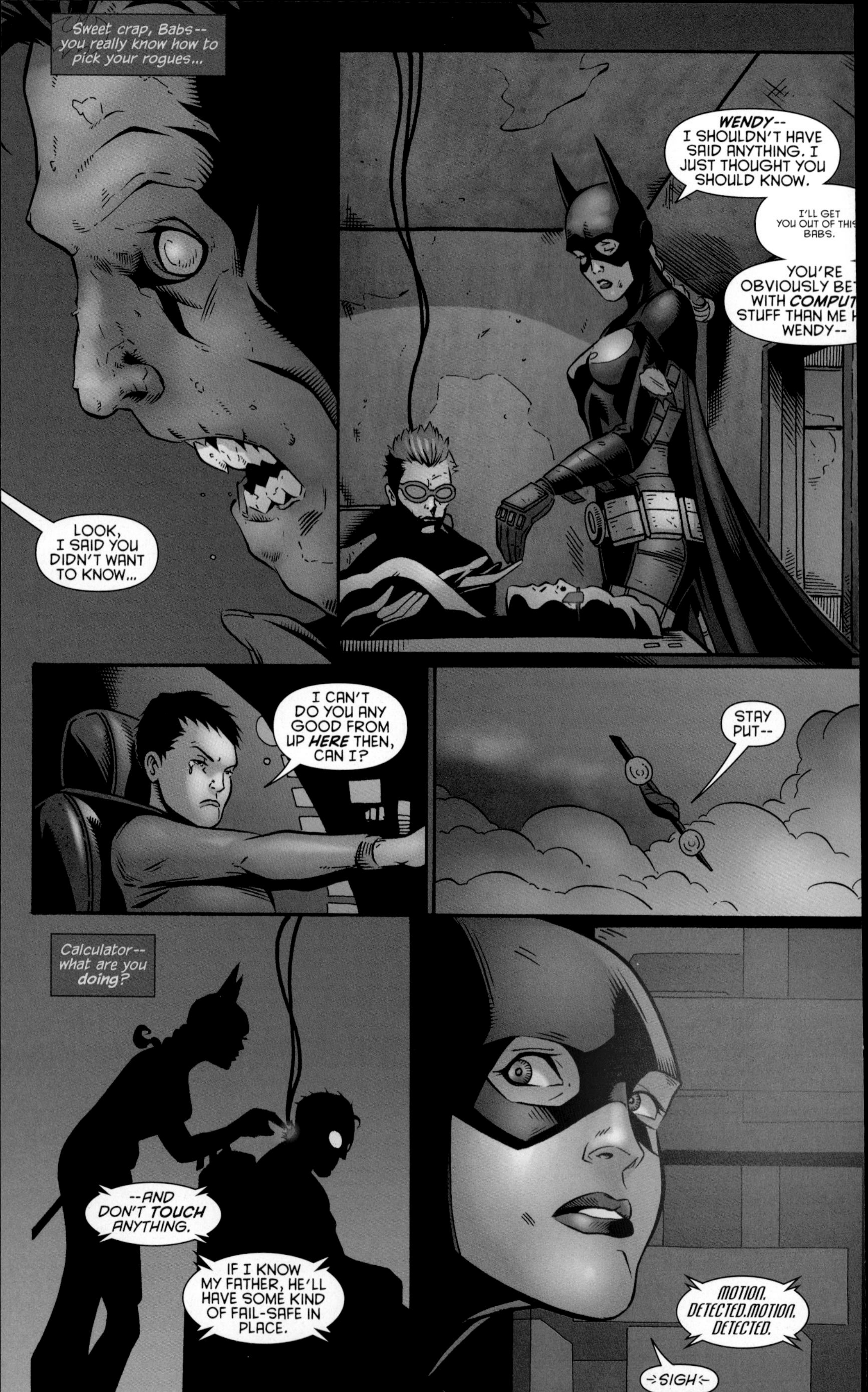
Sweet crap, Babs-- you really know how to pick your rogues...
WENDY-- I SHOULDN'T HAVE SAID ANYTHING. I JUST THOUGHT YOU SHOULD KNOW.
I'LL GET YOU OUT OF THIS BABS.
YOU'RE OBVIOUSLY BET WITH COMPUT STUFF THAN ME H WENDY--
LOOK, I SAID YOU DIDN'T WANT TO KNOW...
I CAN'T DO YOU ANY GOOD FROM UP HERE THEN, CAN I?
STAY PUT--
Calculator-- what are you doing?
--AND DON'T TOUCH ANYTHING.
IF I KNOW MY FATHER, HE'LL HAVE SOME KIND OF FAIL-SAFE IN PLACE.
MOTION. DETECTED.MOTION. DETECTED.
SIGH

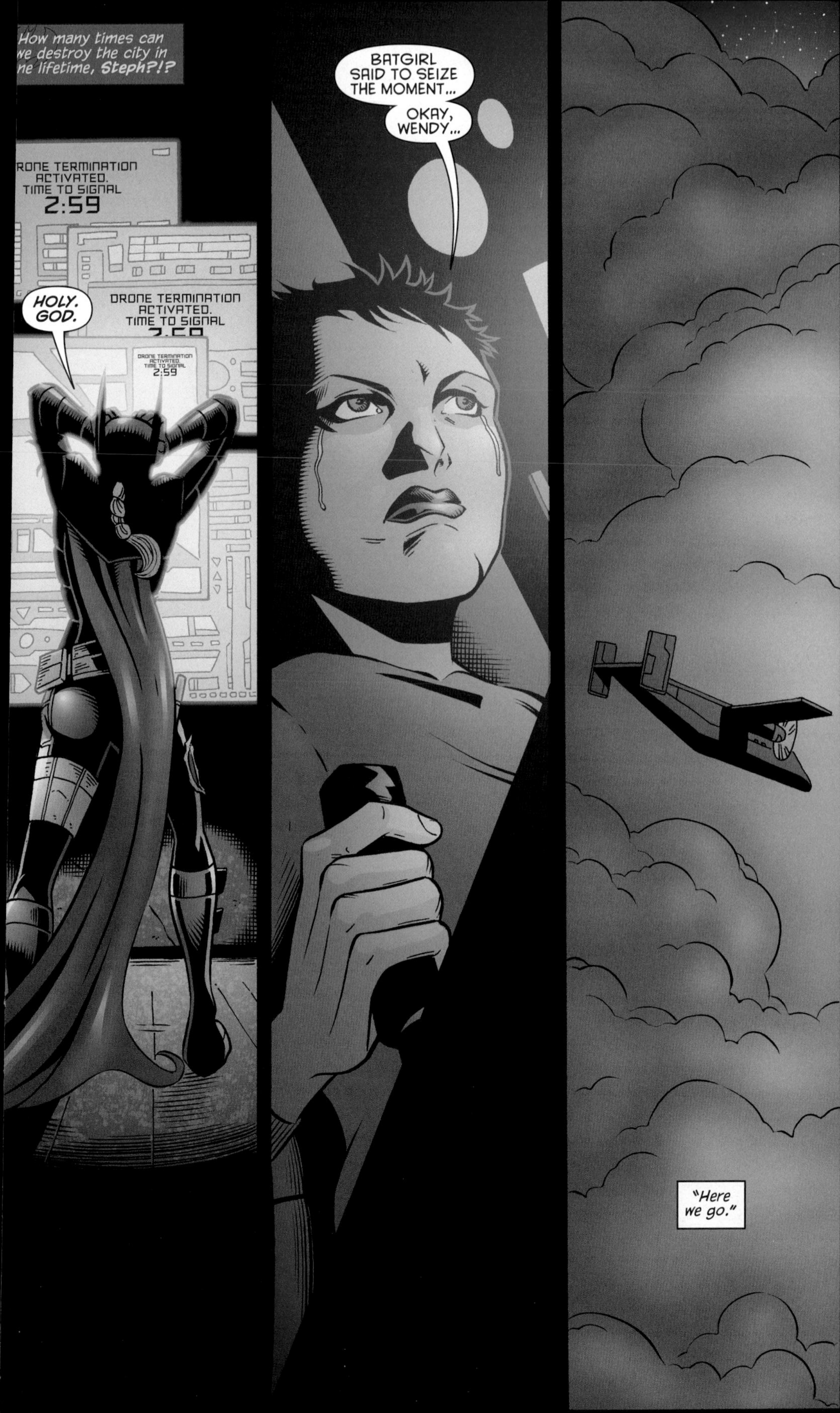
How many times can we destroy the city in one lifetime, Steph?!?
DRONE TERMINATION ACTIVATED. TIME TO SIGNAL 2:59
HOLY. GOD.
BATGIRL SAID TO SEIZE THE MOMENT...
OKAY, WENDY...
"Here we go."

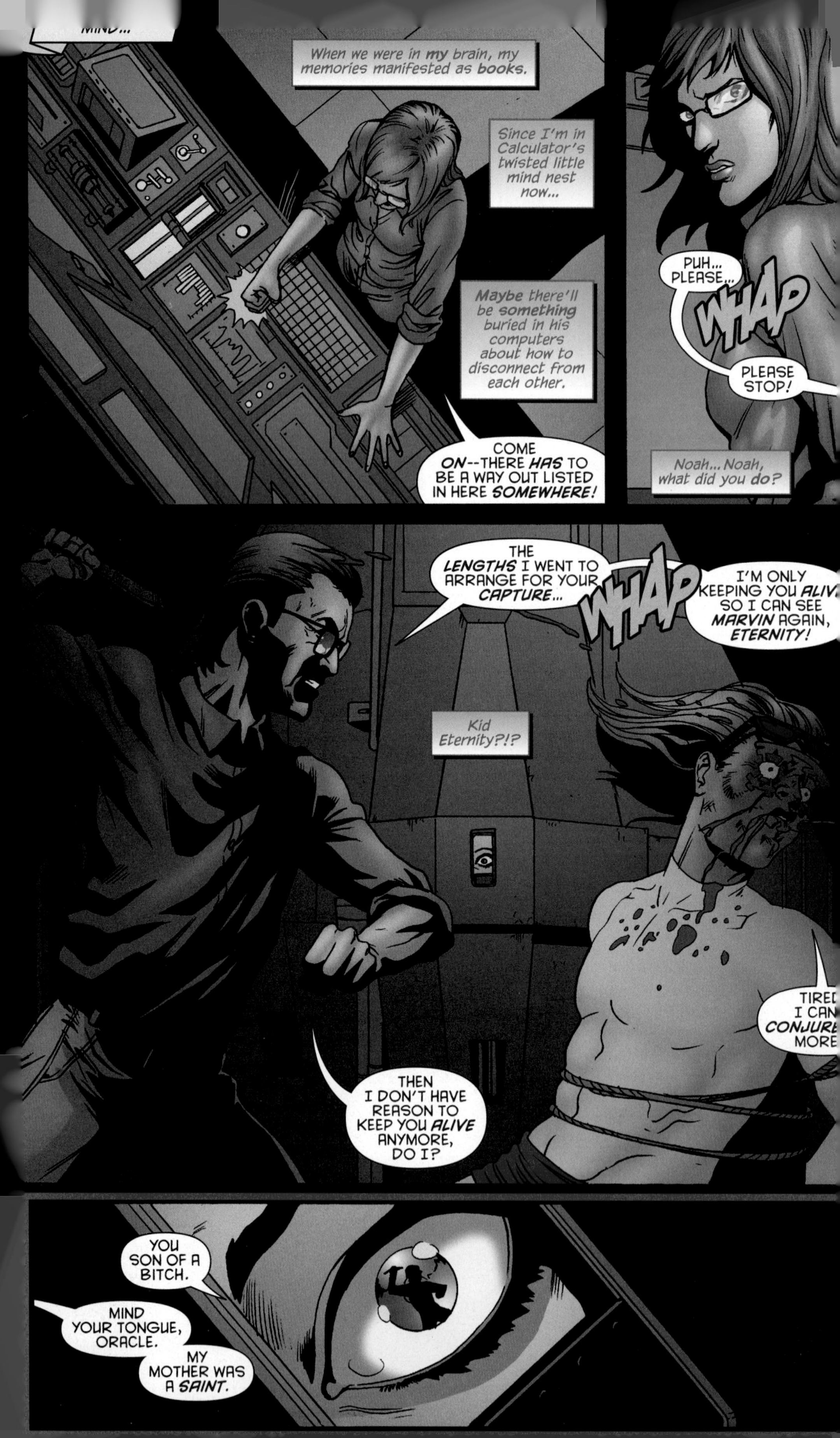
MIND...
When we were in my brain, my memories manifested as books.
Since I'm in Calculator's twisted little mind nest now...
Maybe there'll be something buried in his computers about how to disconnect from each other.
COME ON--THERE HAS TO BE A WAY OUT LISTED IN HERE SOMEWHERE!
PUH... PLEASE...
WHAP
PLEASE STOP!
Noah... Noah, what did you do?
THE LENGTHS I WENT TO ARRANGE FOR YOUR CAPTURE...
WHAP
I'M ONLY KEEPING YOU ALIV SO I CAN SEE MARVIN AGAIN, ETERNITY!
Kid Eternity?!?
TIRED I CAN CONJURE MORE
THEN I DON'T HAVE REASON TO KEEP YOU ALIVE ANYMORE, DO I?
YOU SON OF A BITCH.
MIND YOUR TONGUE, ORACLE.
MY MOTHER WAS A SAINT.

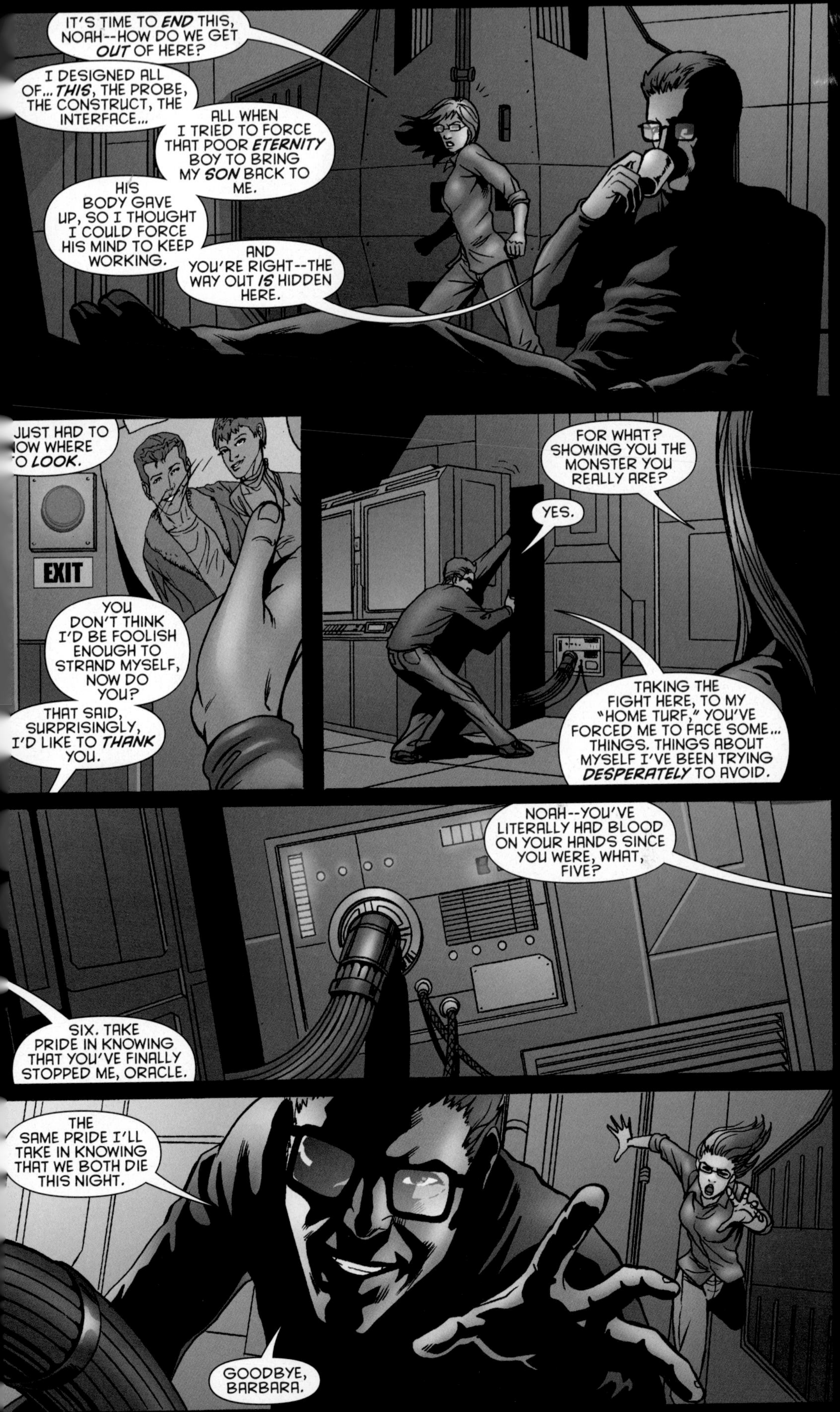

IT'S TIME TO END THIS, NOAH--HOW DO WE GET OUT OF HERE?
I DESIGNED ALL OF... THIS, THE PROBE, THE CONSTRUCT, THE INTERFACE...
ALL WHEN I TRIED TO FORCE THAT POOR ETERNITY BOY TO BRING MY SON BACK TO ME.
HIS BODY GAVE UP, SO I THOUGHT I COULD FORCE HIS MIND TO KEEP WORKING.
AND YOU'RE RIGHT--THE WAY OUT IS HIDDEN HERE.
JUST HAD TO IOW WHERE O LOOK.
EXIT
YOU DON'T THINK I'D BE FOOLISH ENOUGH TO STRAND MYSELF, NOW DO YOU?
THAT SAID, SURPRISINGLY, I'D LIKE TO THANK YOU.
FOR WHAT? SHOWING YOU THE MONSTER YOU REALLY ARE?
YES.
TAKING THE FIGHT HERE, TO MY "HOME TURF," YOU'VE FORCED ME TO FACE SOME... THINGS. THINGS ABOUT MYSELF I'VE BEEN TRYING DESPERATELY TO AVOID.
NOAH--YOU'VE LITERALLY HAD BLOOD ON YOUR HANDS SINCE YOU WERE, WHAT, FIVE?
SIX. TAKE PRIDE IN KNOWING THAT YOU'VE FINALLY STOPPED ME, ORACLE.
THE SAME PRIDE I'LL TAKE IN KNOWING THAT WE BOTH DIE THIS NIGHT.
GOODBYE, BARBARA.

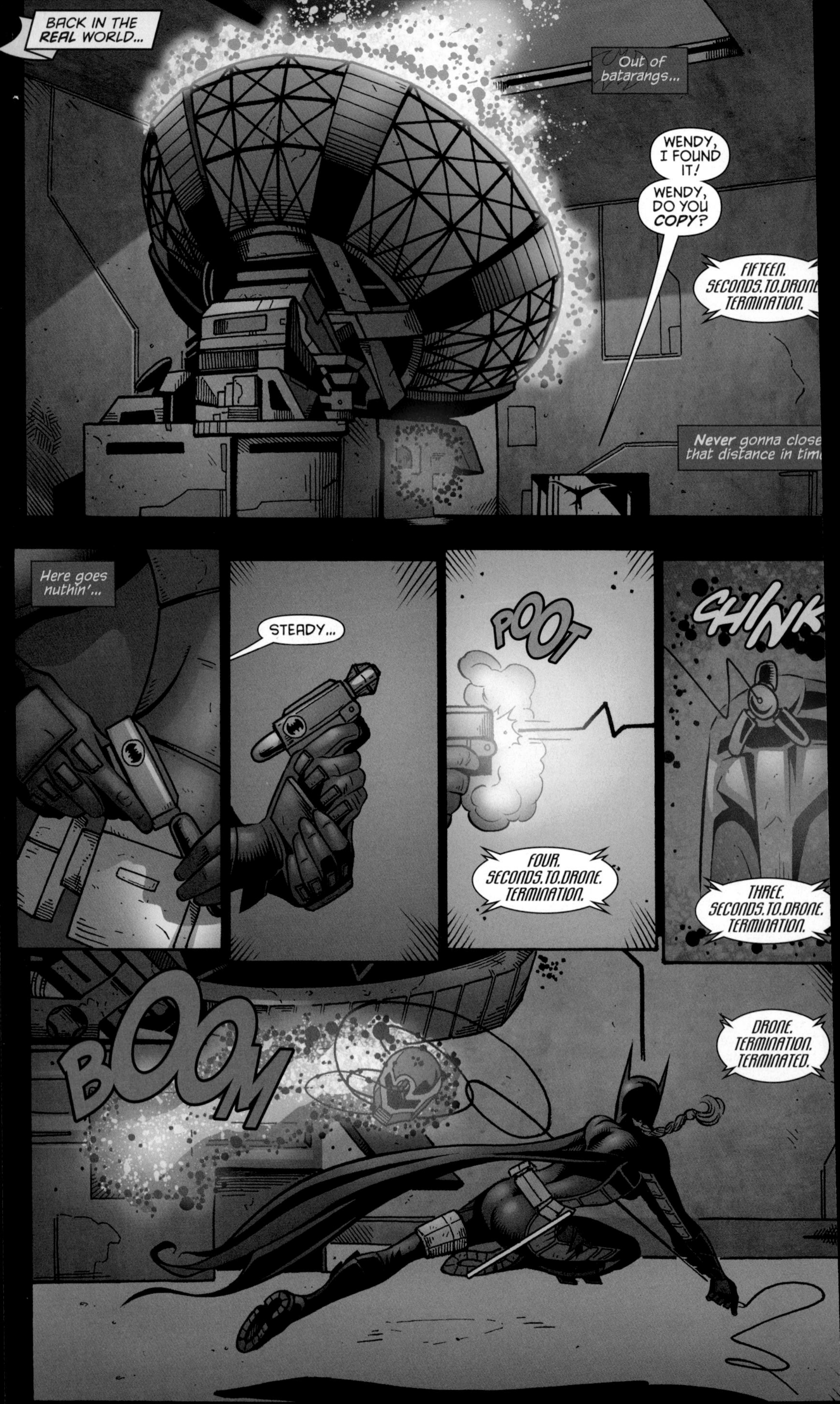

BACK IN THE REAL WORLD...
Out of batarangs...
WENDY, I FOUND IT!
WENDY, DO YOU COPY?
FIFTEEN. SECONDS.TO.DRONE TERMINATION.
Never gonna close that distance in tim
Here goes nuthin'...
STEADY...
POOT
FOUR. SECONDS.TO.DRONE. TERMINATION.
CHINK
THREE. SECONDS.TO.DRONE. TERMINATION.
BOOM
DRONE. TERMINATION. TERMINATED.

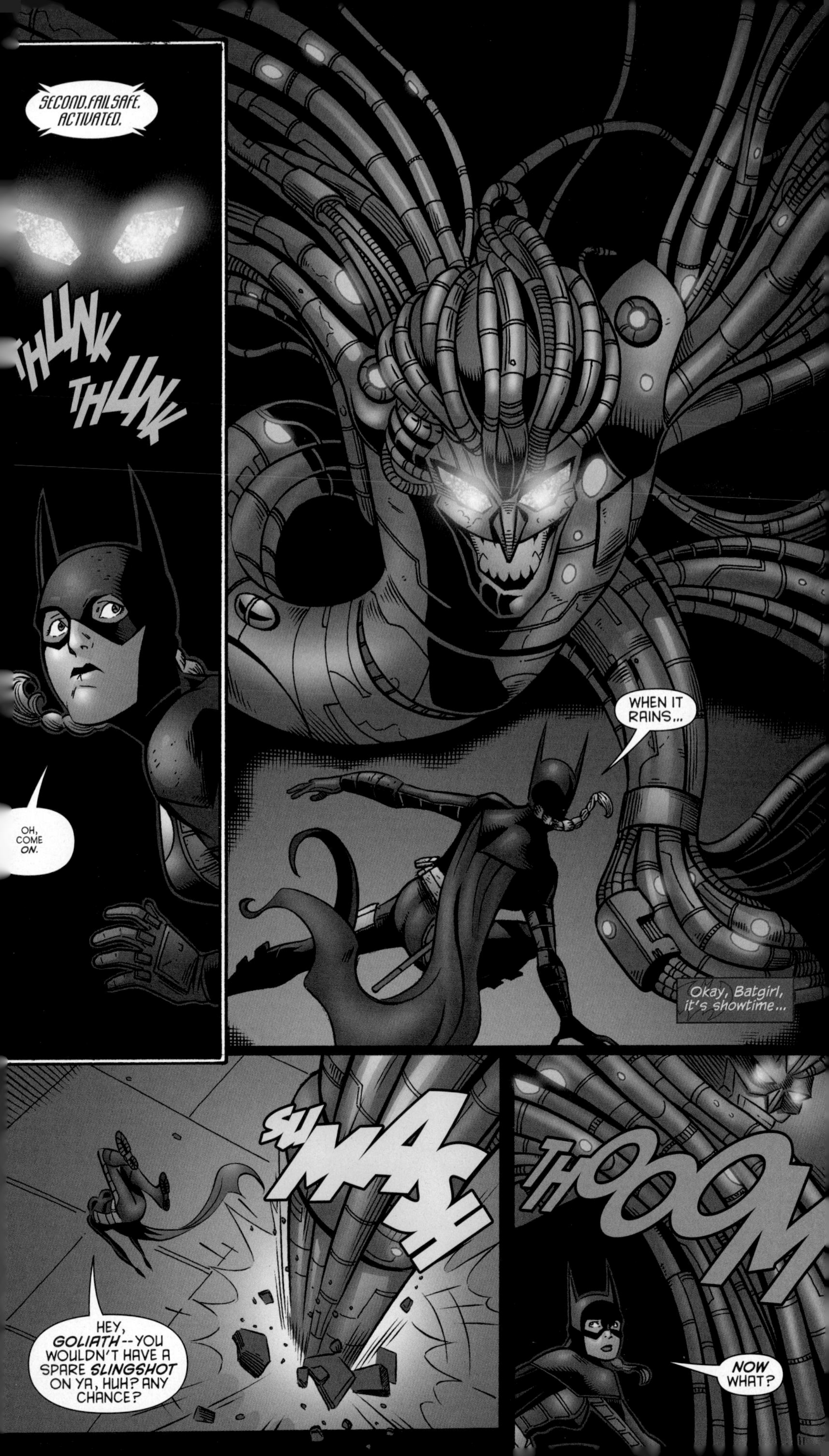
SECOND.FAILSAFE.
ACTIVATED.
THUNK THUNK
OH, COME ON.
WHEN IT RAINS...
Okay, Batgirl, it's showtime...
SMASH
HEY, GOLIATH--YOU WOULDN'T HAVE A SPARE SLINGSHOT ON YA, HUH? ANY CHANCE?
THOOOM
NOW WHAT?

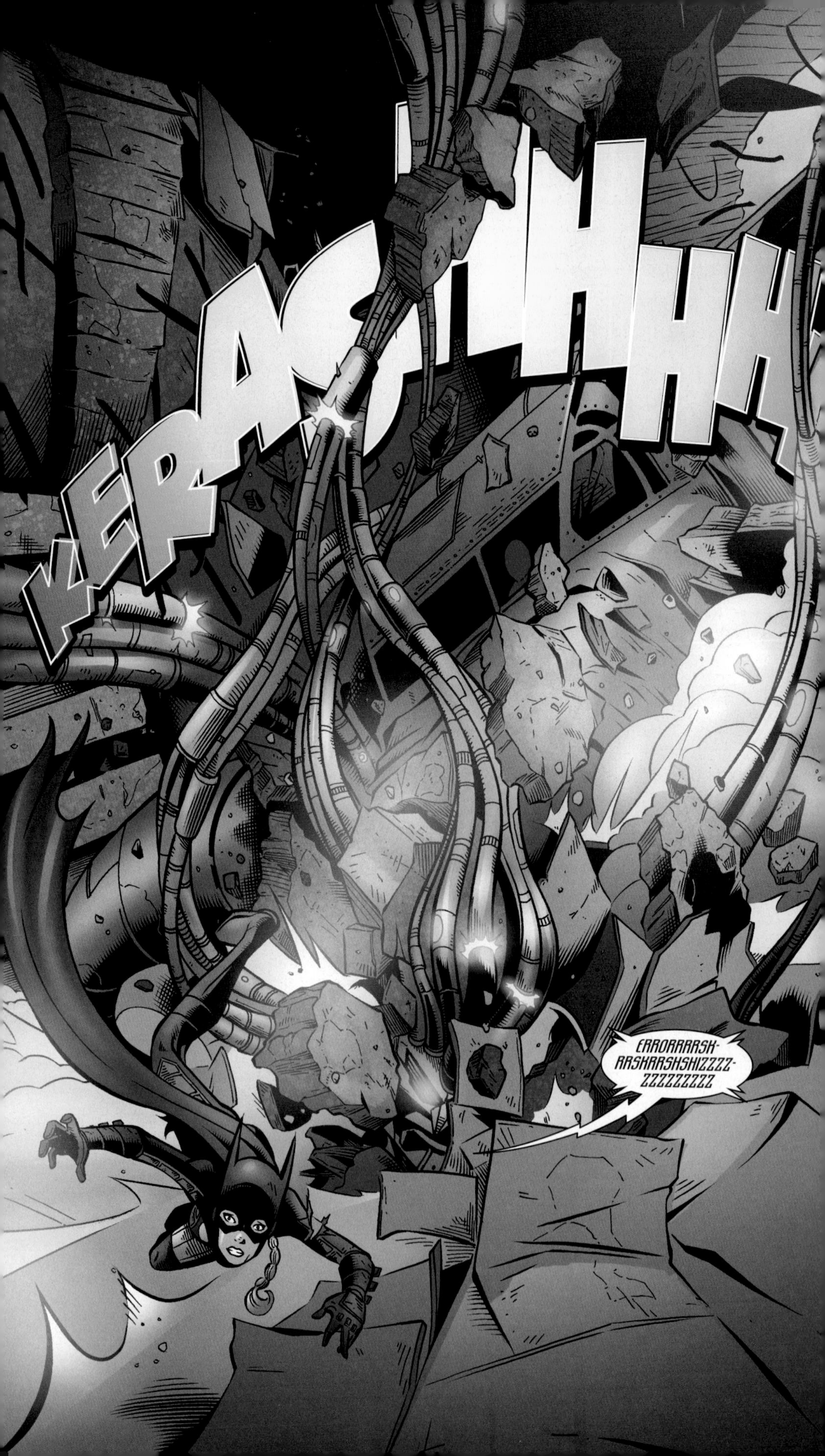
KERASHHHH
ERRORRRRRSK-
RRSKRRSHSHIZZZZ-
ZZZZZZZZZ

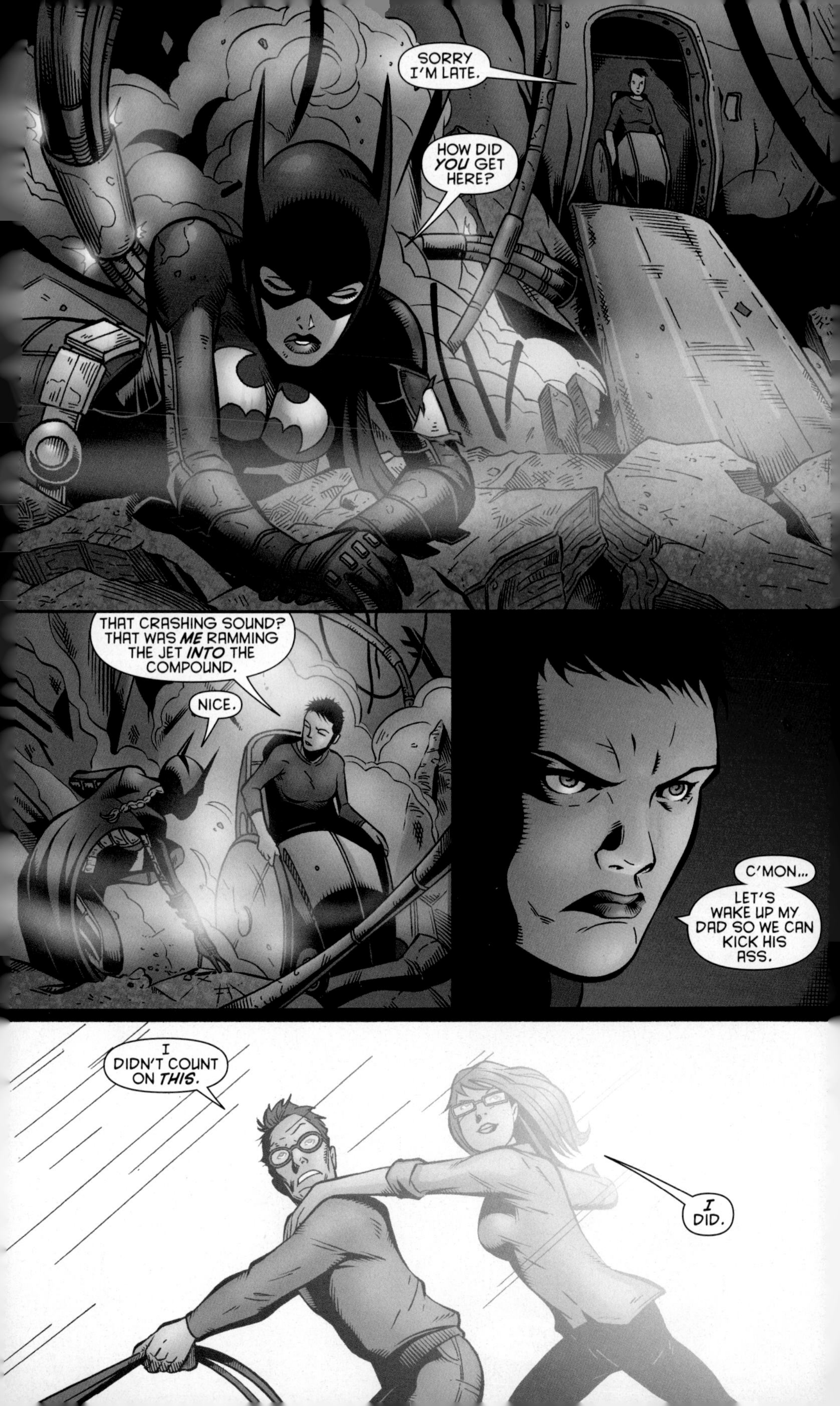
SORRY I'M LATE.
HOW DID *YOU* GET HERE?
THAT CRASHING SOUND? THAT WAS *ME* RAMMING THE JET *INTO* THE COMPOUND.
NICE.
C'MON...
LET'S WAKE UP MY DAD SO WE CAN KICK HIS ASS.
I DIDN'T COUNT ON *THIS*.
I DID.

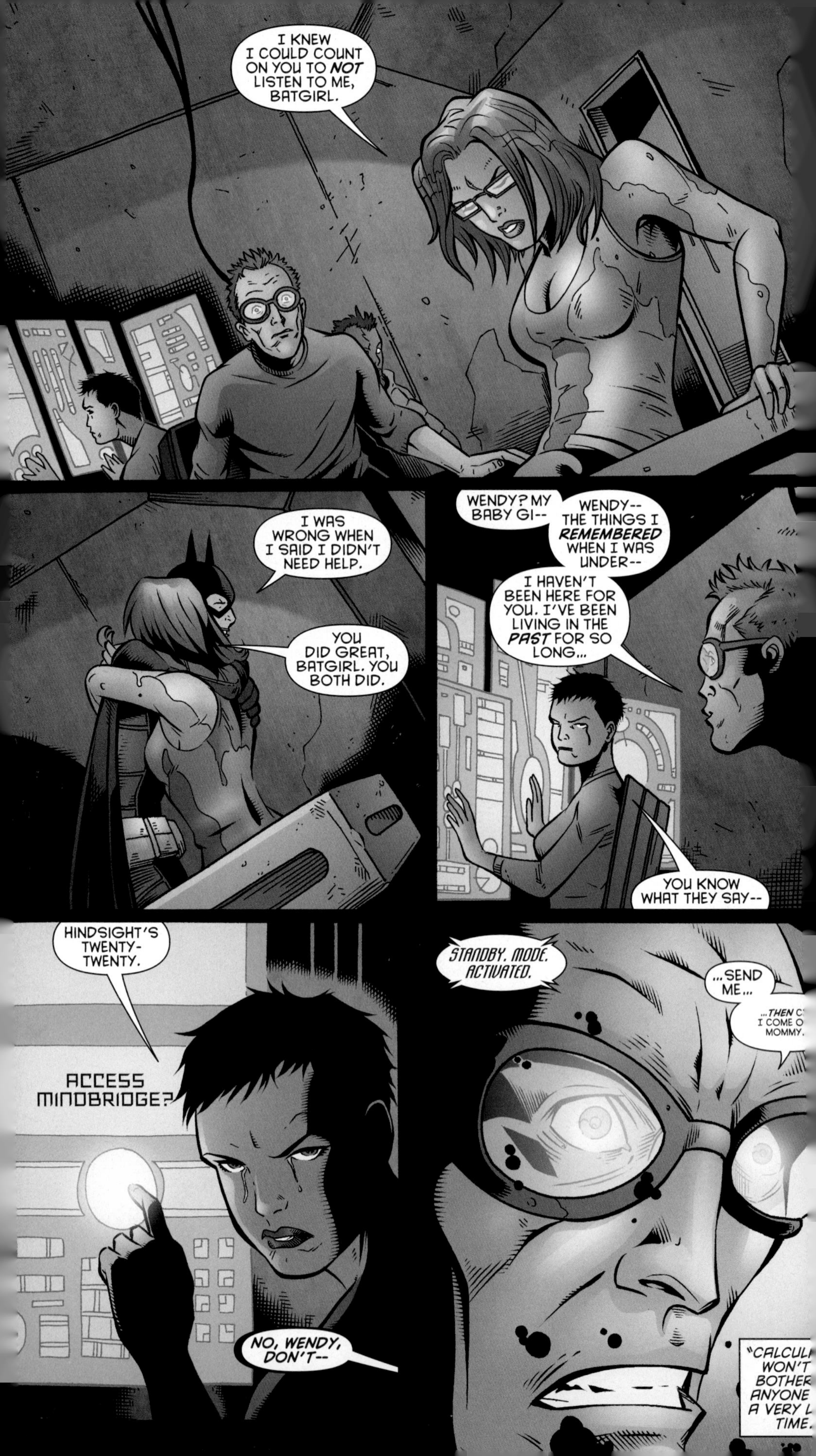
I KNEW I COULD COUNT ON YOU TO NOT LISTEN TO ME, BATGIRL.
I WAS WRONG WHEN I SAID I DIDN'T NEED HELP.
YOU DID GREAT, BATGIRL. YOU BOTH DID.
WENDY? MY BABY GI--
WENDY-- THE THINGS I REMEMBERED WHEN I WAS UNDER--
I HAVEN'T BEEN HERE FOR YOU. I'VE BEEN LIVING IN THE PAST FOR SO LONG...
YOU KNOW WHAT THEY SAY--
HINDSIGHT'S TWENTY-TWENTY.
ACCESS MINDBRIDGE?
NO, WENDY, DON'T--
STANDBY. MODE. ACTIVATED.
...SEND ME...

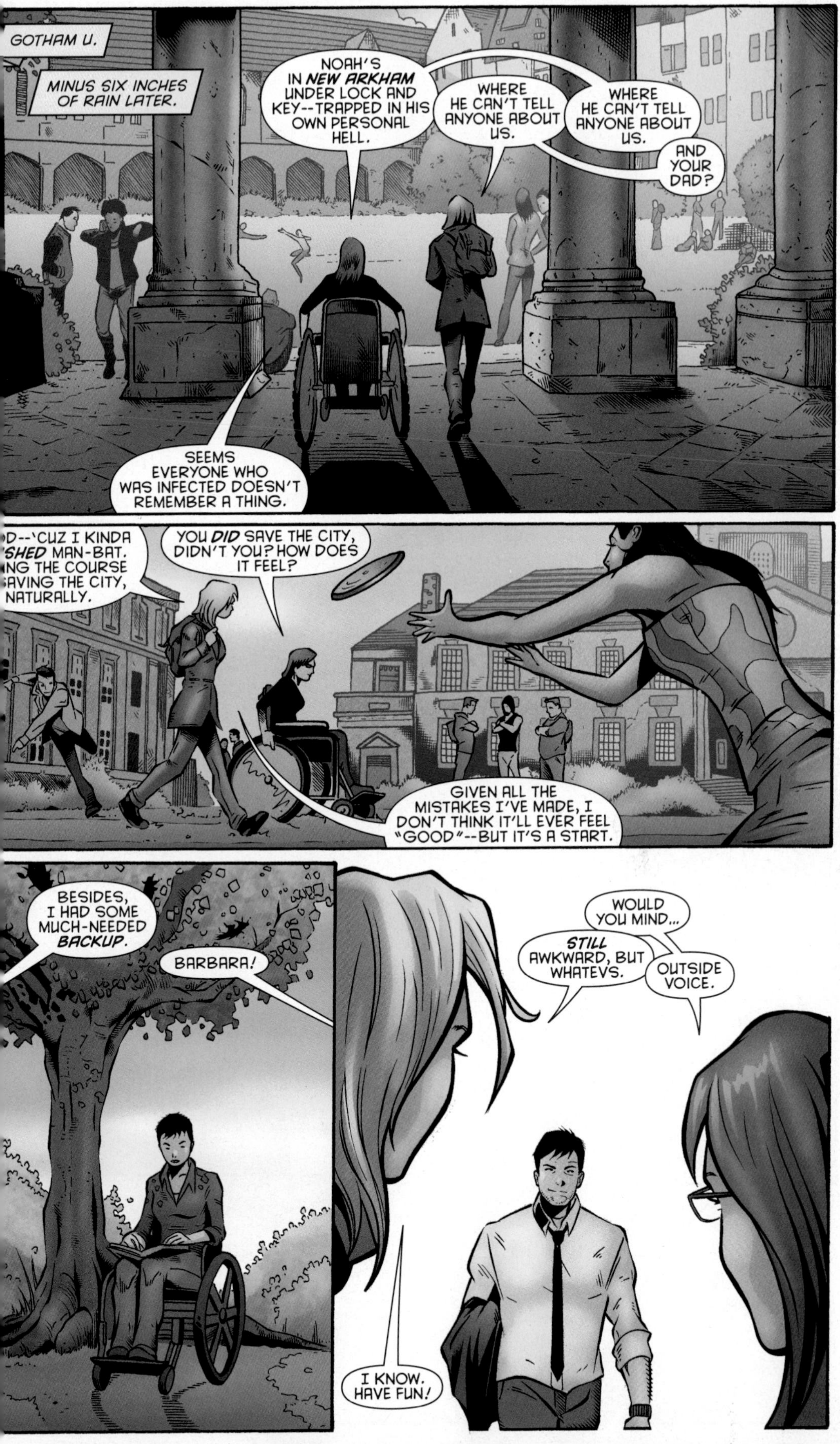

GOTHAM U.
MINUS SIX INCHES OF RAIN LATER.
NOAH'S IN NEW ARKHAM UNDER LOCK AND KEY--TRAPPED IN HIS OWN PERSONAL HELL.
WHERE HE CAN'T TELL ANYONE ABOUT US.
WHERE HE CAN'T TELL ANYONE ABOUT US.
AND YOUR DAD?
SEEMS EVERYONE WHO WAS INFECTED DOESN'T REMEMBER A THING.
D--'CUZ I KINDA SHED MAN-BAT. NG THE COURSE SAVING THE CITY, NATURALLY.
YOU DID SAVE THE CITY, DIDN'T YOU? HOW DOES IT FEEL?
GIVEN ALL THE MISTAKES I'VE MADE, I DON'T THINK IT'LL EVER FEEL "GOOD"--BUT IT'S A START.
BESIDES, I HAD SOME MUCH-NEEDED BACKUP.
BARBARA!
WOULD YOU MIND...
STILL AWKWARD, BUT WHATEVS.
OUTSIDE VOICE.
I KNOW. HAVE FUN!

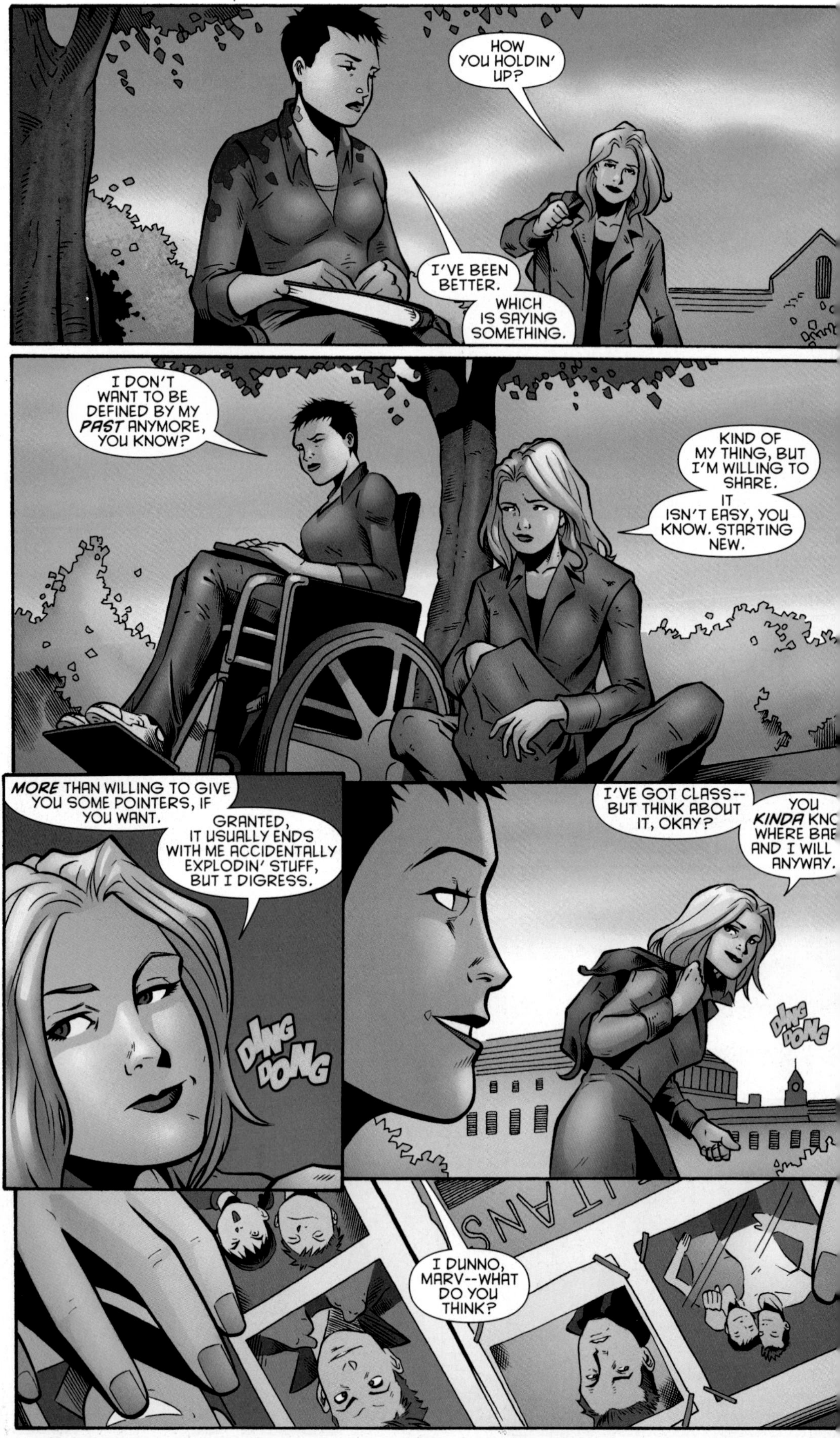
HOW YOU HOLDIN' UP?
I'VE BEEN BETTER.
WHICH IS SAYING SOMETHING.
I DON'T WANT TO BE DEFINED BY MY PAST ANYMORE, YOU KNOW?
KIND OF MY THING, BUT I'M WILLING TO SHARE.
IT ISN'T EASY, YOU KNOW. STARTING NEW.
MORE THAN WILLING TO GIVE YOU SOME POINTERS, IF YOU WANT.
GRANTED, IT USUALLY ENDS WITH ME ACCIDENTALLY EXPLODIN' STUFF, BUT I DIGRESS.
DING DONG
I'VE GOT CLASS-- BUT THINK ABOUT IT, OKAY?
YOU KINDA KNO WHERE BAE AND I WILL ANYWAY.
DING DONG
I DUNNO, MARV--WHAT DO YOU THINK?

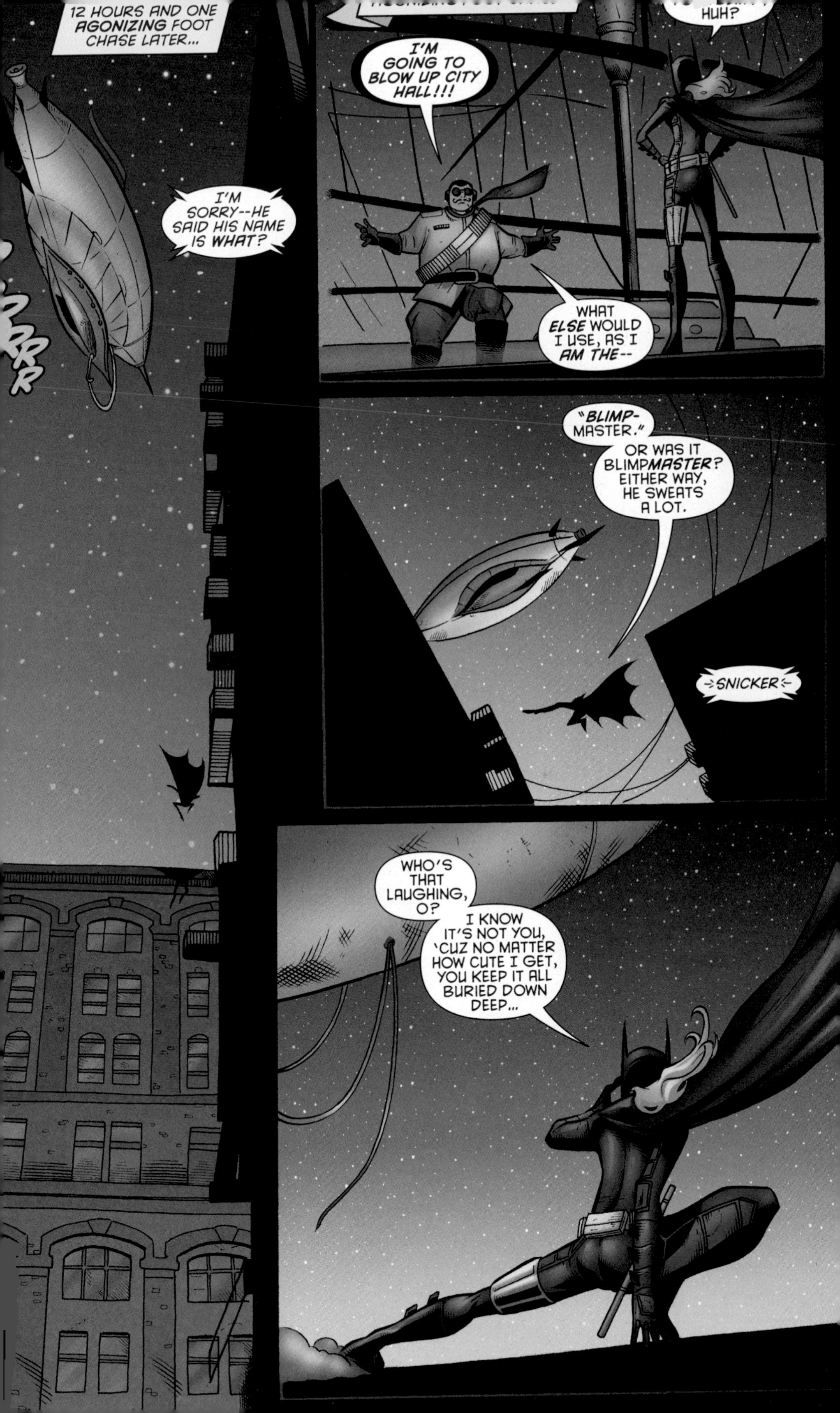

12 HOURS AND ONE AGONIZING FOOT CHASE LATER...
HUH?
I'M GOING TO BLOW UP CITY HALL!!!
I'M SORRY--HE SAID HIS NAME IS WHAT?
WHAT ELSE WOULD I USE, AS I AM THE--
"BLIMP-MASTER."
OR WAS IT BLIMPMASTER? EITHER WAY, HE SWEATS A LOT.
SNICKER
WHO'S THAT LAUGHING, O?
I KNOW IT'S NOT YOU, 'CUZ NO MATTER HOW CUTE I GET, YOU KEEP IT ALL BURIED DOWN DEEP...

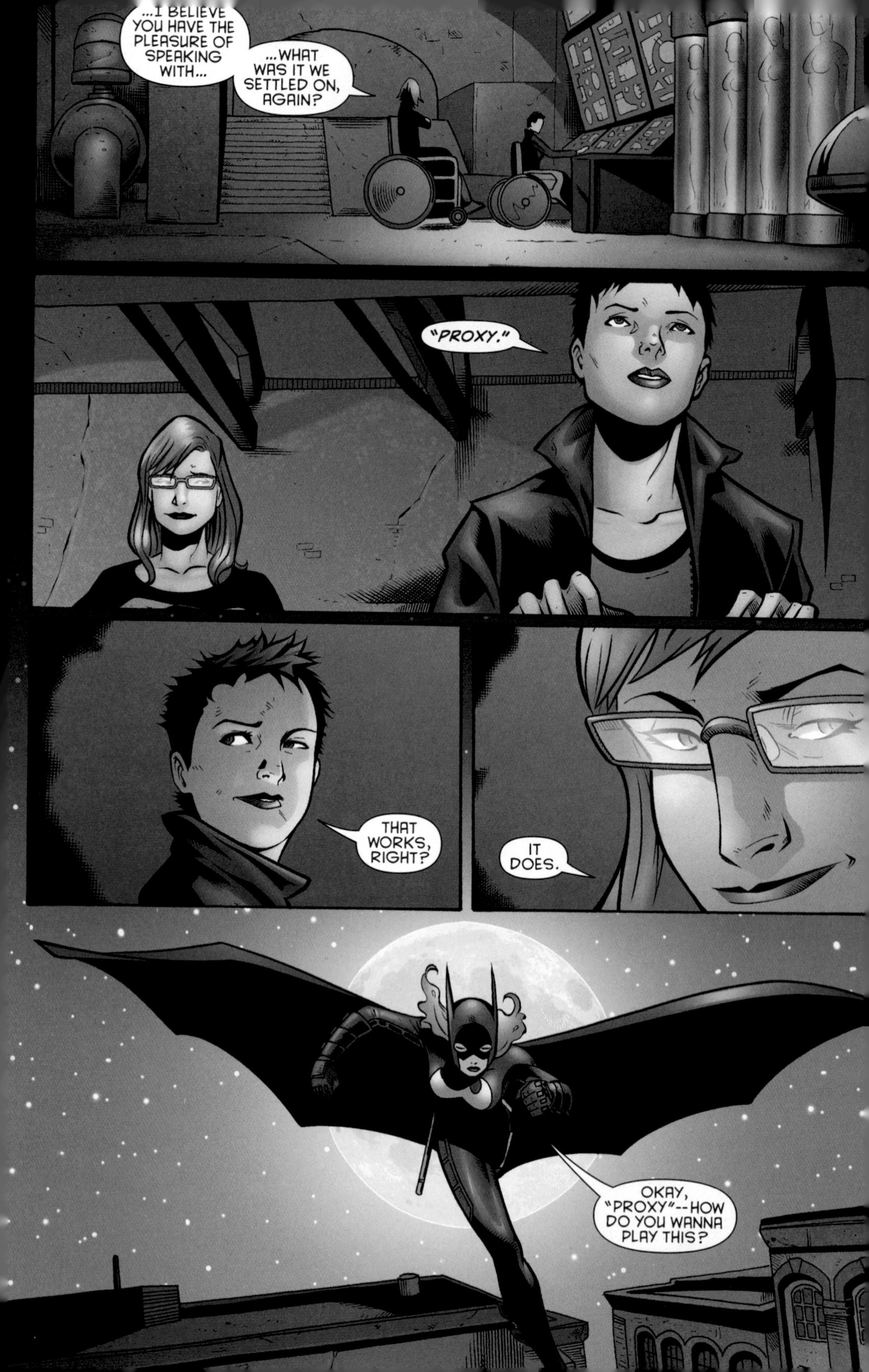
...I BELIEVE YOU HAVE THE PLEASURE OF SPEAKING WITH...
...WHAT WAS IT WE SETTLED ON, AGAIN?
"PROXY."
THAT WORKS, RIGHT?
IT DOES.
OKAY, "PROXY"--HOW DO YOU WANNA PLAY THIS?

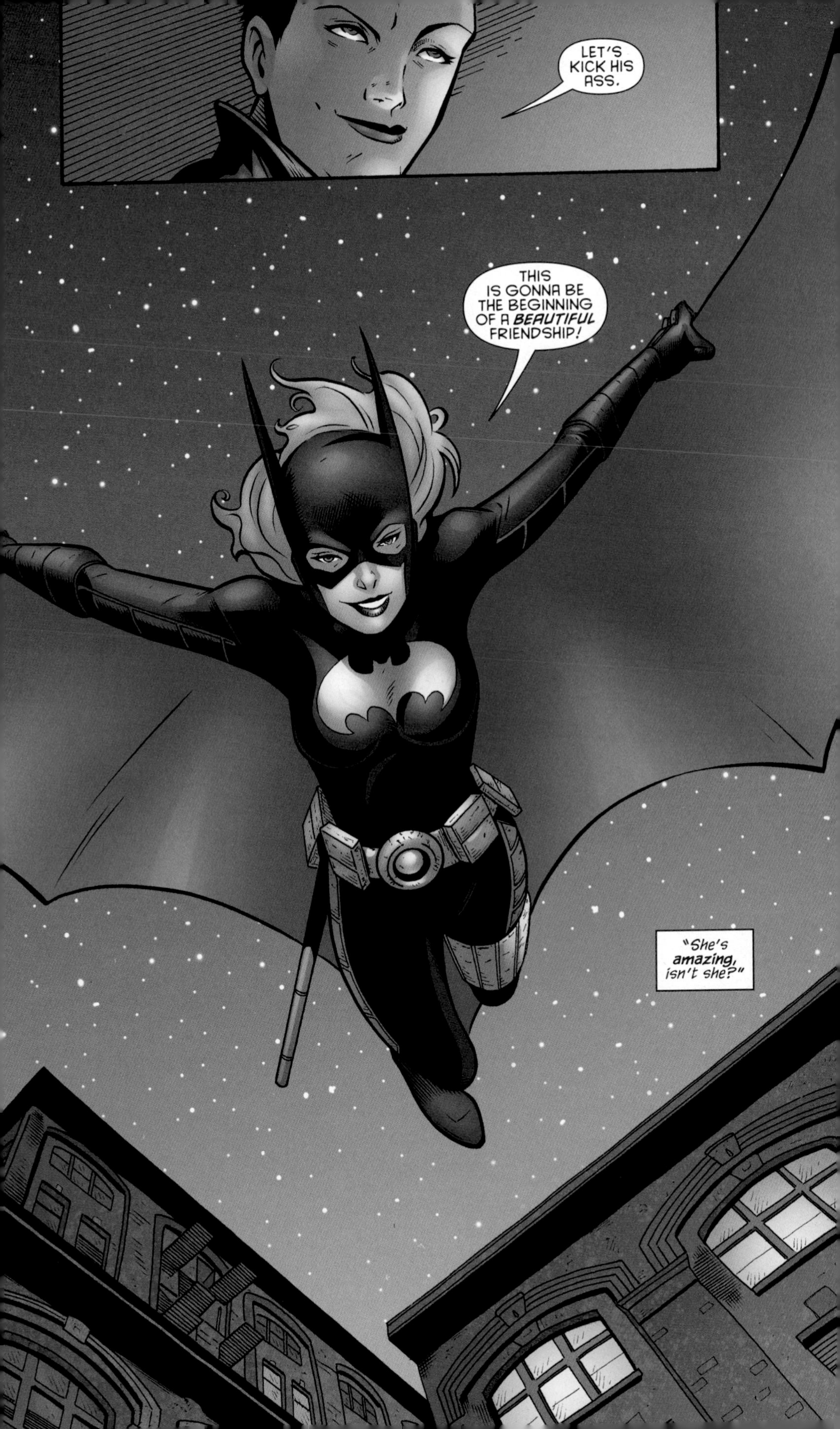
LET'S KICK HIS ASS.
THIS IS GONNA BE THE BEGINNING OF A BEAUTIFUL FRIENDSHIP!
"She's amazing, isn't she?"

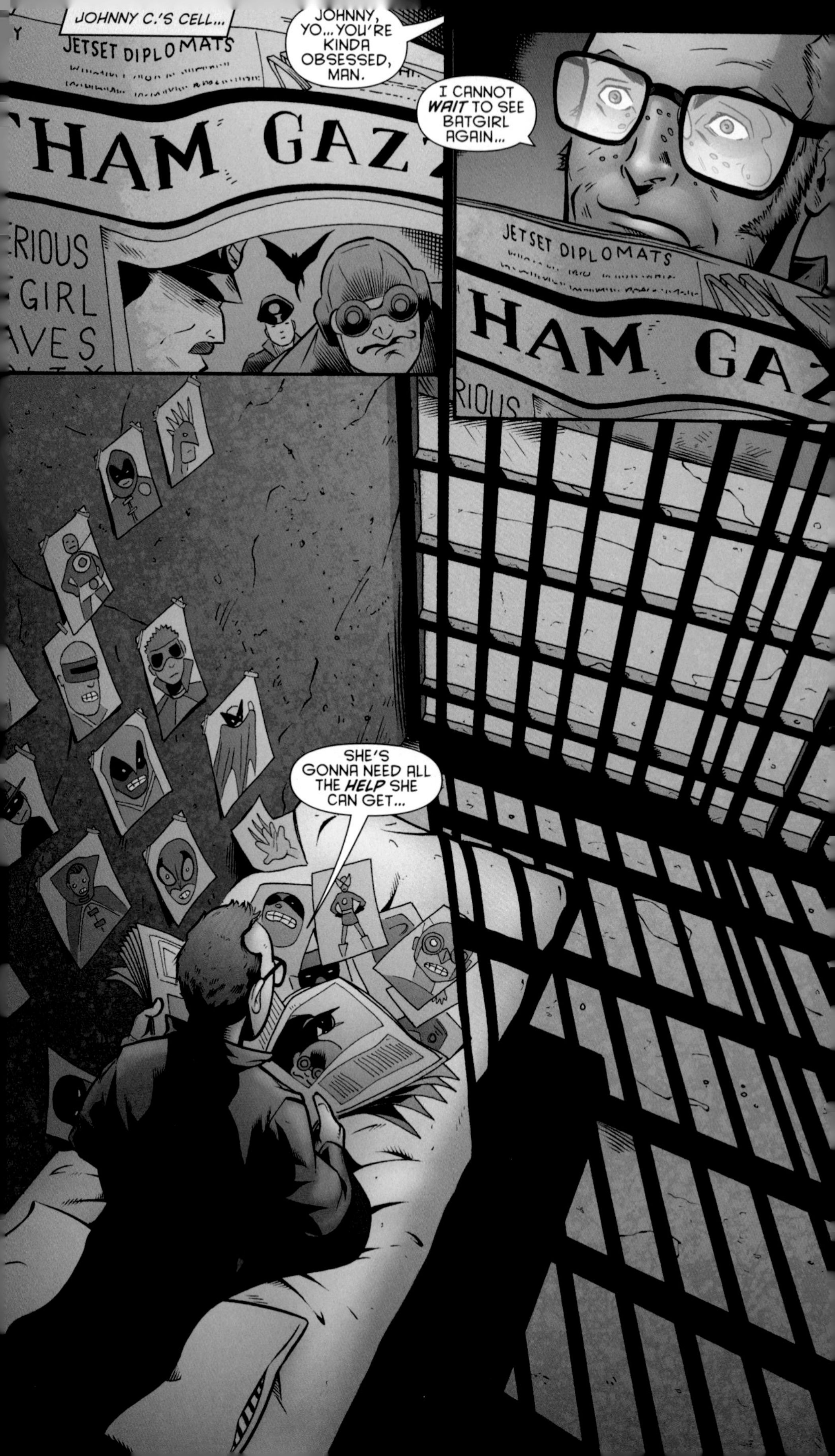
JOHNNY C.'S CELL...
JOHNNY, YO... YOU'RE KINDA OBSESSED, MAN.
I CANNOT WAIT TO SEE BATGIRL AGAIN...
SHE'S GONNA NEED ALL THE HELP SHE CAN GET...

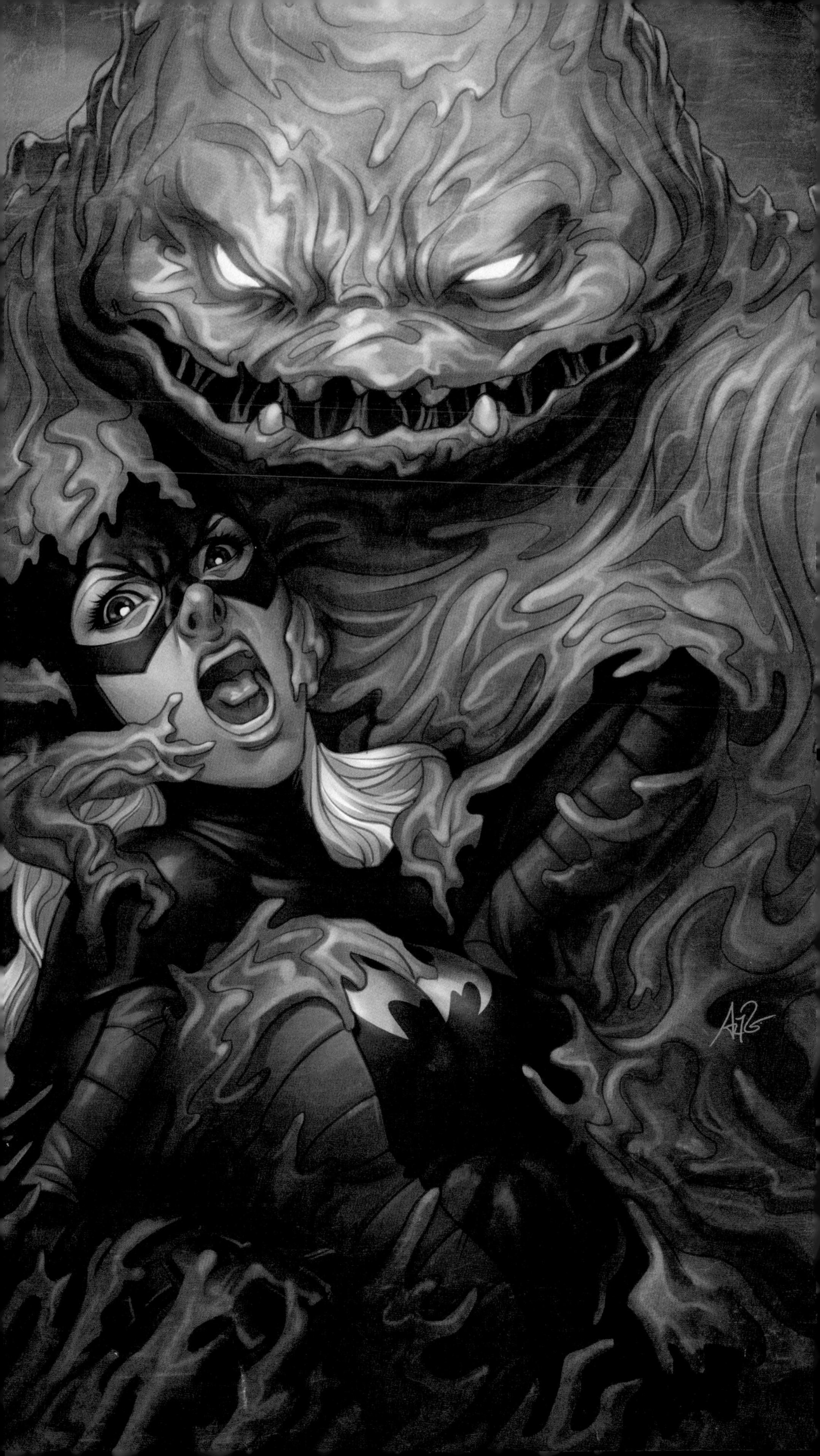

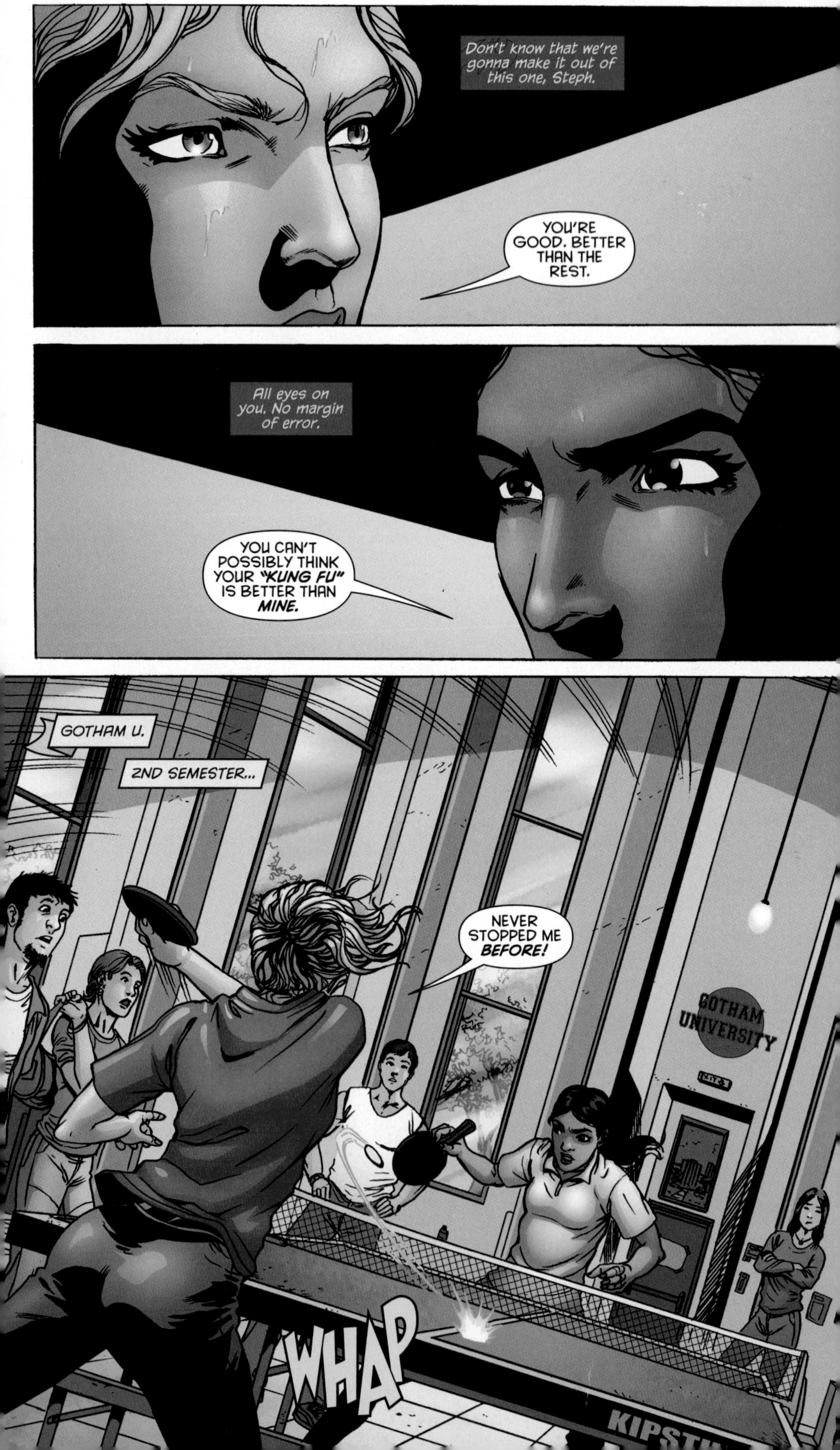

Don't know that we're gonna make it out of this one, Steph.
YOU'RE GOOD. BETTER THAN THE REST.
All eyes on you. No margin of error.
YOU CAN'T POSSIBLY THINK YOUR "KUNG FU" IS BETTER THAN MINE.
GOTHAM U.
2ND SEMESTER...
NEVER STOPPED ME BEFORE!
GOTHAM UNIVERSITY
WHAP

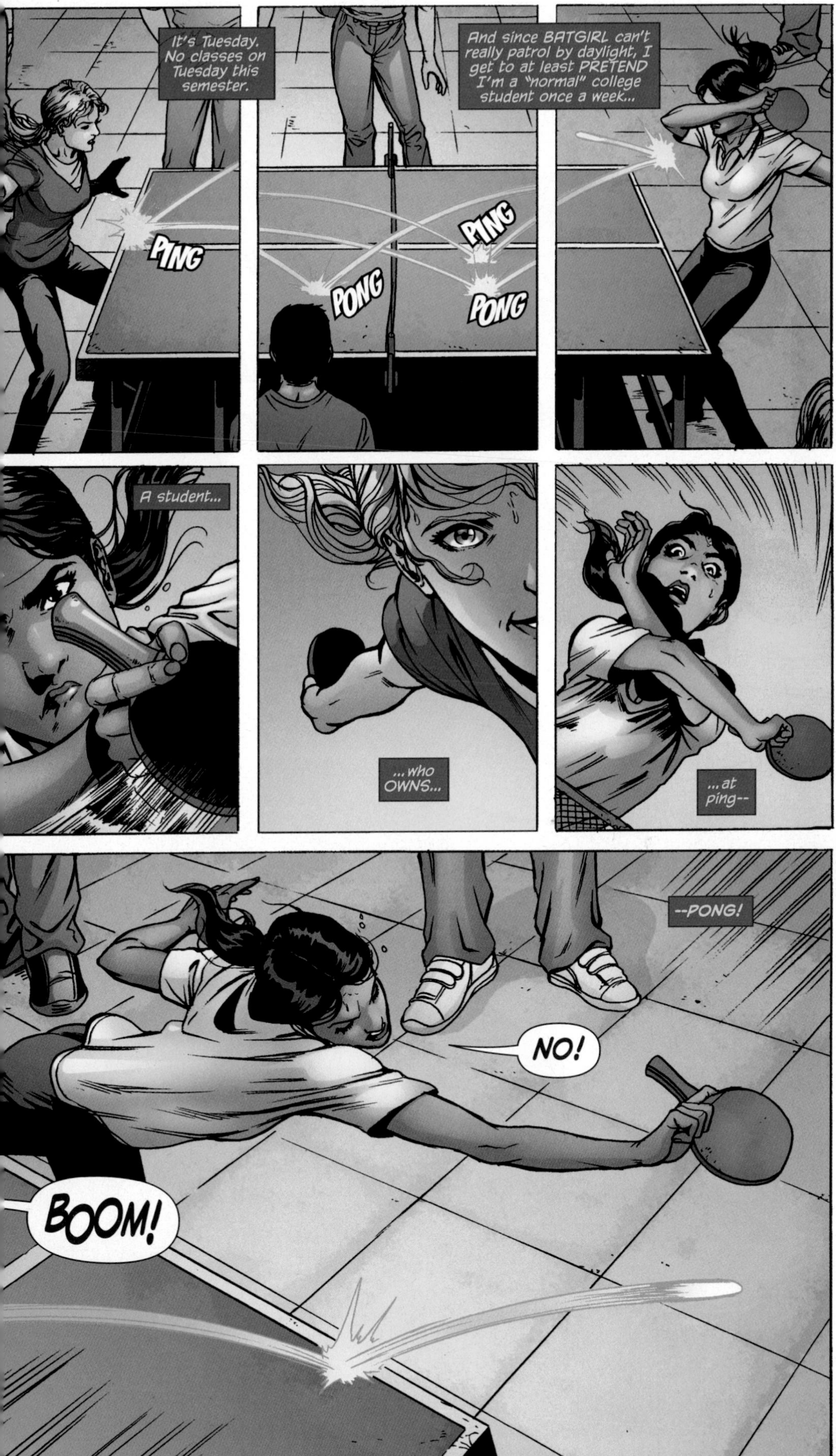

It's Tuesday. No classes on Tuesday this semester.
PING
PONG
PING
PONG
And since BATGIRL can't really patrol by daylight, I get to at least PRETEND I'm a "normal" college student once a week...
A student...
...who OWNS...
...at ping--
--PONG!
NO!
BOOM!

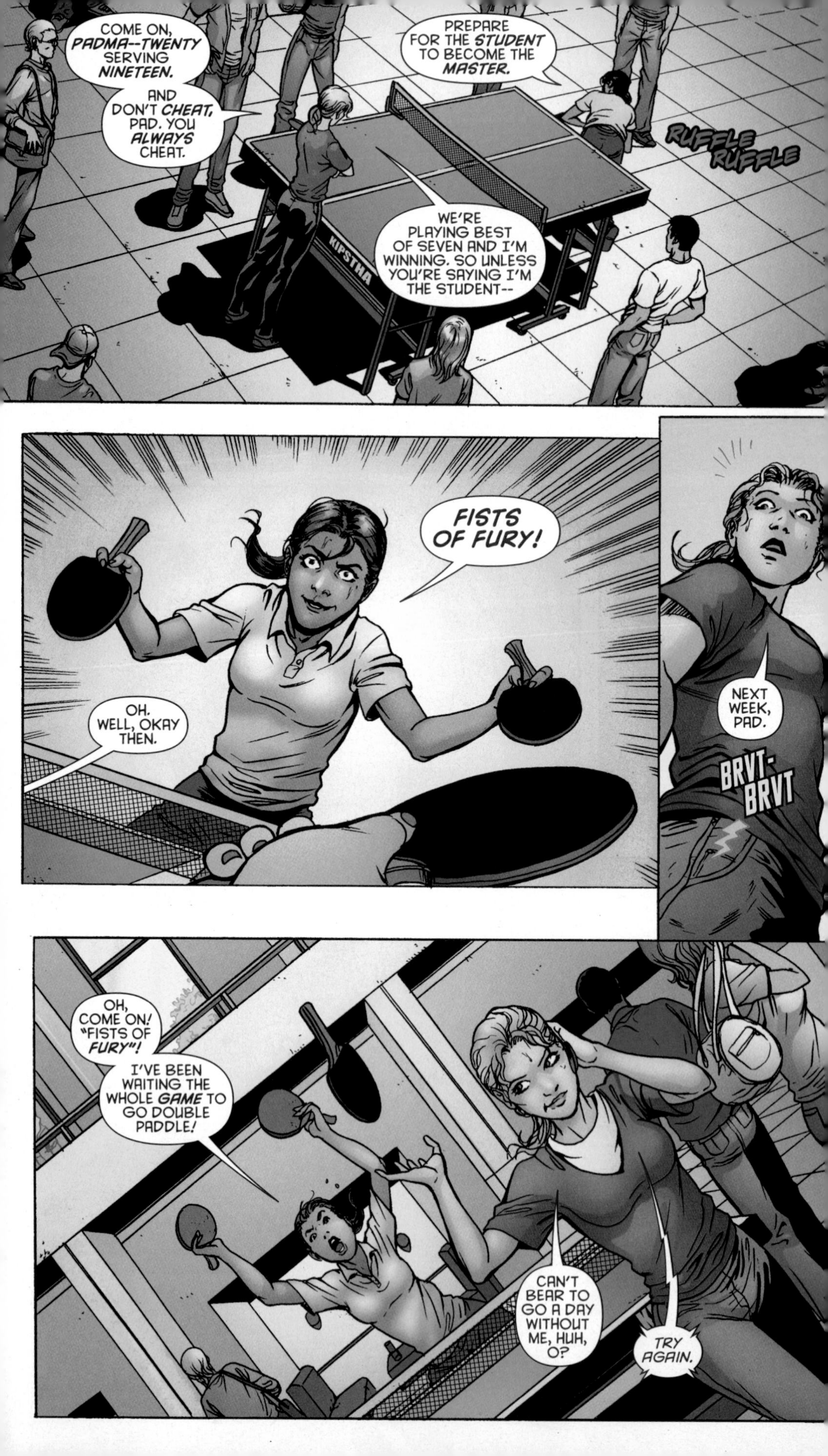
COME ON, PADMA--TWENTY SERVING NINETEEN.
AND DON'T CHEAT, PAD. YOU ALWAYS CHEAT.
PREPARE FOR THE STUDENT TO BECOME THE MASTER.
RUFFLE RUFFLE
KIPSTHA
WE'RE PLAYING BEST OF SEVEN AND I'M WINNING. SO UNLESS YOU'RE SAYING I'M THE STUDENT--
FISTS OF FURY!
OH. WELL, OKAY THEN.
NEXT WEEK, PAD.
BRVT-BRVT
OH, COME ON! "FISTS OF FURY"!
I'VE BEEN WAITING THE WHOLE GAME TO GO DOUBLE PADDLE!
CAN'T BEAR TO GO A DAY WITHOUT ME, HUH, O?
TRY AGAIN.

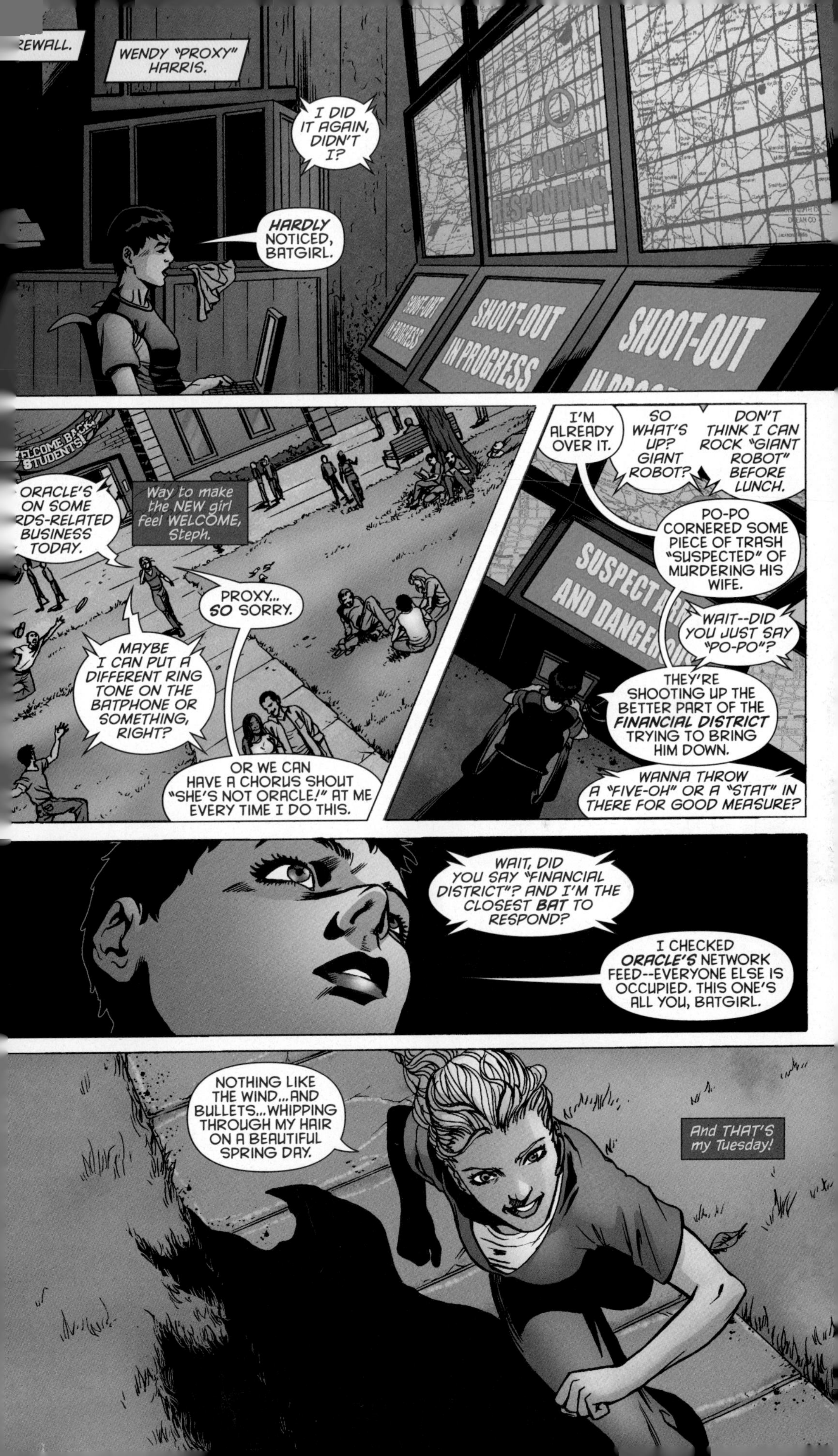

REWALL.
WENDY "PROXY" HARRIS.
I DID IT AGAIN, DIDN'T I?
HARDLY NOTICED, BATGIRL.
POLICE RESPONDING
SHOOT-OUT IN PROGRESS
SHOOT-OUT IN PROGRESS
SHOOT-OUT
WELCOME BACK STUDENTS!
ORACLE'S ON SOME RDS-RELATED BUSINESS TODAY.
Way to make the NEW girl feel WELCOME, Steph.
PROXY... SO SORRY.
MAYBE I CAN PUT A DIFFERENT RING TONE ON THE BATPHONE OR SOMETHING, RIGHT?
OR WE CAN HAVE A CHORUS SHOUT "SHE'S NOT ORACLE!" AT ME EVERY TIME I DO THIS.
I'M ALREADY OVER IT.
SO WHAT'S UP? GIANT ROBOT?
DON'T THINK I CAN ROCK "GIANT ROBOT" BEFORE LUNCH.
PO-PO CORNERED SOME PIECE OF TRASH "SUSPECTED" OF MURDERING HIS WIFE.
WAIT--DID YOU JUST SAY "PO-PO"?
THEY'RE SHOOTING UP THE BETTER PART OF THE FINANCIAL DISTRICT TRYING TO BRING HIM DOWN.
WANNA THROW A "FIVE-OH" OR A "STAT" IN THERE FOR GOOD MEASURE?
WAIT, DID YOU SAY "FINANCIAL DISTRICT"? AND I'M THE CLOSEST BAT TO RESPOND?
I CHECKED ORACLE'S NETWORK FEED--EVERYONE ELSE IS OCCUPIED. THIS ONE'S ALL YOU, BATGIRL.
NOTHING LIKE THE WIND...AND BULLETS...WHIPPING THROUGH MY HAIR ON A BEAUTIFUL SPRING DAY.
And THAT'S my Tuesday!

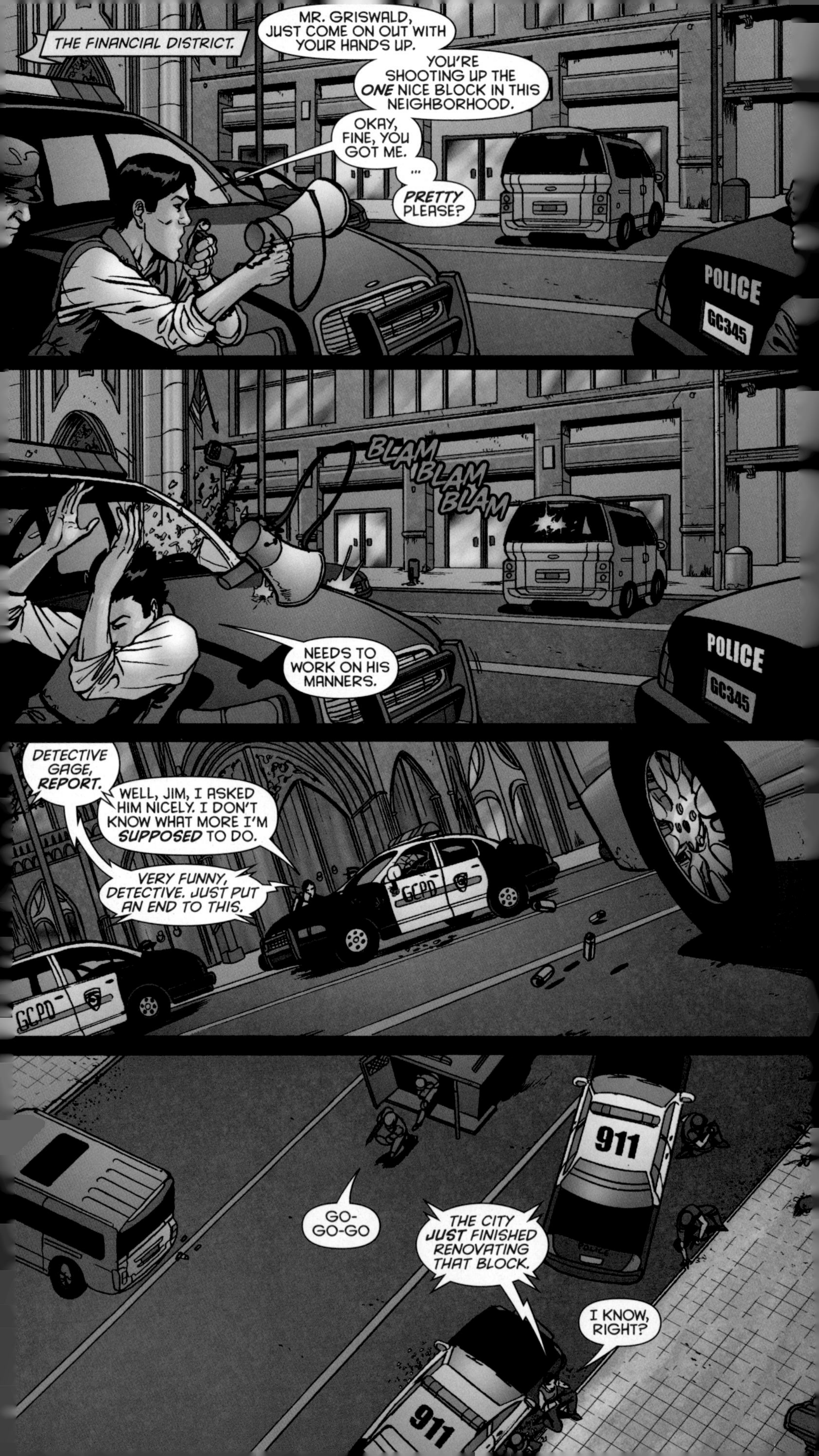
THE FINANCIAL DISTRICT.
MR. GRISWALD, JUST COME ON OUT WITH YOUR HANDS UP.
YOU'RE SHOOTING UP THE ONE NICE BLOCK IN THIS NEIGHBORHOOD.
OKAY, FINE, YOU GOT ME.
...
PRETTY PLEASE?
POLICE
GC345
BLAM BLAM BLAM
NEEDS TO WORK ON HIS MANNERS.
POLICE
GC345
DETECTIVE GAGE, REPORT.
WELL, JIM, I ASKED HIM NICELY. I DON'T KNOW WHAT MORE I'M SUPPOSED TO DO.
VERY FUNNY, DETECTIVE. JUST PUT AN END TO THIS.
GCPD
GCPD
911
GO-GO-GO
THE CITY JUST FINISHED RENOVATING THAT BLOCK.
I KNOW, RIGHT?
911

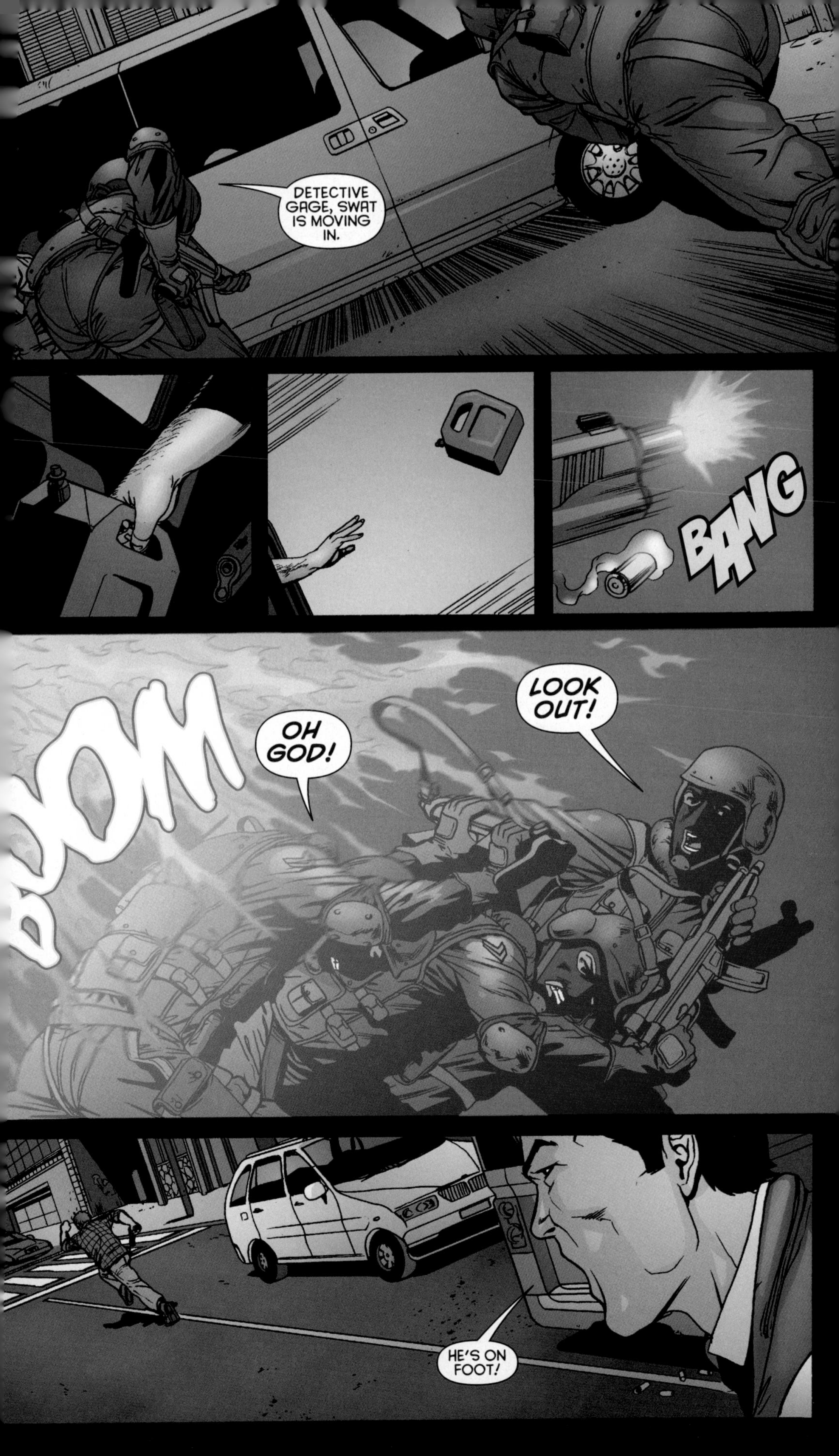
DETECTIVE GAGE, SWAT IS MOVING IN.
BANG
BOOM
OH GOD!
LOOK OUT!
HE'S ON FOOT!

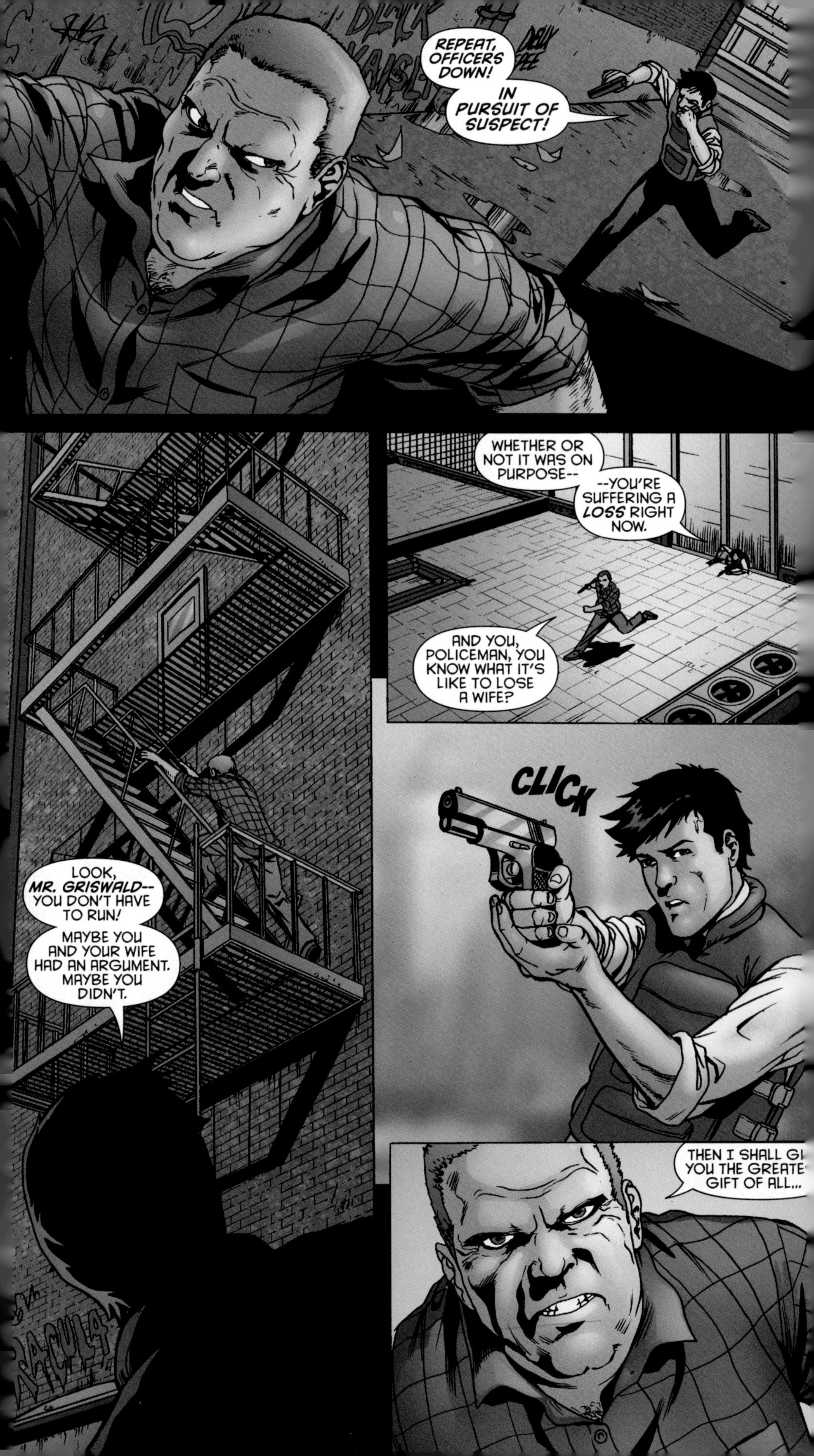

REPEAT, OFFICERS DOWN!
IN PURSUIT OF SUSPECT!
LOOK, MR. GRISWALD-- YOU DON'T HAVE TO RUN!
MAYBE YOU AND YOUR WIFE HAD AN ARGUMENT. MAYBE YOU DIDN'T.
WHETHER OR NOT IT WAS ON PURPOSE--
--YOU'RE SUFFERING A LOSS RIGHT NOW.
AND YOU, POLICEMAN, YOU KNOW WHAT IT'S LIKE TO LOSE A WIFE?
CLICK
THEN I SHALL GI
YOU THE GREATE
GIFT OF ALL...

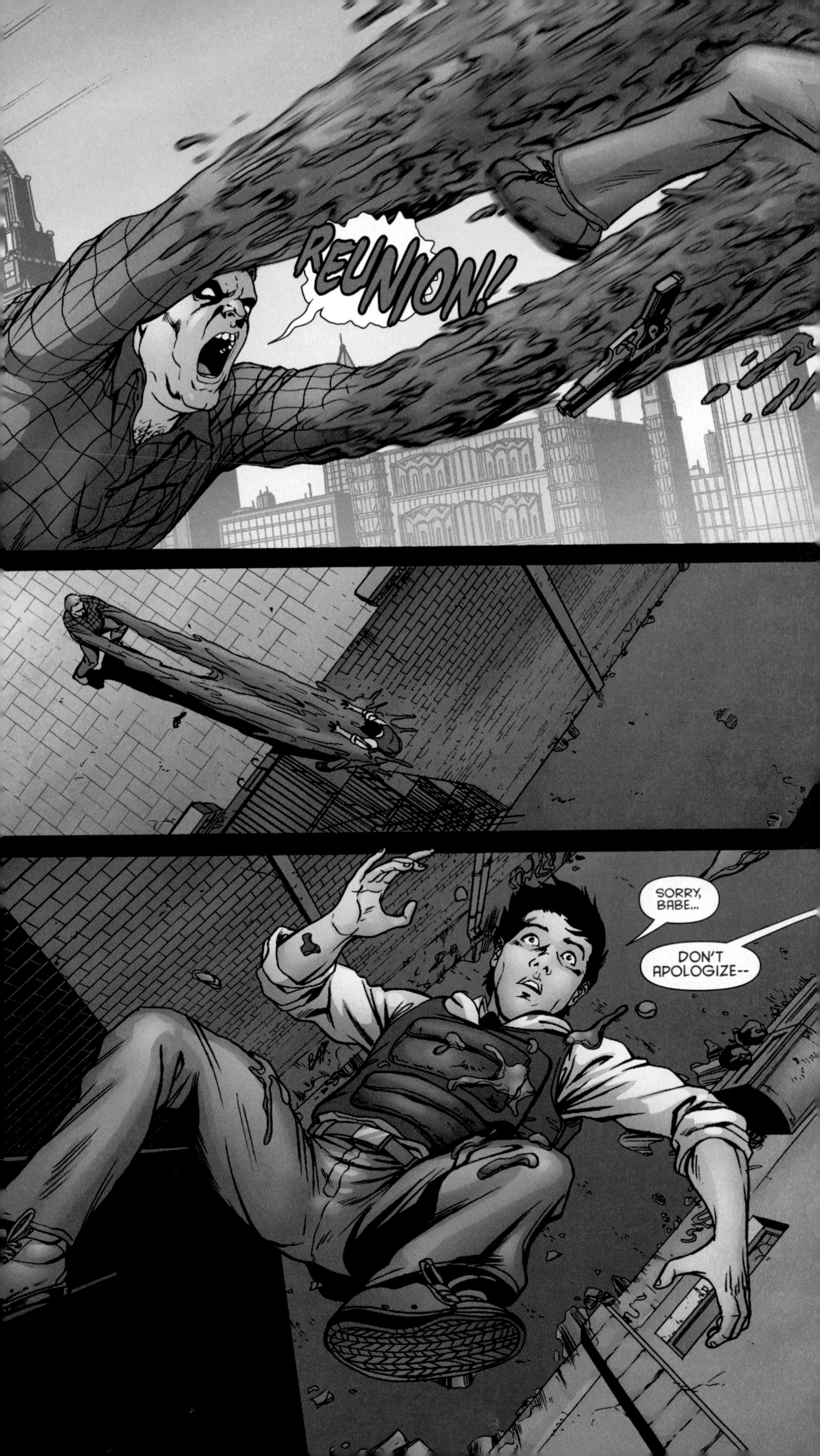
REUNION!
SORRY, BABE...
DON'T APOLOGIZE--

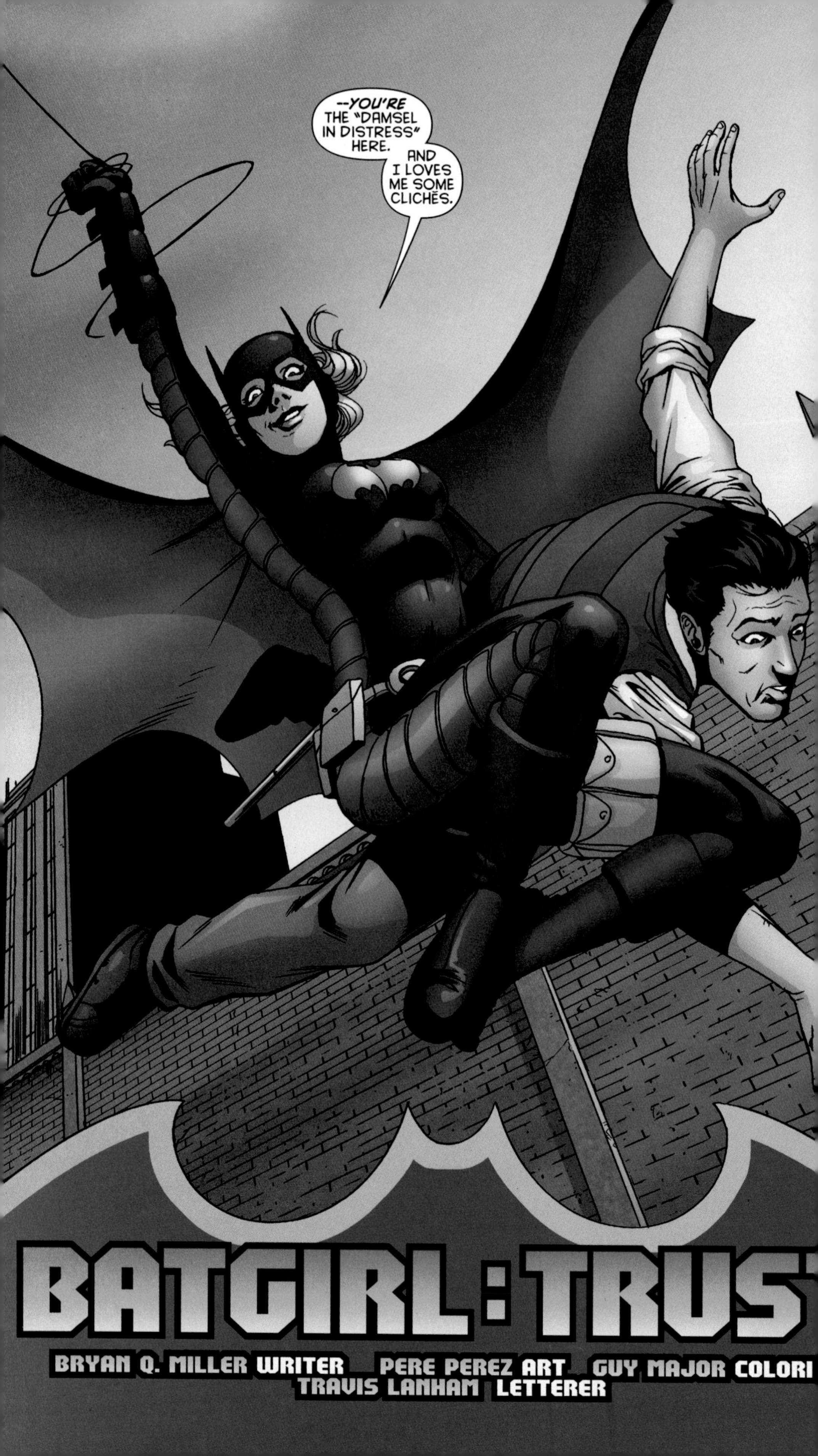
--YOU'RE THE "DAMSEL IN DISTRESS" HERE.
AND I LOVES ME SOME CLICHÉS.
BATGIRL: TRUS
BRYAN Q. MILLER WRITER PERE PEREZ ART GUY MAJOR COLORI
TRAVIS LANHAM LETTERER

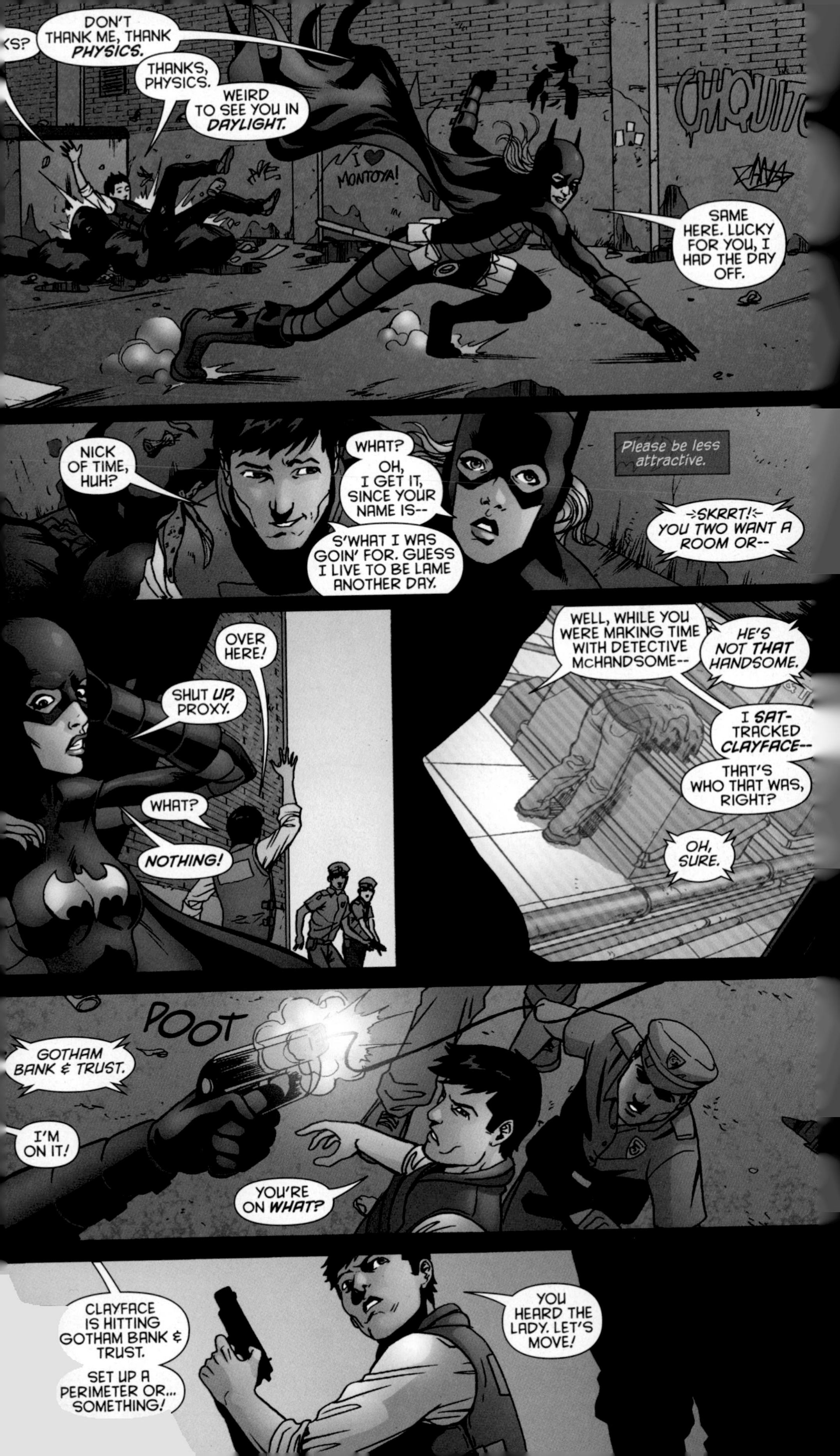

...KS?
DON'T THANK ME, THANK PHYSICS.
THANKS, PHYSICS.
WEIRD TO SEE YOU IN DAYLIGHT.
I ♥ MONTOYA!
CHQUITO
SAME HERE. LUCKY FOR YOU, I HAD THE DAY OFF.
NICK OF TIME, HUH?
WHAT?
OH, I GET IT, SINCE YOUR NAME IS--
S'WHAT I WAS GOIN' FOR. GUESS I LIVE TO BE LAME ANOTHER DAY.
Please be less attractive.
-SKRRT!- YOU TWO WANT A ROOM OR--
OVER HERE!
SHUT UP, PROXY.
WHAT?
NOTHING!
WELL, WHILE YOU WERE MAKING TIME WITH DETECTIVE McHANDSOME--
HE'S NOT THAT HANDSOME.
I SAT-TRACKED CLAYFACE--
THAT'S WHO THAT WAS, RIGHT?
OH, SURE.
POOT
GOTHAM BANK & TRUST.
I'M ON IT!
YOU'RE ON WHAT?
CLAYFACE IS HITTING GOTHAM BANK & TRUST.
SET UP A PERIMETER OR... SOMETHING!
YOU HEARD THE LADY. LET'S MOVE!

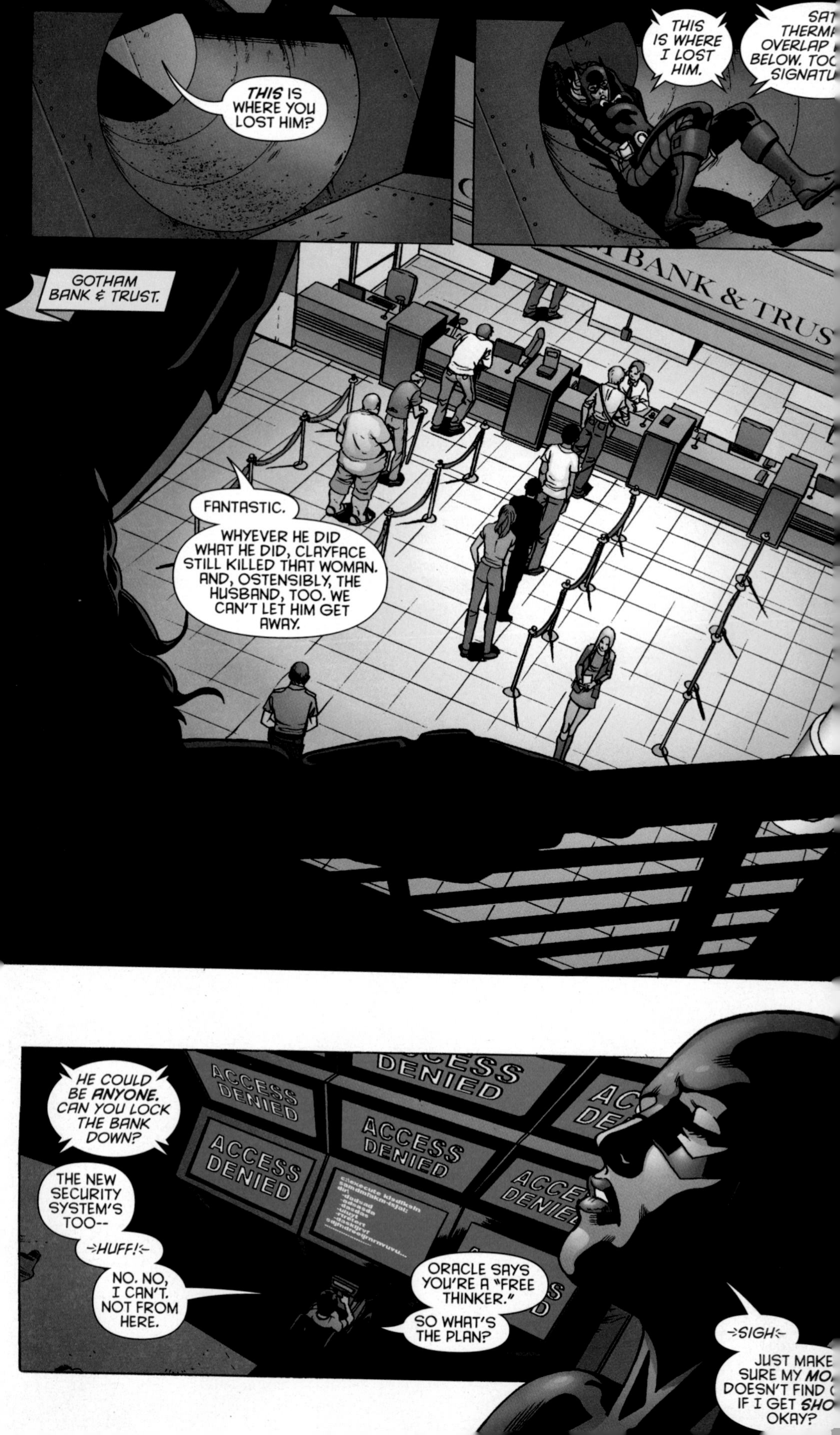

THIS IS WHERE YOU LOST HIM?
THIS IS WHERE I LOST HIM.
SAT THERM OVERLAP BELOW. TOO SIGNATU
GOTHAM BANK & TRUST.
BANK & TRUS
FANTASTIC.
WHYEVER HE DID WHAT HE DID, CLAYFACE STILL KILLED THAT WOMAN. AND, OSTENSIBLY, THE HUSBAND, TOO. WE CAN'T LET HIM GET AWAY.
HE COULD BE ANYONE. CAN YOU LOCK THE BANK DOWN?
THE NEW SECURITY SYSTEM'S TOO--
HUFF!
NO. NO, I CAN'T. NOT FROM HERE.
ACCESS DENIED
ORACLE SAYS YOU'RE A "FREE THINKER."
SO WHAT'S THE PLAN?
SIGH
JUST MAKE SURE MY MO DOESN'T FIND IF I GET SHO OKAY?

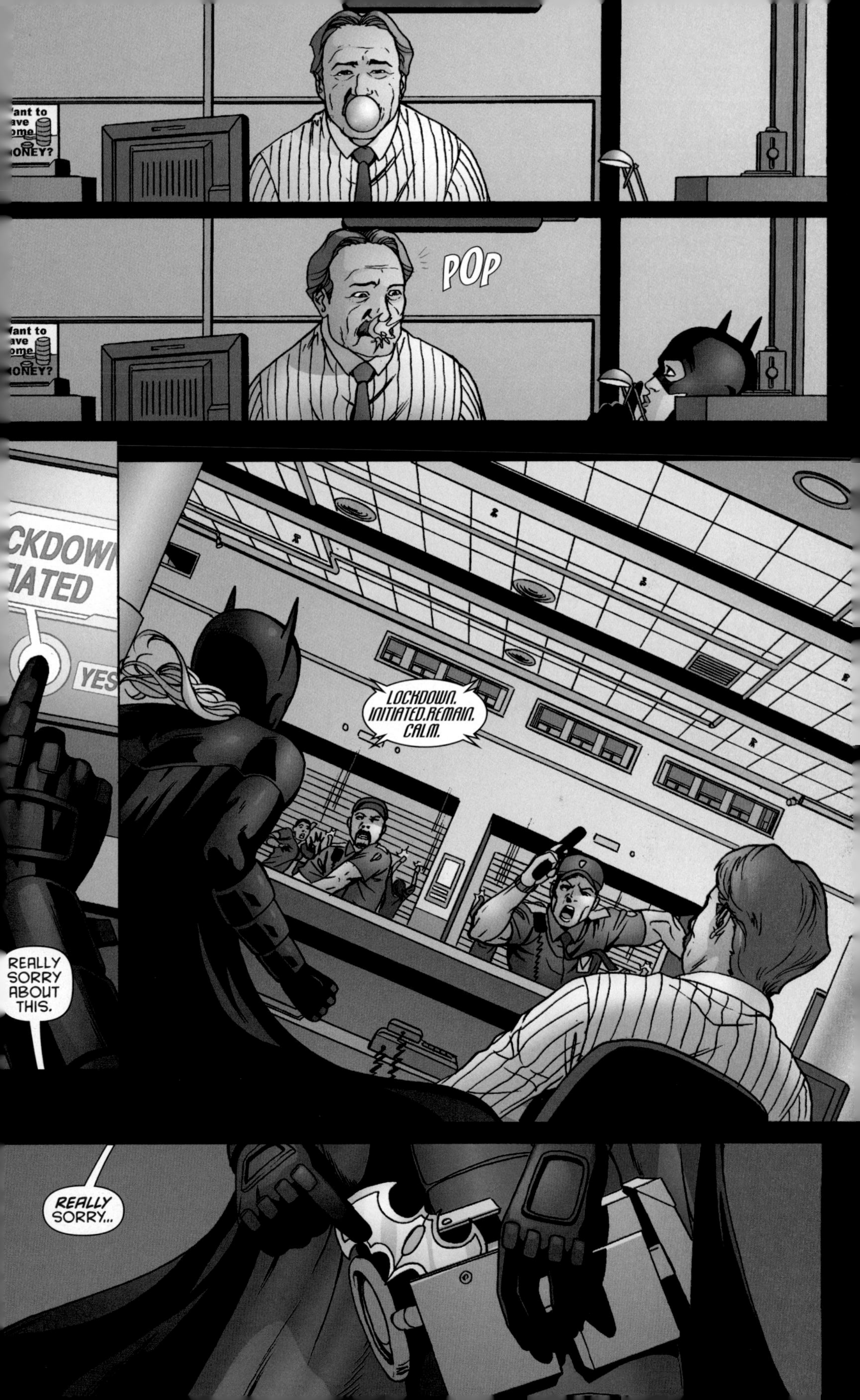
Want to save some MONEY?
POP
Want to save some MONEY?
LOCKDOWN INITIATED
YES
LOCKDOWN. INITIATED.REMAIN. CALM.
REALLY SORRY ABOUT THIS.
REALLY SORRY...

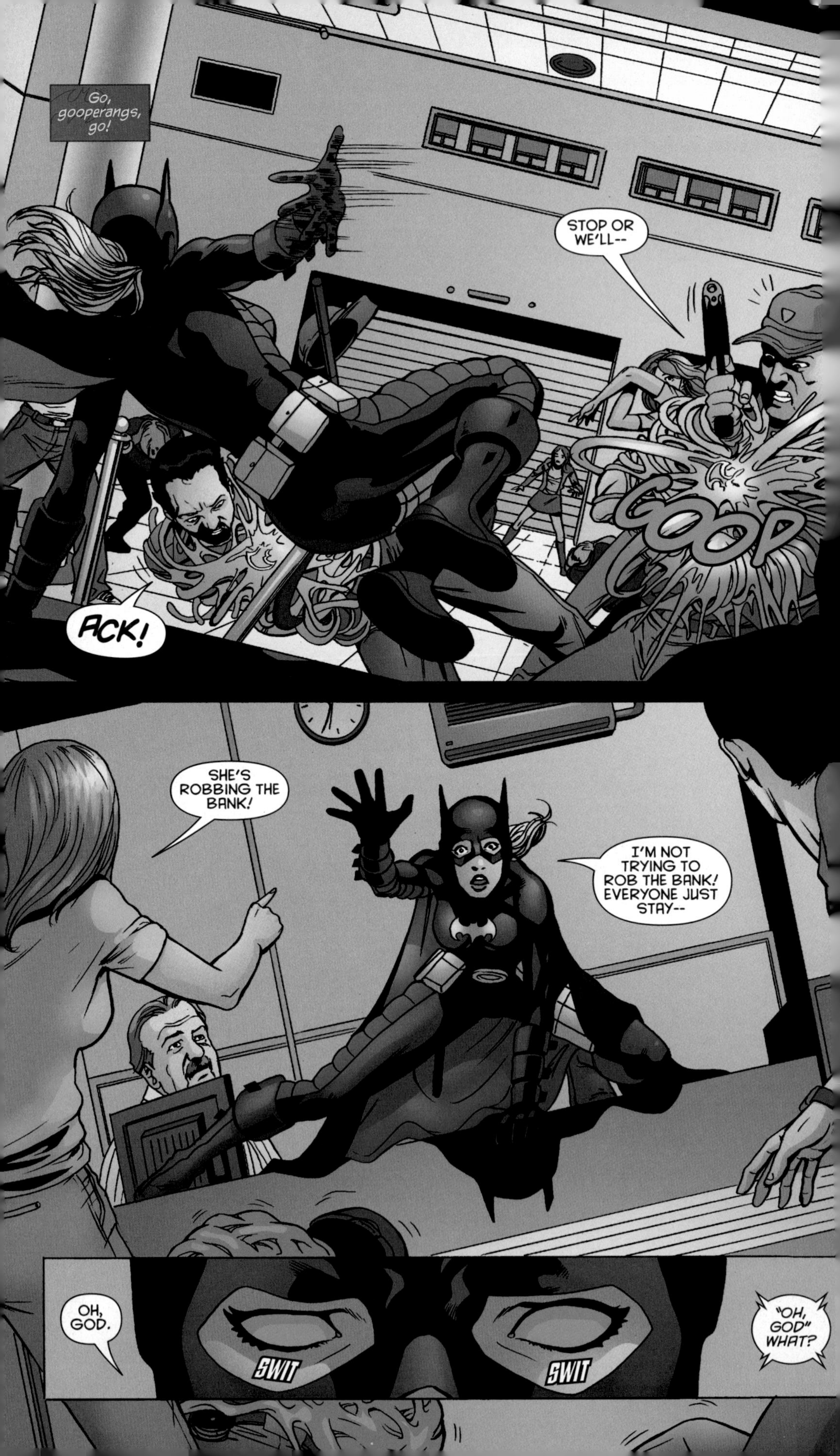

Go, gooperangs, go!
STOP OR WE'LL--
GOOP
ACK!
SHE'S ROBBING THE BANK!
I'M NOT TRYING TO ROB THE BANK! EVERYONE JUST STAY--
OH, GOD.
SWIT
SWIT
"OH, GOD" WHAT?

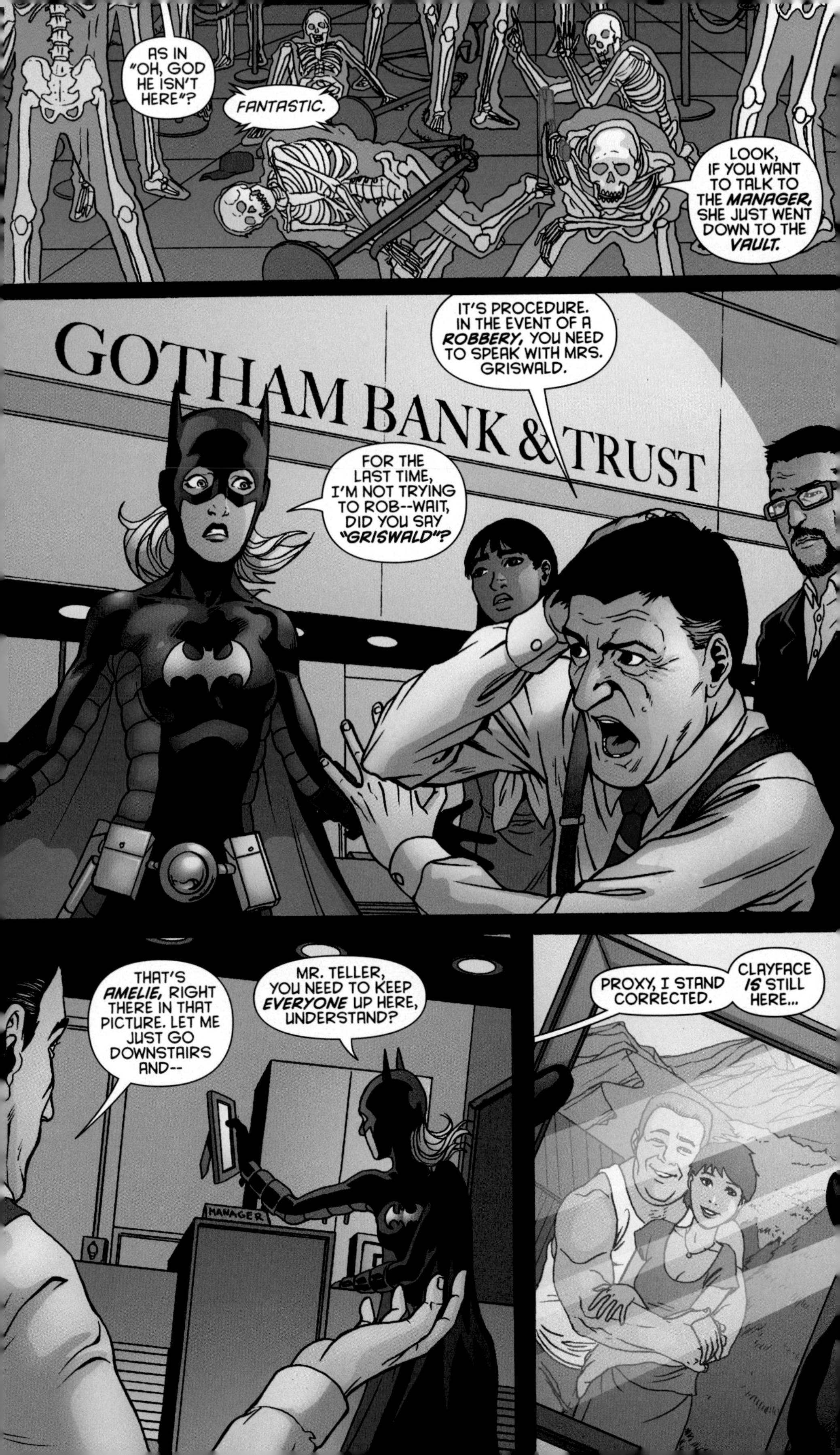
AS IN "OH, GOD HE ISN'T HERE"?
FANTASTIC.
LOOK, IF YOU WANT TO TALK TO THE **MANAGER,** SHE JUST WENT DOWN TO THE **VAULT.**
GOTHAM BANK & TRUST
IT'S PROCEDURE. IN THE EVENT OF A **ROBBERY,** YOU NEED TO SPEAK WITH MRS. GRISWALD.
FOR THE LAST TIME, I'M NOT TRYING TO ROB--WAIT, DID YOU SAY **"GRISWALD"?**
THAT'S **AMELIE,** RIGHT THERE IN THAT PICTURE. LET ME JUST GO DOWNSTAIRS AND--
MR. TELLER, YOU NEED TO KEEP **EVERYONE** UP HERE, UNDERSTAND?
MANAGER
PROXY, I STAND CORRECTED.
CLAYFACE **IS** STILL HERE...

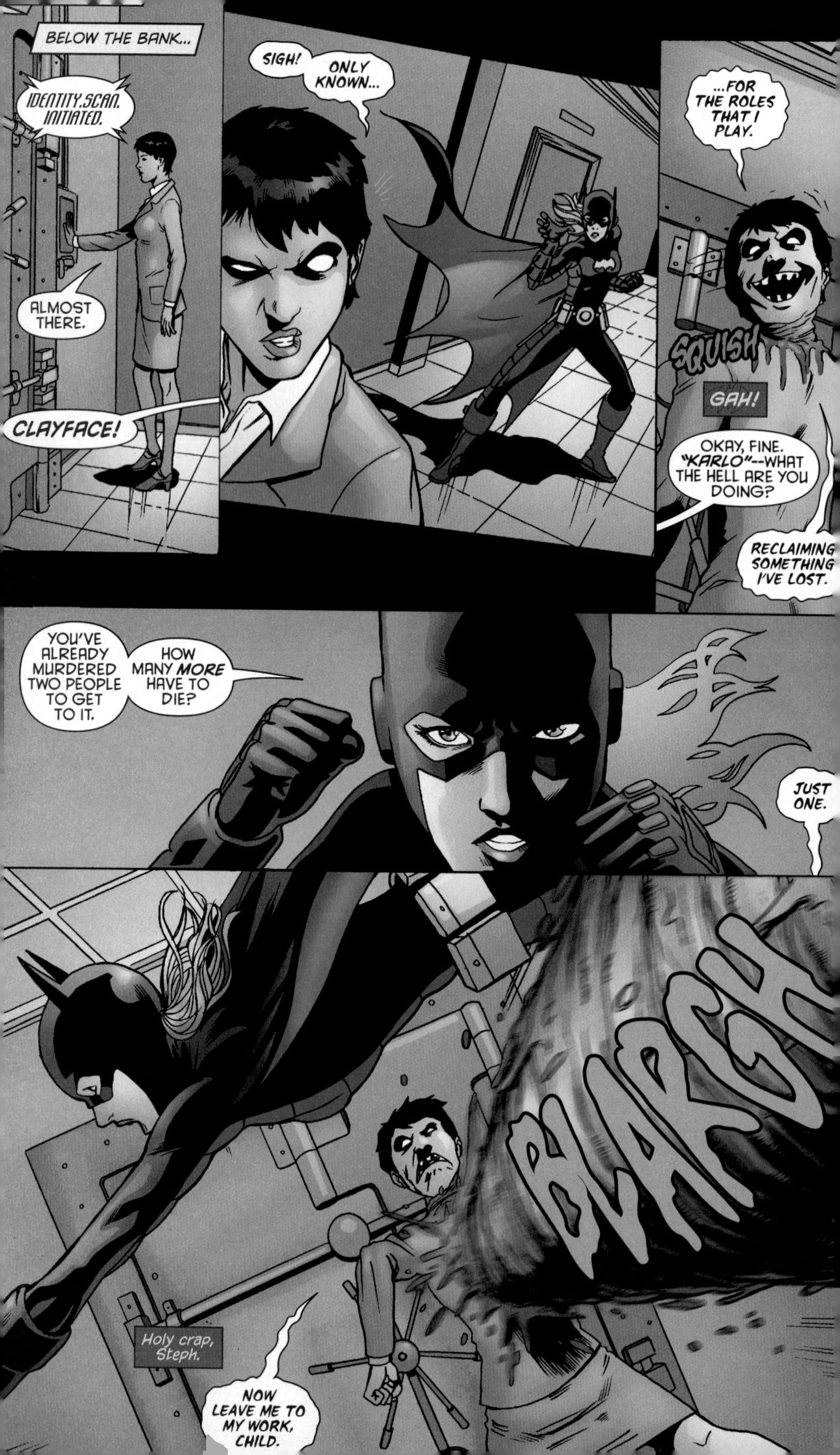
BELOW THE BANK...
IDENTITY.SCAN. INITIATED.
ALMOST THERE.
CLAYFACE!
SIGH!
ONLY KNOWN...
...FOR THE ROLES THAT I PLAY.
SQUISH
GAH!
OKAY, FINE. "KARLO"--WHAT THE HELL ARE YOU DOING?
RECLAIMING SOMETHING I'VE LOST.
YOU'VE ALREADY MURDERED TWO PEOPLE TO GET TO IT.
HOW MANY MORE HAVE TO DIE?
JUST ONE.
BLARGH
Holy crap, Steph.
NOW LEAVE ME TO MY WORK, CHILD.

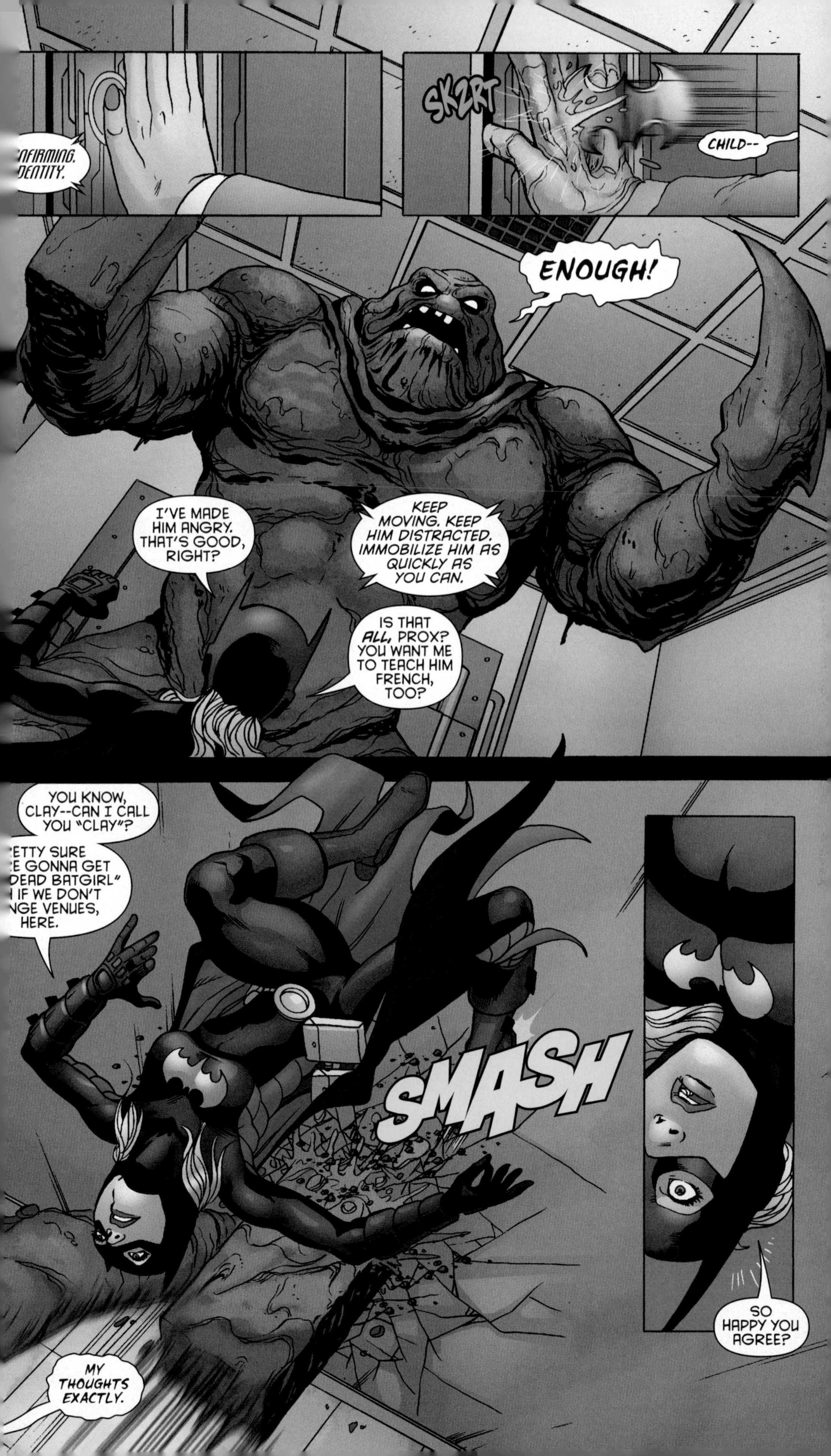

NFIRMING.
DENTITY.
SK2RT
CHILD--
ENOUGH!
I'VE MADE HIM ANGRY. THAT'S GOOD, RIGHT?
KEEP MOVING. KEEP HIM DISTRACTED. IMMOBILIZE HIM AS QUICKLY AS YOU CAN.
IS THAT ALL, PROX? YOU WANT ME TO TEACH HIM FRENCH, TOO?
YOU KNOW, CLAY--CAN I CALL YOU "CLAY"?
ETTY SURE
E GONNA GET
DEAD BATGIRL"
IF WE DON'T
NGE VENUES,
HERE.
SMASH
SO HAPPY YOU AGREE?
MY THOUGHTS EXACTLY.

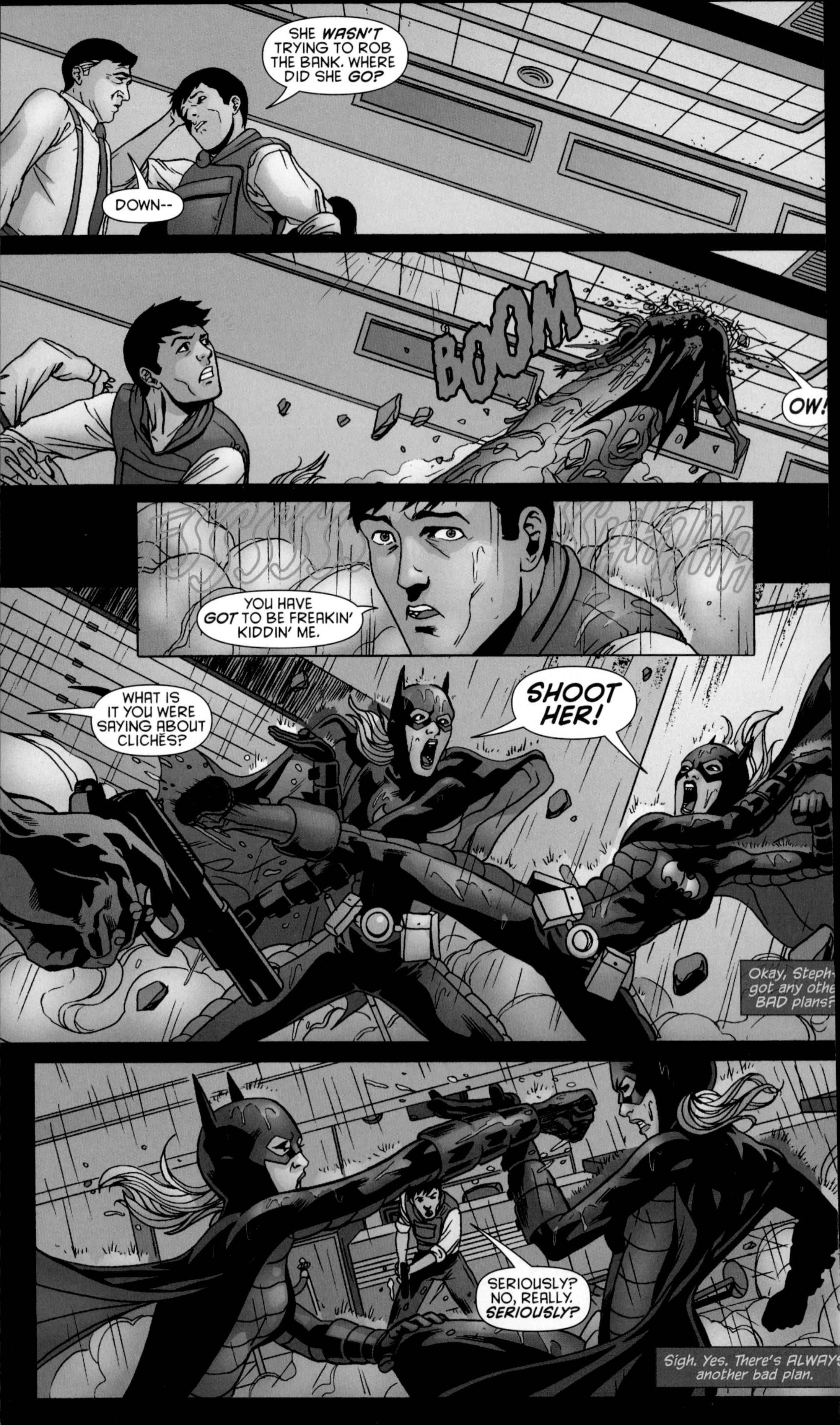

SHE WASN'T TRYING TO ROB THE BANK. WHERE DID SHE GO?
DOWN--
BOOM
OW!
YOU HAVE GOT TO BE FREAKIN' KIDDIN' ME.
WHAT IS IT YOU WERE SAYING ABOUT CLICHÉS?
SHOOT HER!
Okay, Steph-- got any other BAD plans?
SERIOUSLY? NO, REALLY. SERIOUSLY?
Sigh. Yes. There's ALWAYS another bad plan.

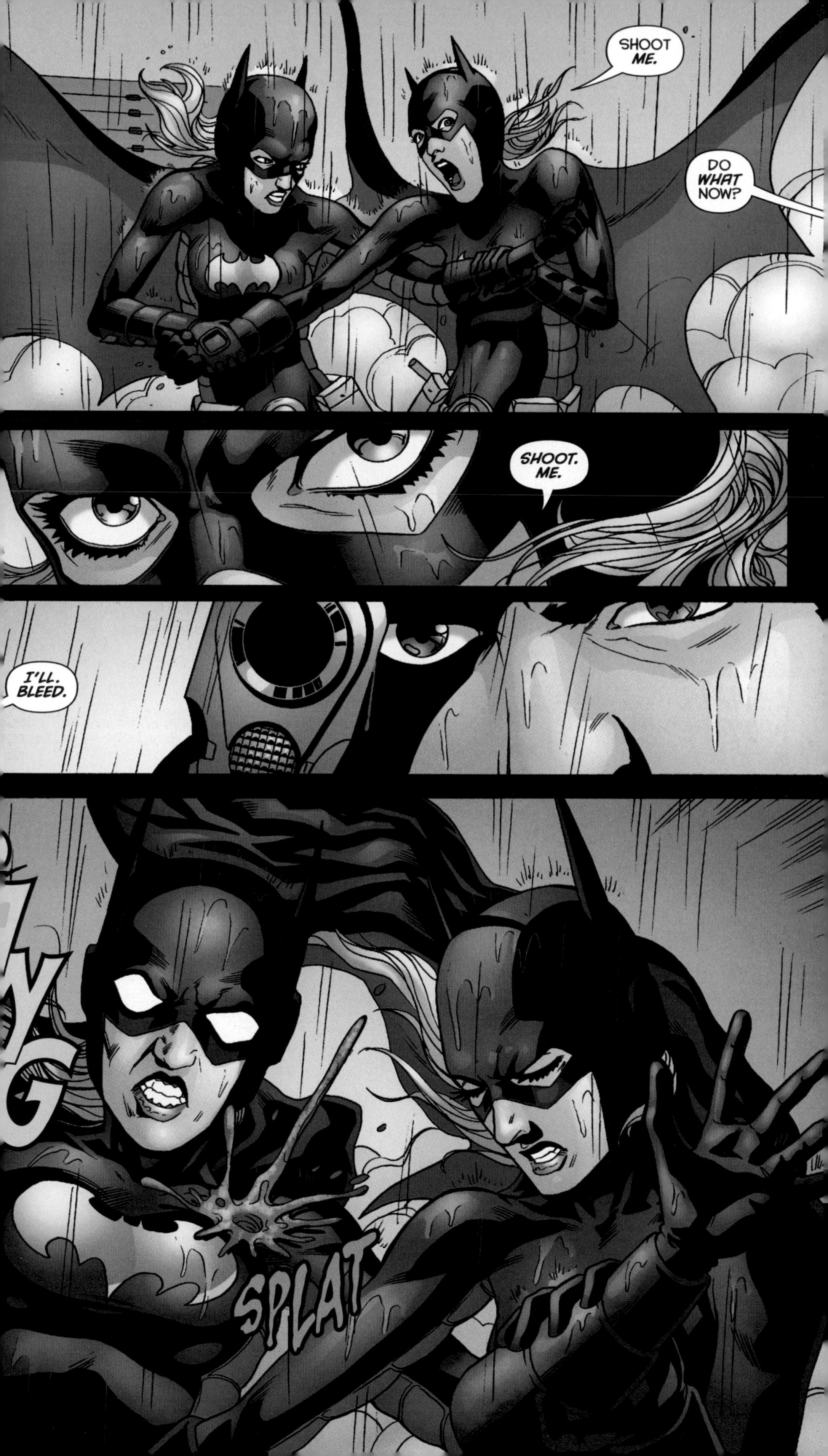
SHOOT ME.
DO WHAT NOW?
SHOOT. ME.
I'LL. BLEED.
SPLAT

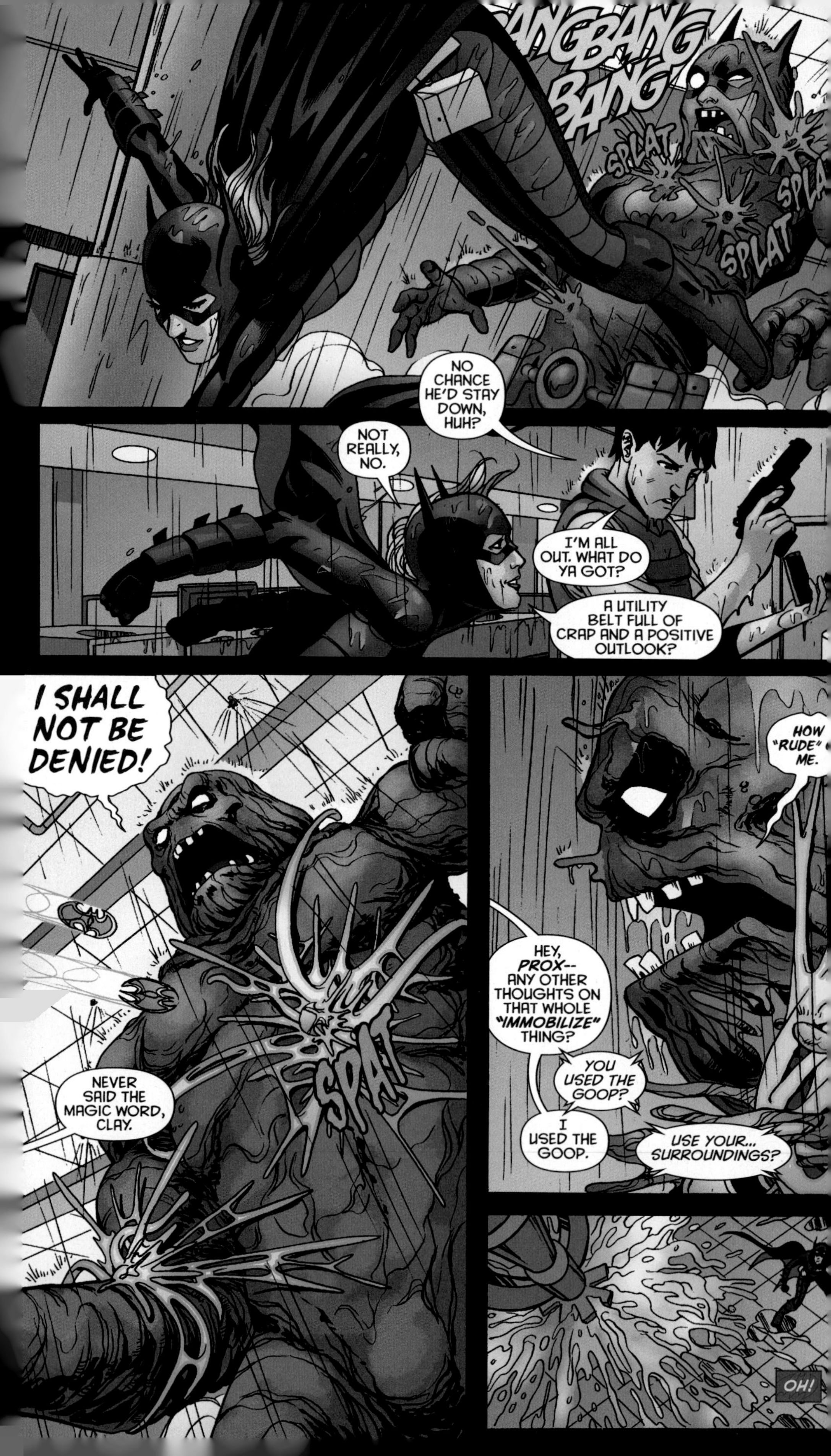
BANGBANG BANG
SPLAT
SPLAT
SPLAT
SPLAT
NO CHANCE HE'D STAY DOWN, HUH?
NOT REALLY, NO.
I'M ALL OUT. WHAT DO YA GOT?
A UTILITY BELT FULL OF CRAP AND A POSITIVE OUTLOOK?
I SHALL NOT BE DENIED!
SPAT
NEVER SAID THE MAGIC WORD, CLAY.
HOW "RUDE" ME.
HEY, *PROX*-- ANY OTHER THOUGHTS ON THAT WHOLE *"IMMOBILIZE"* THING?
YOU USED THE GOOP?
I USED THE GOOP.
USE YOUR... SURROUNDINGS?
OH!

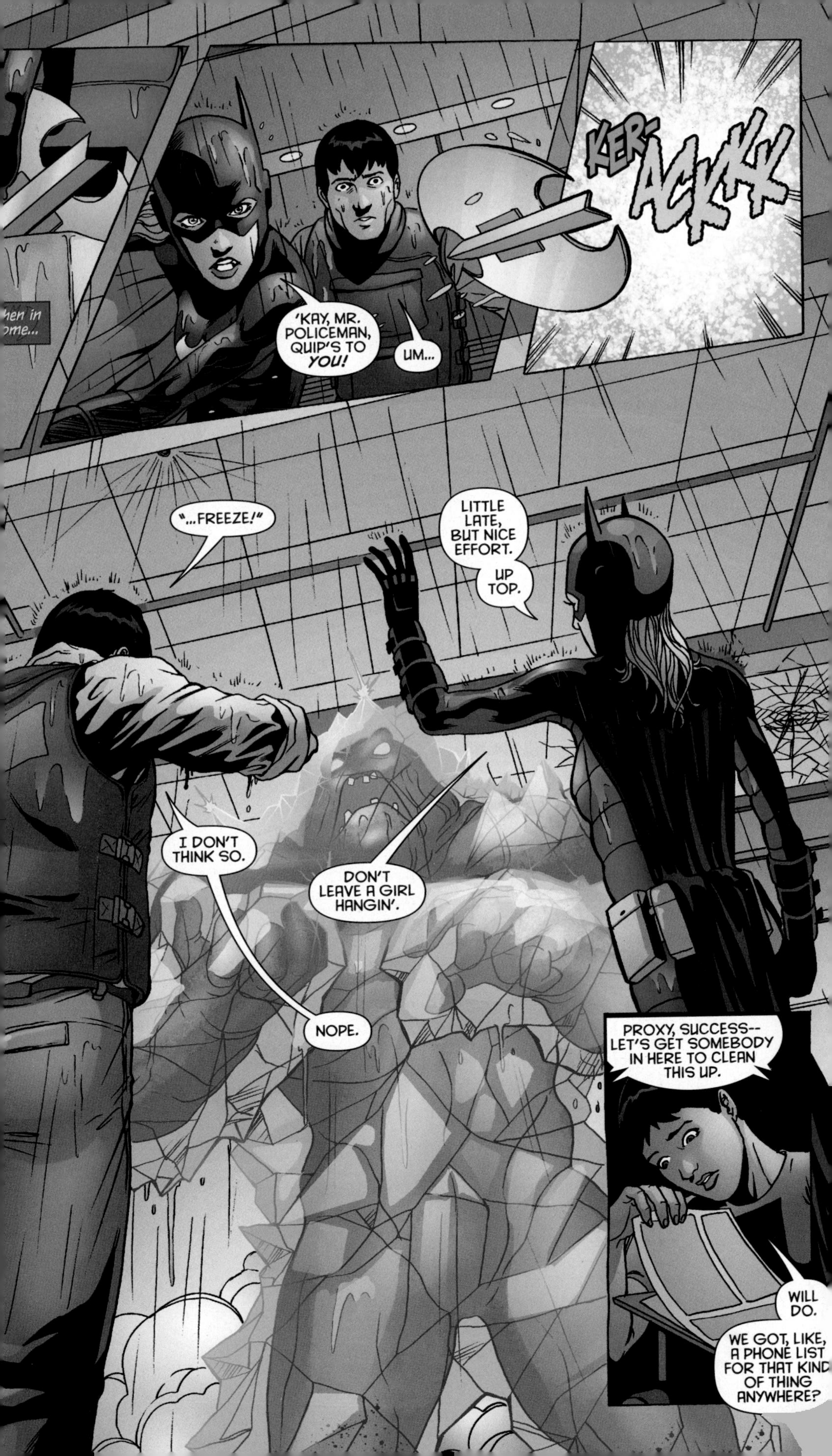

KER-ACKKK
'KAY, MR. POLICEMAN, QUIP'S TO YOU!
UM...
"...FREEZE!"
LITTLE LATE, BUT NICE EFFORT.
UP TOP.
I DON'T THINK SO.
DON'T LEAVE A GIRL HANGIN'.
NOPE.
PROXY, SUCCESS-- LET'S GET SOMEBODY IN HERE TO CLEAN THIS UP.
WILL DO.
WE GOT, LIKE, A PHONE LIST FOR THAT KIND OF THING ANYWHERE?

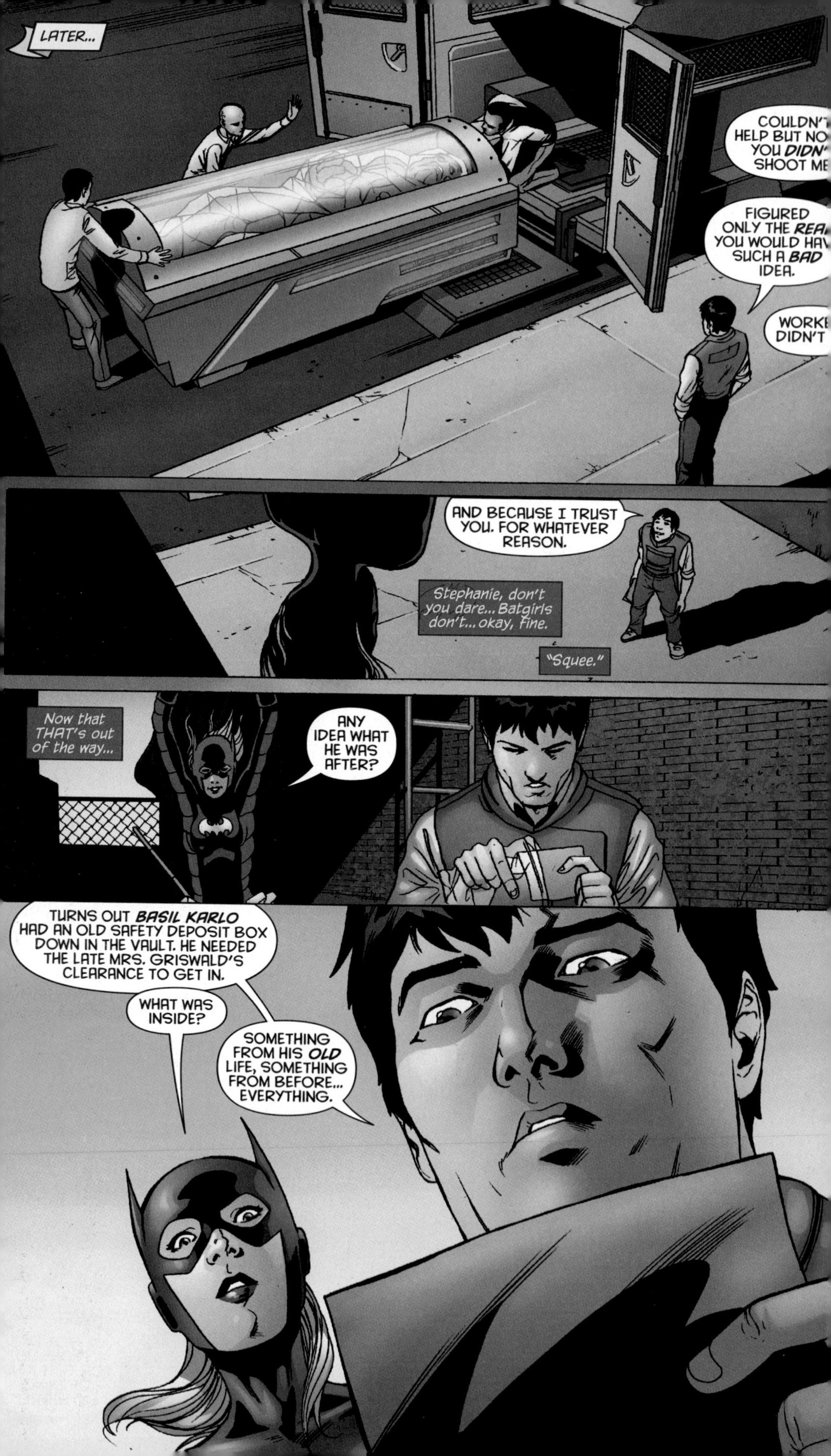
LATER...
COULDN'T HELP BUT NO YOU DIDN' SHOOT ME
FIGURED ONLY THE REA YOU WOULD HAV SUCH A BAD IDEA.
WORKE DIDN'T
AND BECAUSE I TRUST YOU. FOR WHATEVER REASON.
Stephanie, don't you dare... Batgirls don't... okay, fine.
"Squee."
Now that THAT's out of the way...
ANY IDEA WHAT HE WAS AFTER?
TURNS OUT BASIL KARLO HAD AN OLD SAFETY DEPOSIT BOX DOWN IN THE VAULT. HE NEEDED THE LATE MRS. GRISWALD'S CLEARANCE TO GET IN.
WHAT WAS INSIDE?
SOMETHING FROM HIS OLD LIFE, SOMETHING FROM BEFORE... EVERYTHING.

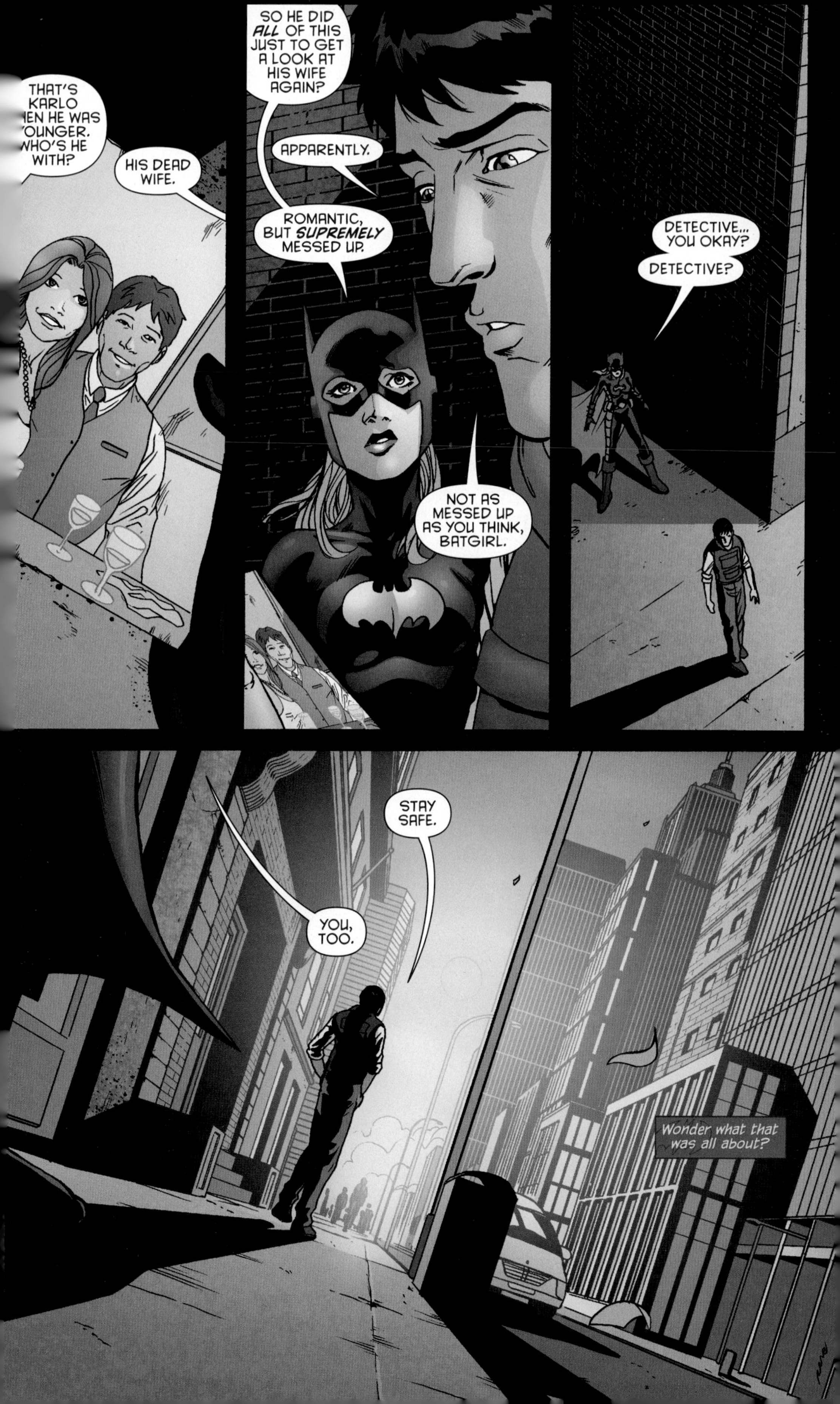
THAT'S KARLO HEN HE WAS YOUNGER. WHO'S HE WITH?
HIS DEAD WIFE.
SO HE DID ALL OF THIS JUST TO GET A LOOK AT HIS WIFE AGAIN?
APPARENTLY.
ROMANTIC, BUT SUPREMELY MESSED UP.
NOT AS MESSED UP AS YOU THINK, BATGIRL.
DETECTIVE... YOU OKAY?
DETECTIVE?
STAY SAFE.
YOU, TOO.
Wonder what that was all about?

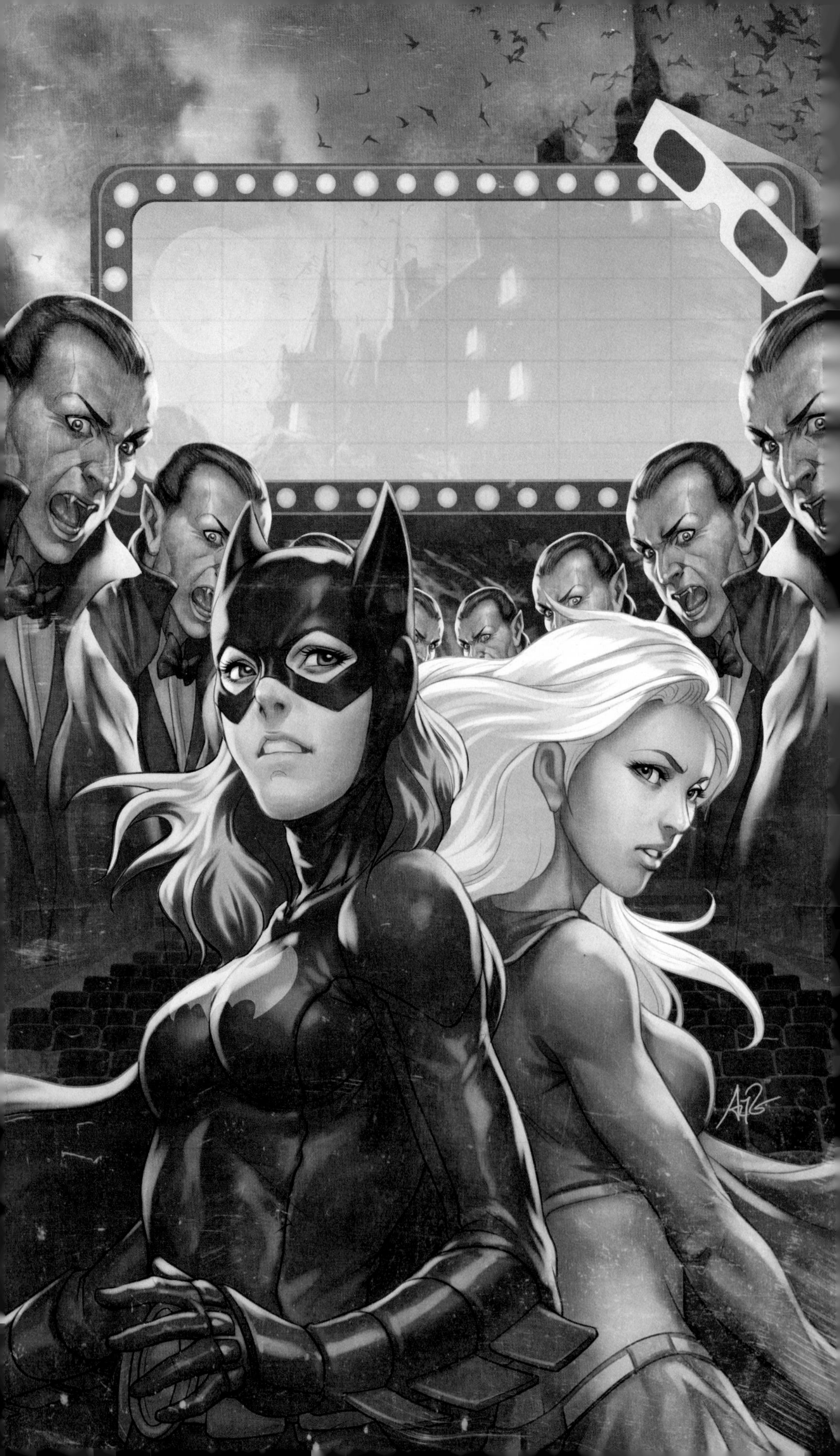

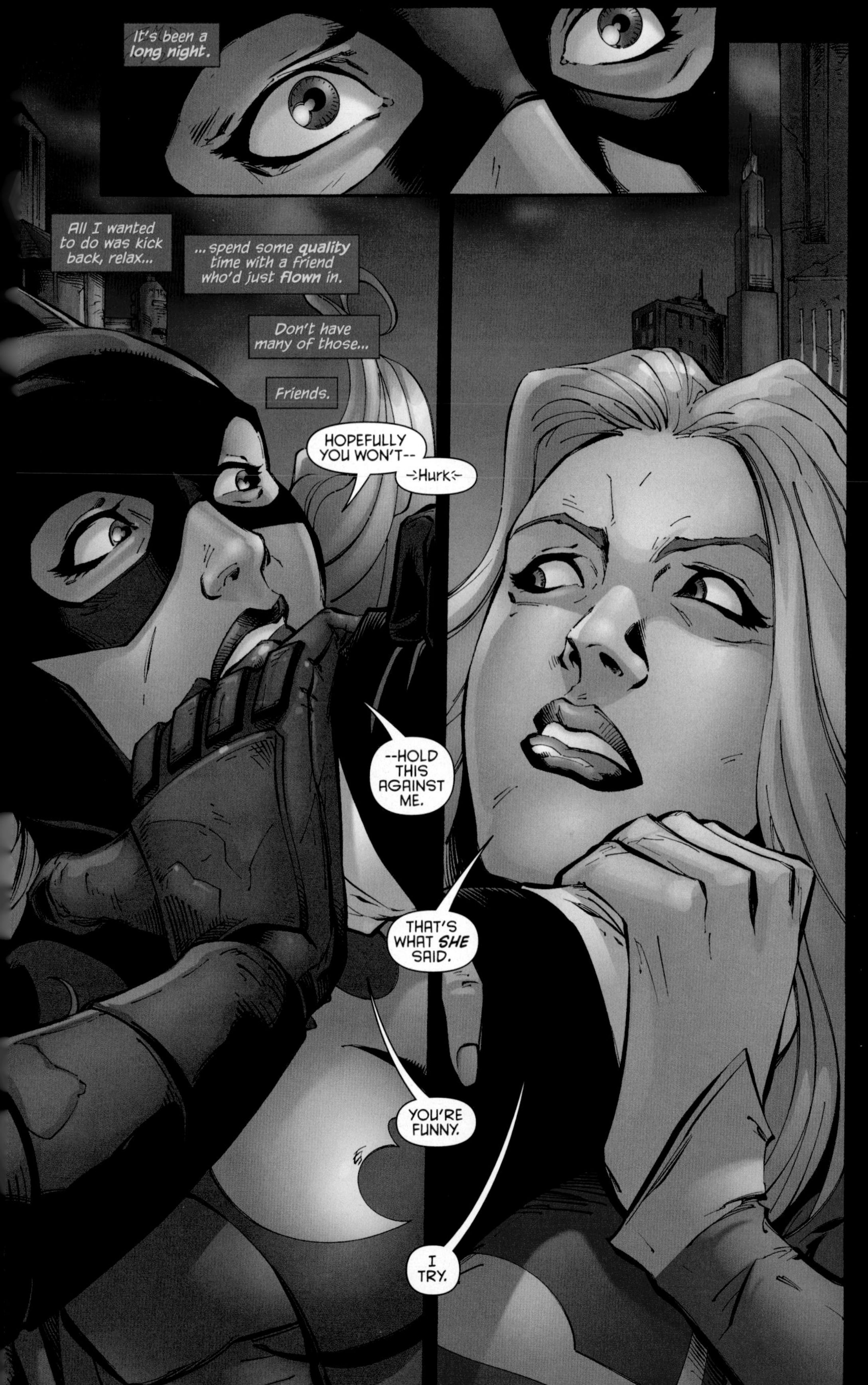
It's been a long night.
All I wanted to do was kick back, relax...
...spend some quality time with a friend who'd just flown in.
Don't have many of those...
Friends.
HOPEFULLY YOU WON'T--
Hurk
--HOLD THIS AGAINST ME.
THAT'S WHAT SHE SAID.
YOU'RE FUNNY.
I TRY.

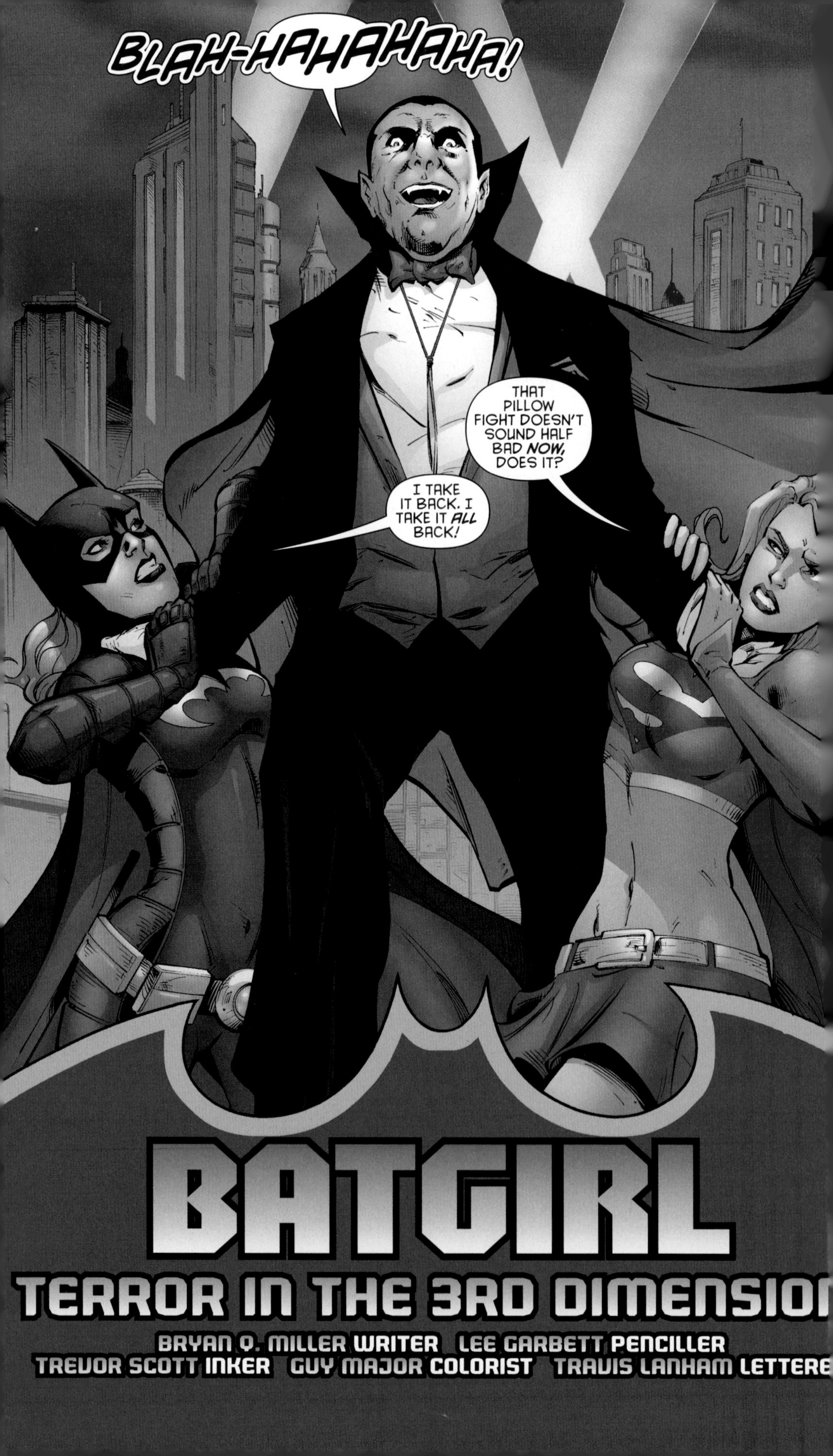

BLAH-HAHAHAHAHA!
THAT PILLOW FIGHT DOESN'T SOUND HALF BAD NOW, DOES IT?
I TAKE IT BACK. I TAKE IT ALL BACK!
BATGIRL
TERROR IN THE 3RD DIMENSION
BRYAN Q. MILLER WRITER LEE GARBETT PENCILLER
TREVOR SCOTT INKER GUY MAJOR COLORIST TRAVIS LANHAM LETTERER

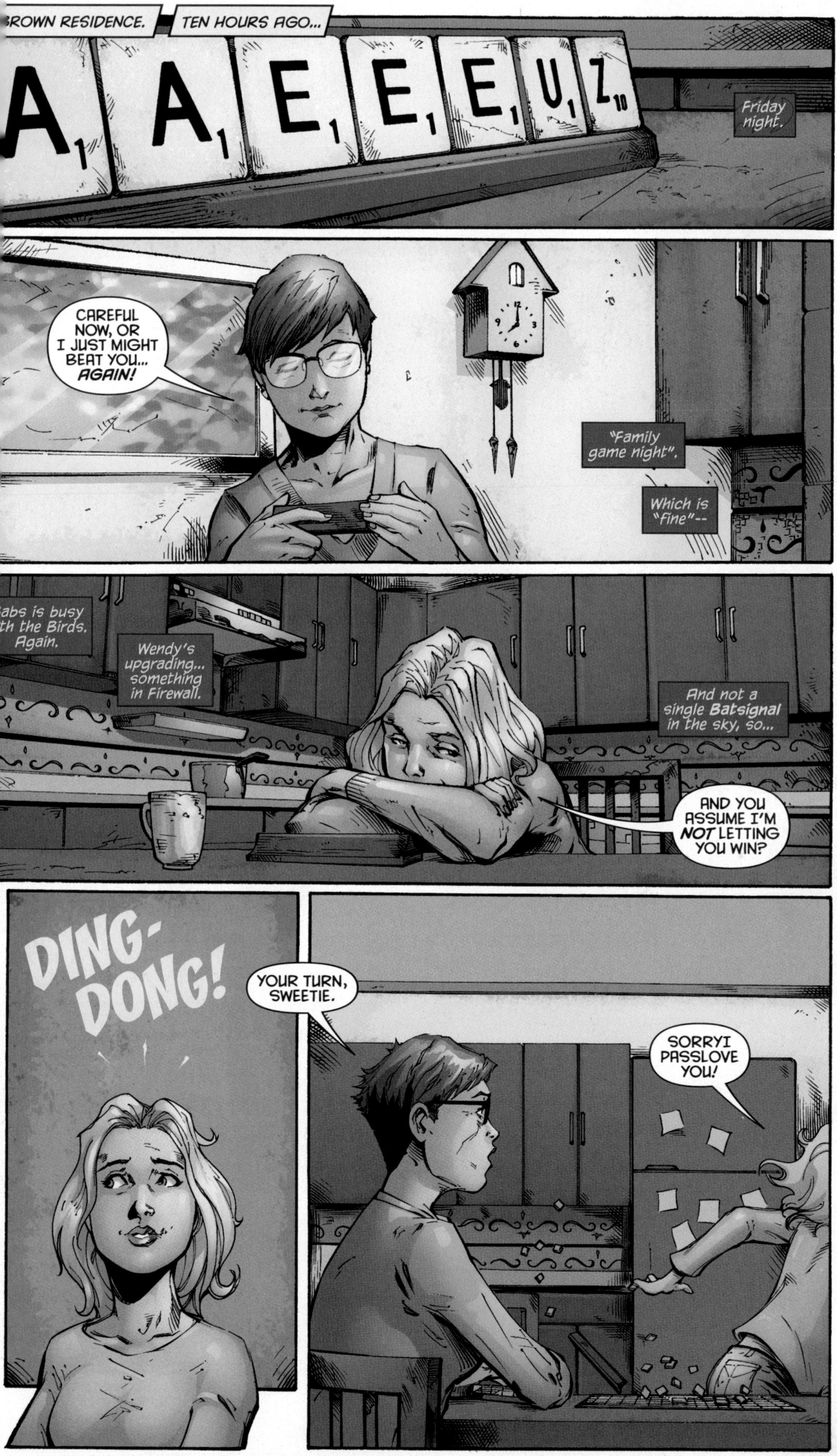
BROWN RESIDENCE.
TEN HOURS AGO...
Friday night.
CAREFUL NOW, OR I JUST MIGHT BEAT YOU... AGAIN!
"Family game night".
Which is "fine"--
abs is busy th the Birds. Again.
Wendy's upgrading... something in Firewall.
And not a single Batsignal in the sky, so...
AND YOU ASSUME I'M NOT LETTING YOU WIN?
DING-DONG!
YOUR TURN, SWEETIE.
SORRYI PASSLOVE YOU!

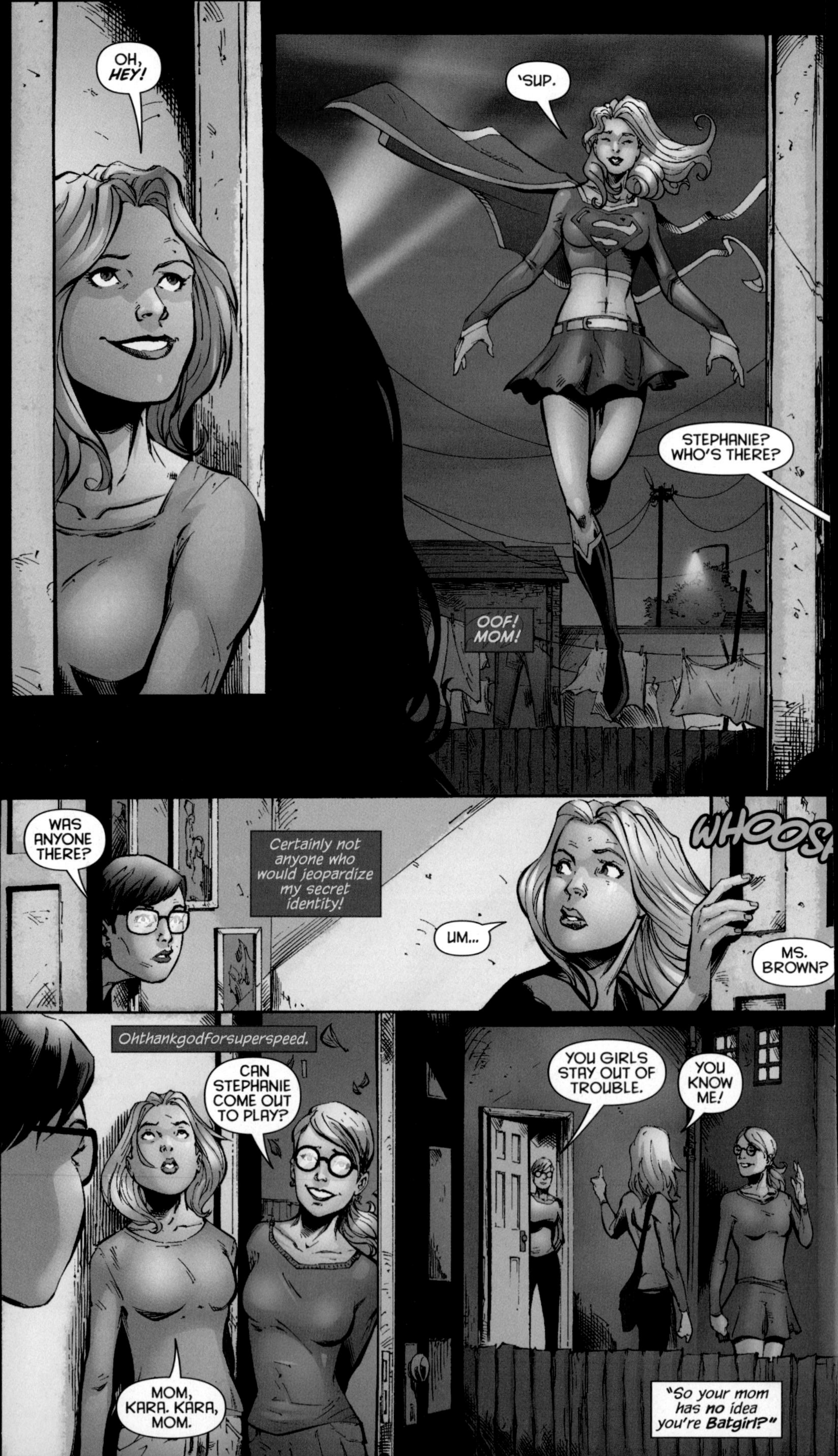

OH, HEY!
'SUP.
STEPHANIE? WHO'S THERE?
OOF! MOM!
WAS ANYONE THERE?
Certainly not anyone who would jeopardize my secret identity!
UM...
WHOOSH
MS. BROWN?
Ohthankgodforsuperspeed.
CAN STEPHANIE COME OUT TO PLAY?
MOM, KARA. KARA, MOM.
YOU GIRLS STAY OUT OF TROUBLE.
YOU KNOW ME!
"So your mom has no idea you're Batgirl?"

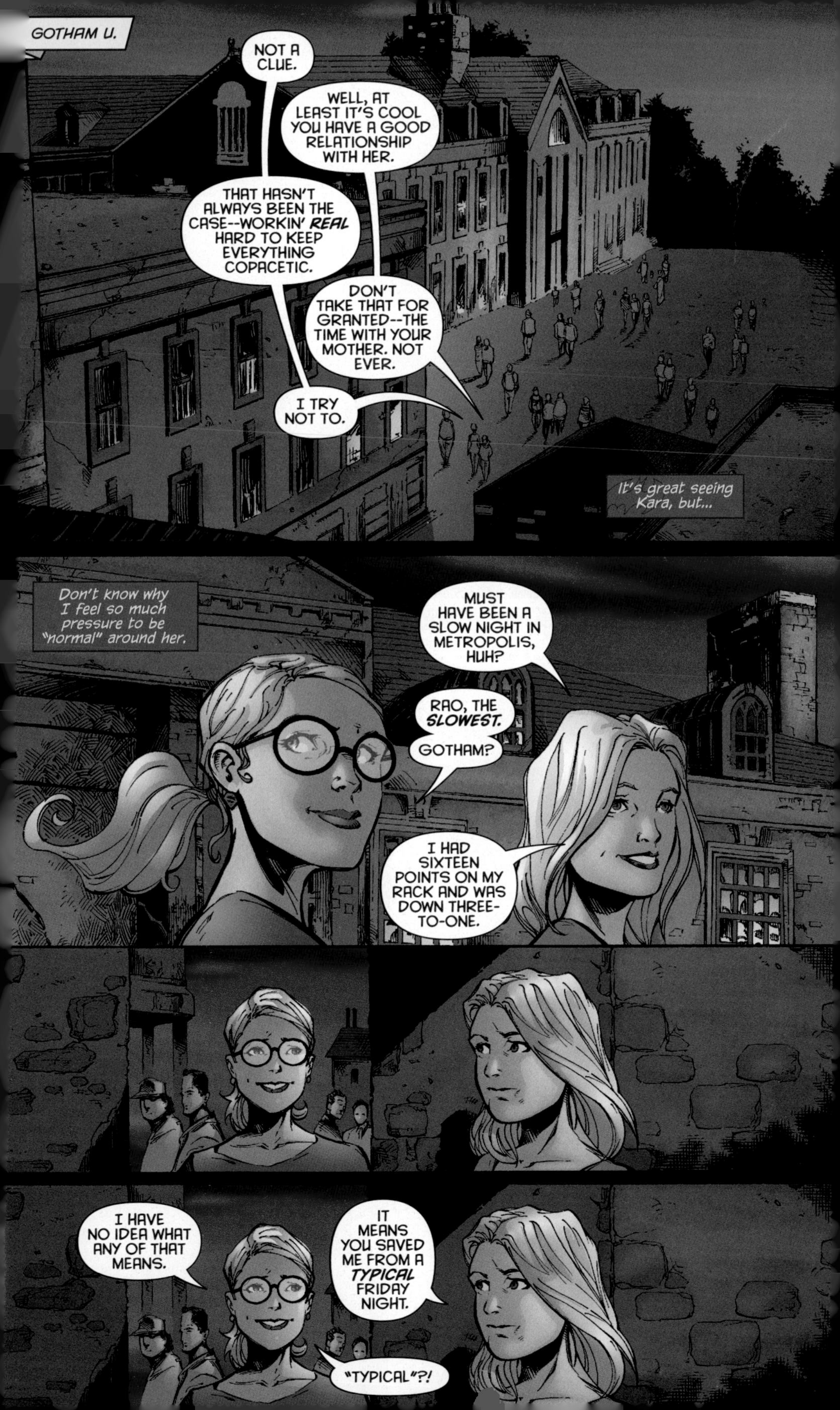
GOTHAM U.
NOT A CLUE.
WELL, AT LEAST IT'S COOL YOU HAVE A GOOD RELATIONSHIP WITH HER.
THAT HASN'T ALWAYS BEEN THE CASE--WORKIN' *REAL* HARD TO KEEP EVERYTHING COPACETIC.
DON'T TAKE THAT FOR GRANTED--THE TIME WITH YOUR MOTHER. NOT EVER.
I TRY NOT TO.
It's great seeing Kara, but...
Don't know why I feel so much pressure to be "normal" around her.
MUST HAVE BEEN A SLOW NIGHT IN METROPOLIS, HUH?
RAO, THE *SLOWEST.*
GOTHAM?
I HAD SIXTEEN POINTS ON MY RACK AND WAS DOWN THREE-TO-ONE.
I HAVE NO IDEA WHAT ANY OF THAT MEANS.
IT MEANS YOU SAVED ME FROM A *TYPICAL* FRIDAY NIGHT.
"TYPICAL"?!

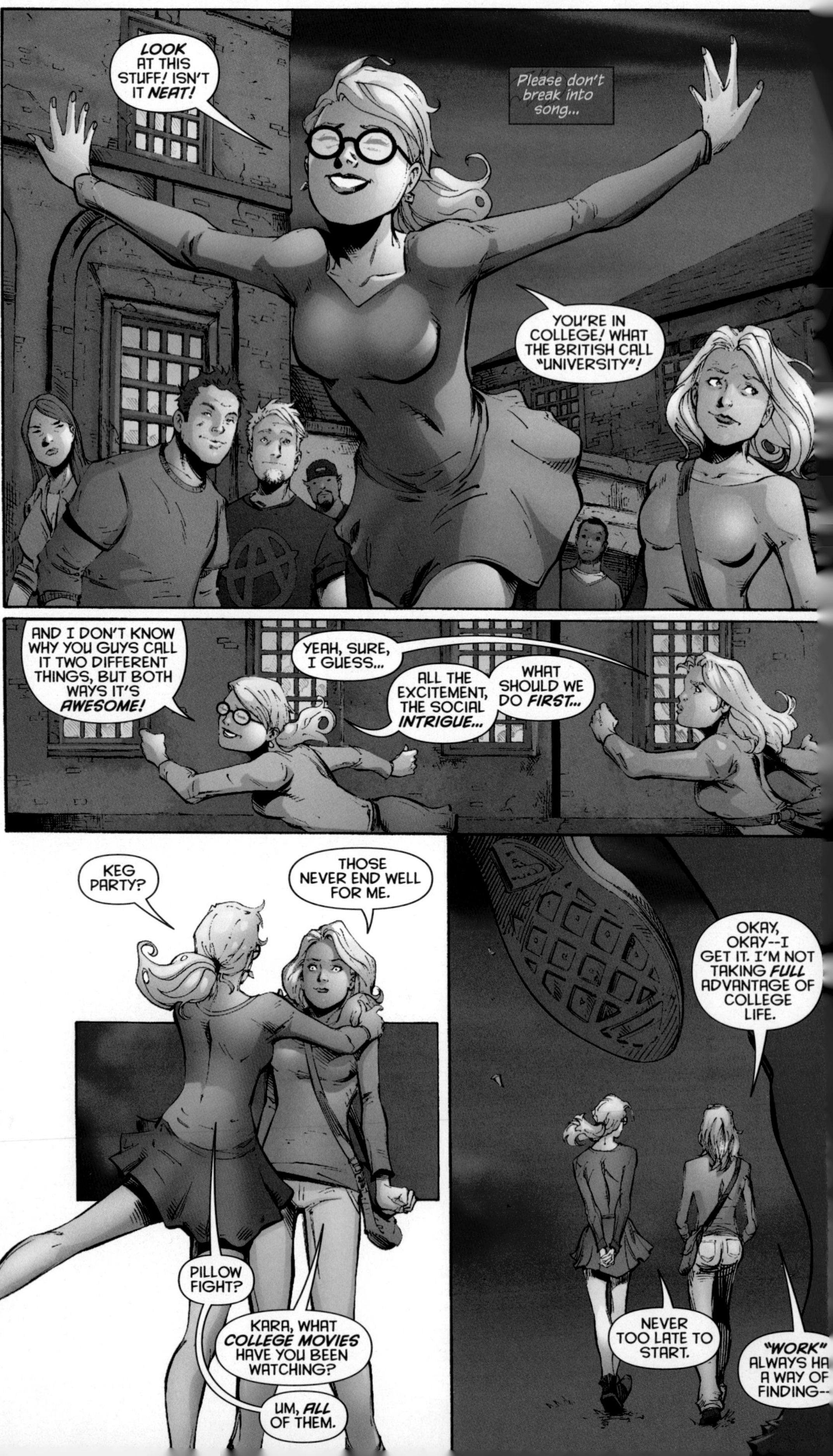

LOOK AT THIS STUFF! ISN'T IT NEAT!
Please don't break into song...
YOU'RE IN COLLEGE! WHAT THE BRITISH CALL "UNIVERSITY"!
AND I DON'T KNOW WHY YOU GUYS CALL IT TWO DIFFERENT THINGS, BUT BOTH WAYS IT'S AWESOME!
YEAH, SURE, I GUESS...
ALL THE EXCITEMENT, THE SOCIAL INTRIGUE...
WHAT SHOULD WE DO FIRST...
KEG PARTY?
THOSE NEVER END WELL FOR ME.
PILLOW FIGHT?
KARA, WHAT COLLEGE MOVIES HAVE YOU BEEN WATCHING?
UM, ALL OF THEM.
OKAY, OKAY--I GET IT. I'M NOT TAKING FULL ADVANTAGE OF COLLEGE LIFE.
NEVER TOO LATE TO START.
"WORK" ALWAYS HA A WAY OF FINDING--

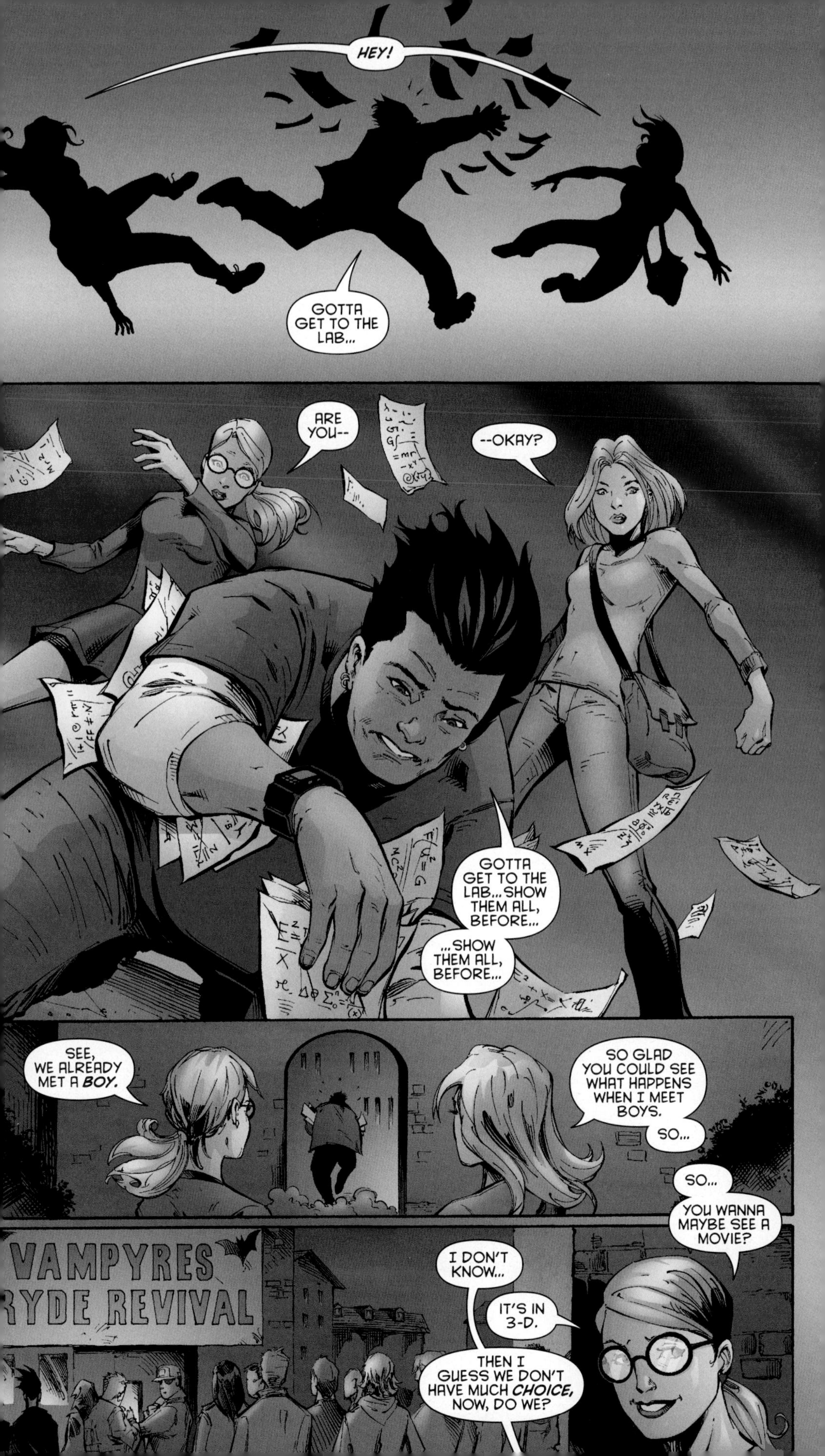
HEY!
GOTTA GET TO THE LAB...
ARE YOU--
--OKAY?
GOTTA GET TO THE LAB... SHOW THEM ALL, BEFORE...
...SHOW THEM ALL, BEFORE...
SEE, WE ALREADY MET A BOY.
SO GLAD YOU COULD SEE WHAT HAPPENS WHEN I MEET BOYS.
SO...
SO...
YOU WANNA MAYBE SEE A MOVIE?
VAMPYRES
RYDE REVIVAL
I DON'T KNOW...
IT'S IN 3-D.
THEN I GUESS WE DON'T HAVE MUCH CHOICE, NOW, DO WE?

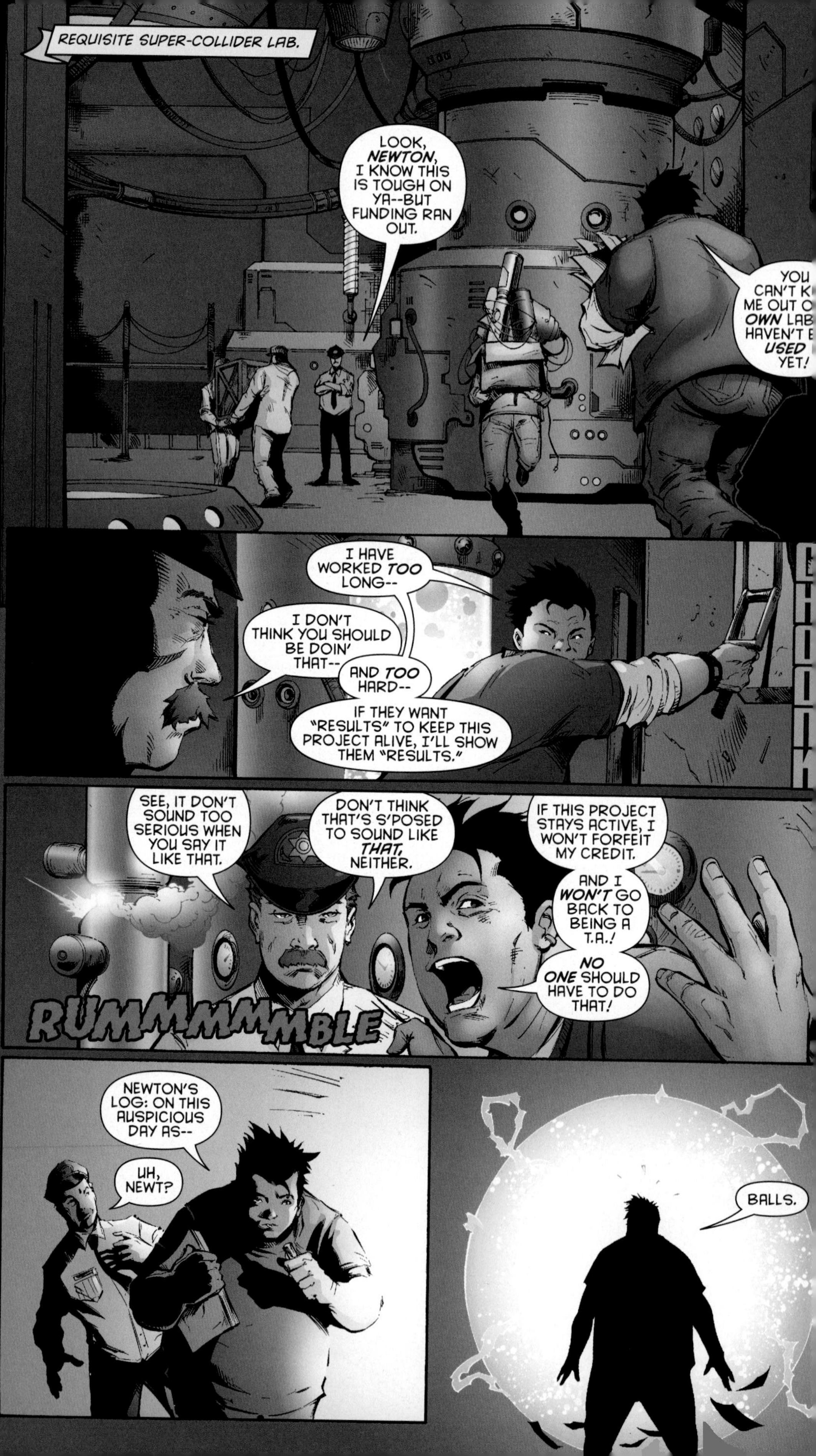
REQUISITE SUPER-COLLIDER LAB.
LOOK, NEWTON, I KNOW THIS IS TOUGH ON YA--BUT FUNDING RAN OUT.
YOU CAN'T K ME OUT O OWN LAB HAVEN'T E USED YET!
I HAVE WORKED TOO LONG--
I DON'T THINK YOU SHOULD BE DOIN' THAT--
AND TOO HARD--
IF THEY WANT "RESULTS" TO KEEP THIS PROJECT ALIVE, I'LL SHOW THEM "RESULTS."
SEE, IT DON'T SOUND TOO SERIOUS WHEN YOU SAY IT LIKE THAT.
DON'T THINK THAT'S S'POSED TO SOUND LIKE THAT, NEITHER.
IF THIS PROJECT STAYS ACTIVE, I WON'T FORFEIT MY CREDIT.
AND I WON'T GO BACK TO BEING A T.A.!
NO ONE SHOULD HAVE TO DO THAT!
RUMMMMMMBLE
NEWTON'S LOG: ON THIS AUSPICIOUS DAY AS--
UH, NEWT?
BALLS.

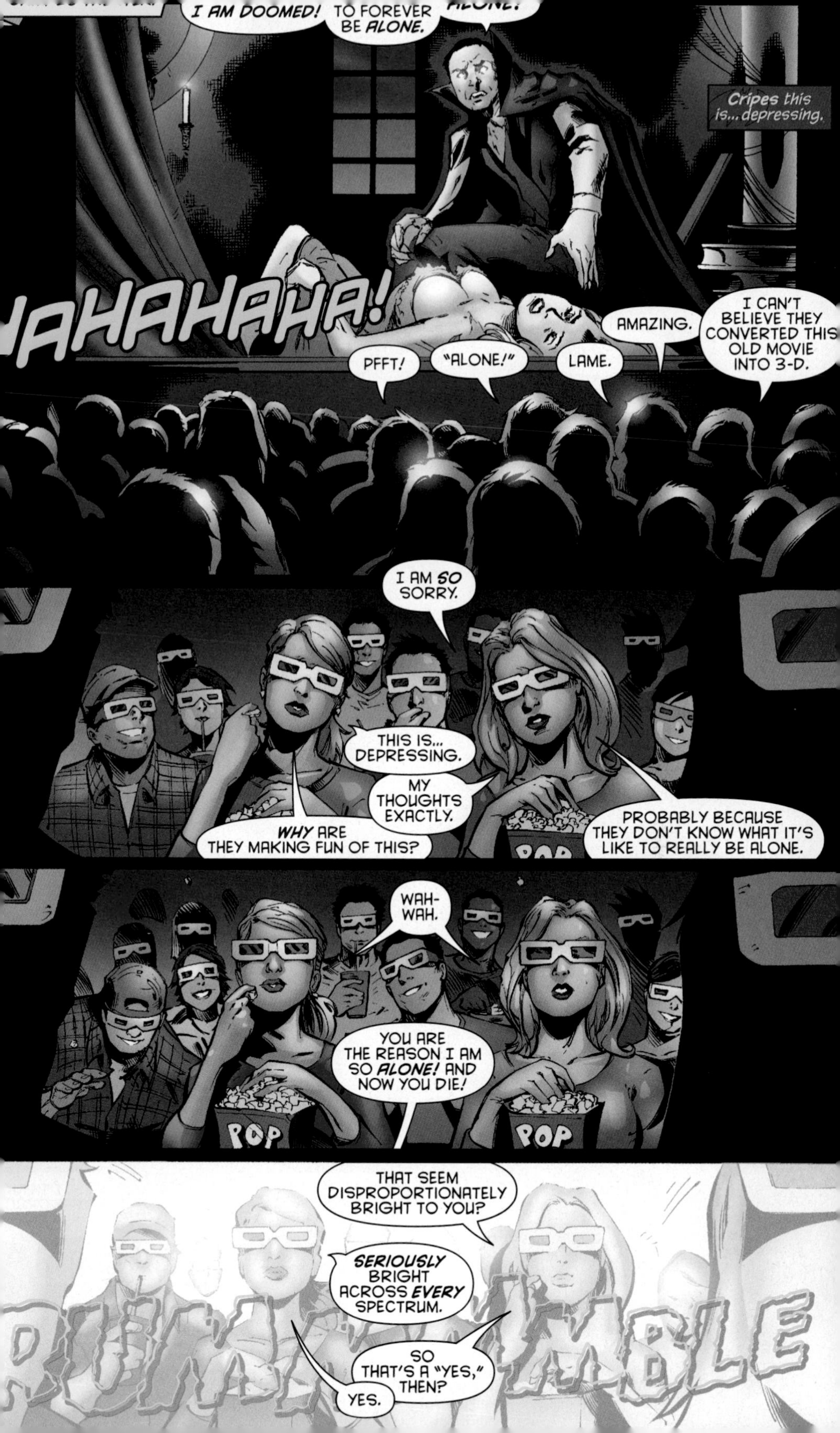
I AM DOOMED!
TO FOREVER BE ALONE.
Cripes this is... depressing.
AHAHAHAHA!
PFFT!
"ALONE!"
LAME.
AMAZING.
I CAN'T BELIEVE THEY CONVERTED THIS OLD MOVIE INTO 3-D.
I AM SO SORRY.
THIS IS... DEPRESSING.
MY THOUGHTS EXACTLY.
WHY ARE THEY MAKING FUN OF THIS?
PROBABLY BECAUSE THEY DON'T KNOW WHAT IT'S LIKE TO REALLY BE ALONE.
WAH-WAH.
YOU ARE THE REASON I AM SO ALONE! AND NOW YOU DIE!
POP
POP
THAT SEEM DISPROPORTIONATELY BRIGHT TO YOU?
SERIOUSLY BRIGHT ACROSS EVERY SPECTRUM.
SO THAT'S A "YES," THEN?
YES.

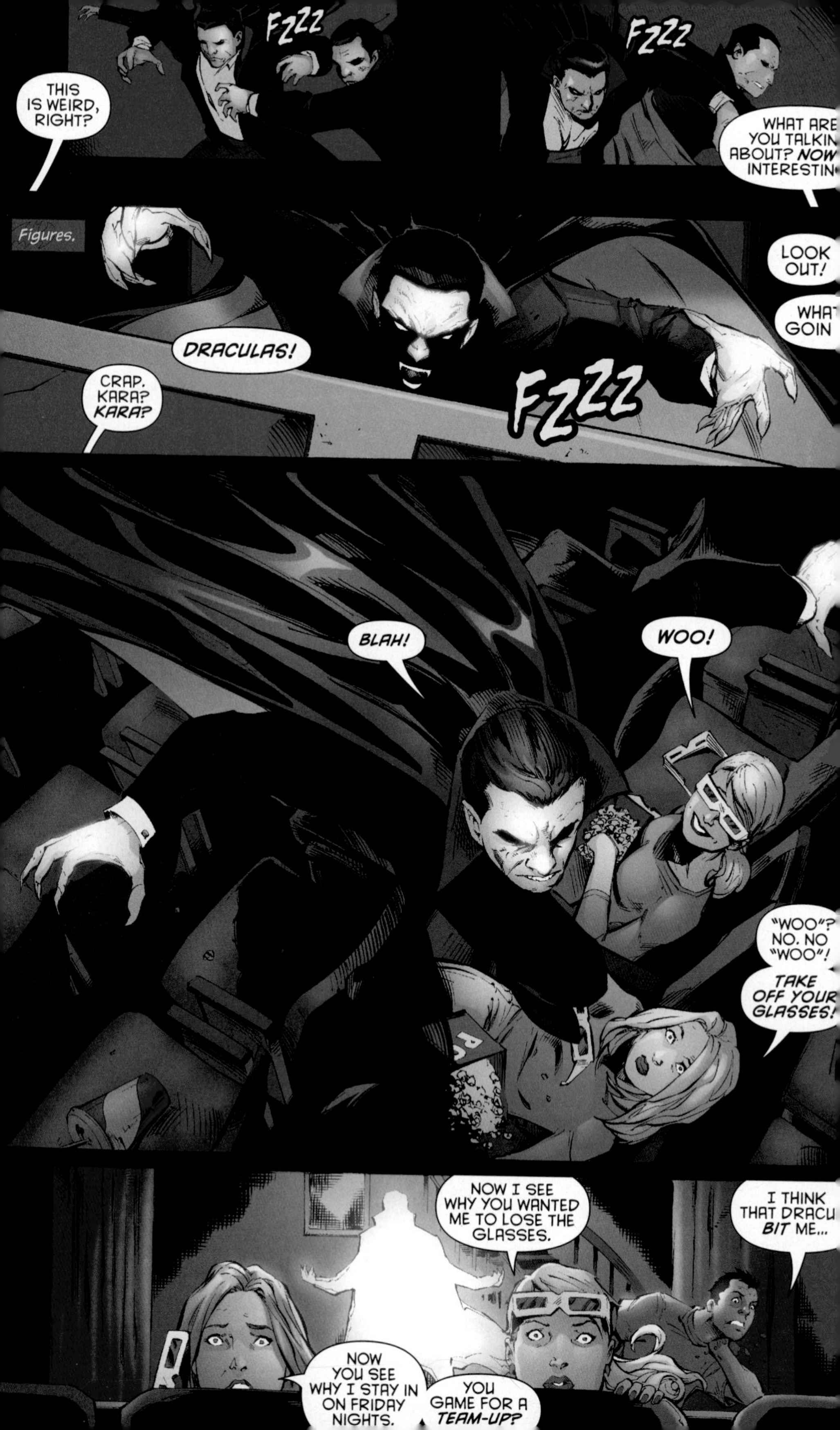
FZZZ
THIS IS WEIRD, RIGHT?
FZZZ
WHAT ARE YOU TALKIN ABOUT? NOW INTERESTIN
Figures.
LOOK OUT!
WHAT GOIN
DRACULAS!
CRAP. KARA? KARA?
FZZZZ
BLAH!
WOO!
"WOO"? NO. NO "WOO"!
TAKE OFF YOUR GLASSES!
NOW I SEE WHY YOU WANTED ME TO LOSE THE GLASSES.
I THINK THAT DRACU BIT ME...
NOW YOU SEE WHY I STAY IN ON FRIDAY NIGHTS.
YOU GAME FOR A TEAM-UP?

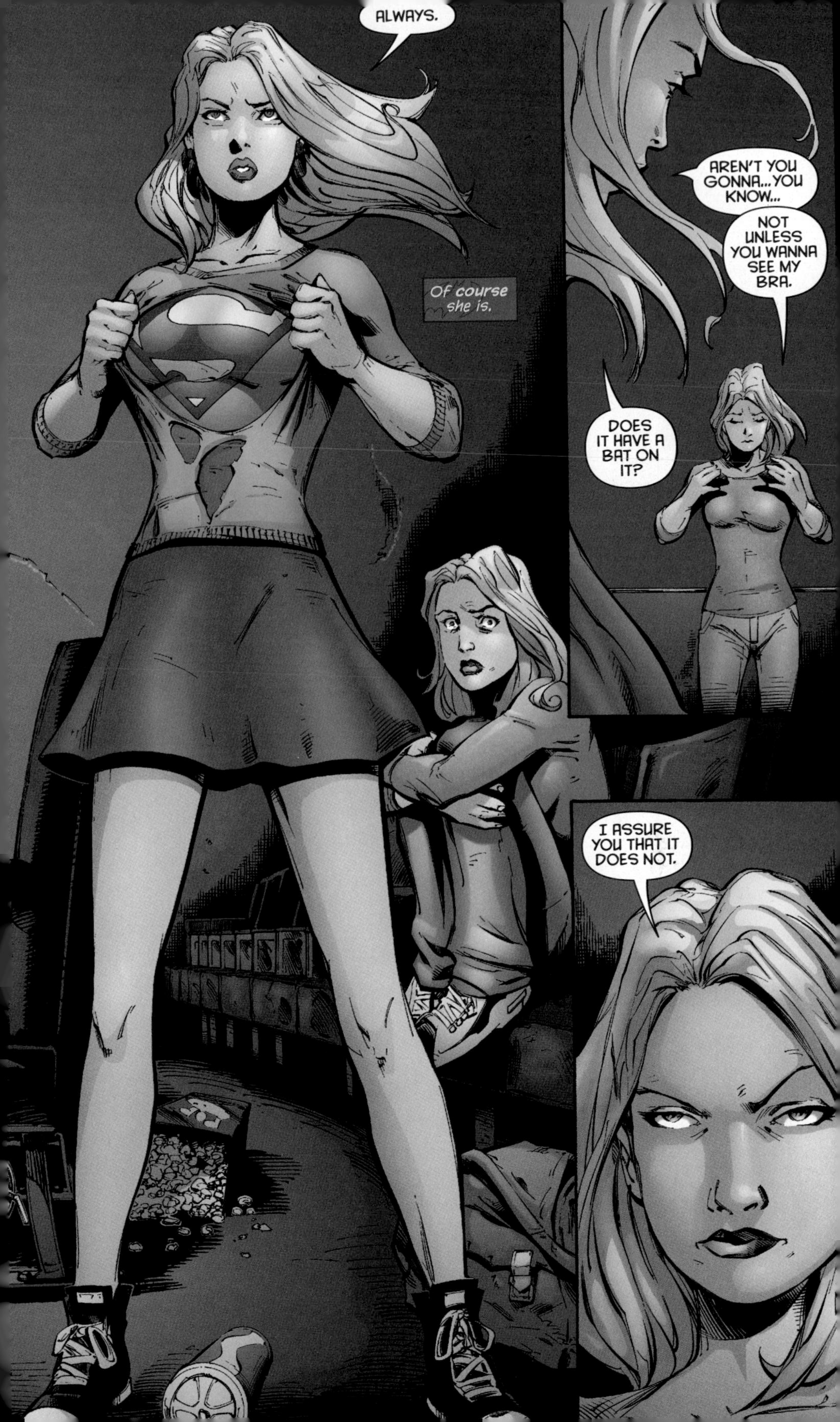
ALWAYS.
Of course she is.
AREN'T YOU GONNA...YOU KNOW...
NOT UNLESS YOU WANNA SEE MY BRA.
DOES IT HAVE A BAT ON IT?
I ASSURE YOU THAT IT DOES NOT.

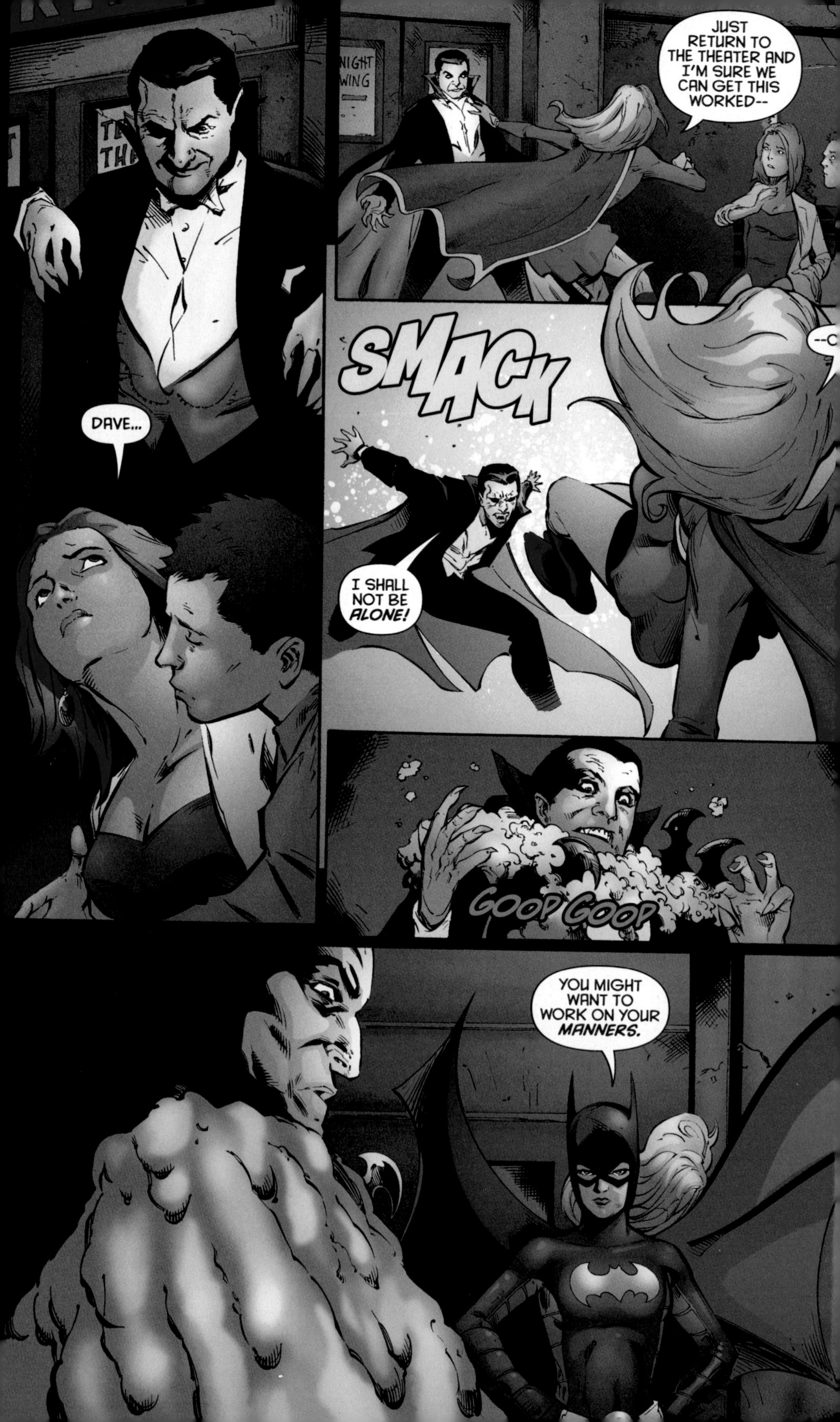
JUST RETURN TO THE THEATER AND I'M SURE WE CAN GET THIS WORKED--
DAVE...
SMACK
--C
I SHALL NOT BE *ALONE!*
GOOP GOOP
YOU MIGHT WANT TO WORK ON YOUR *MANNERS.*

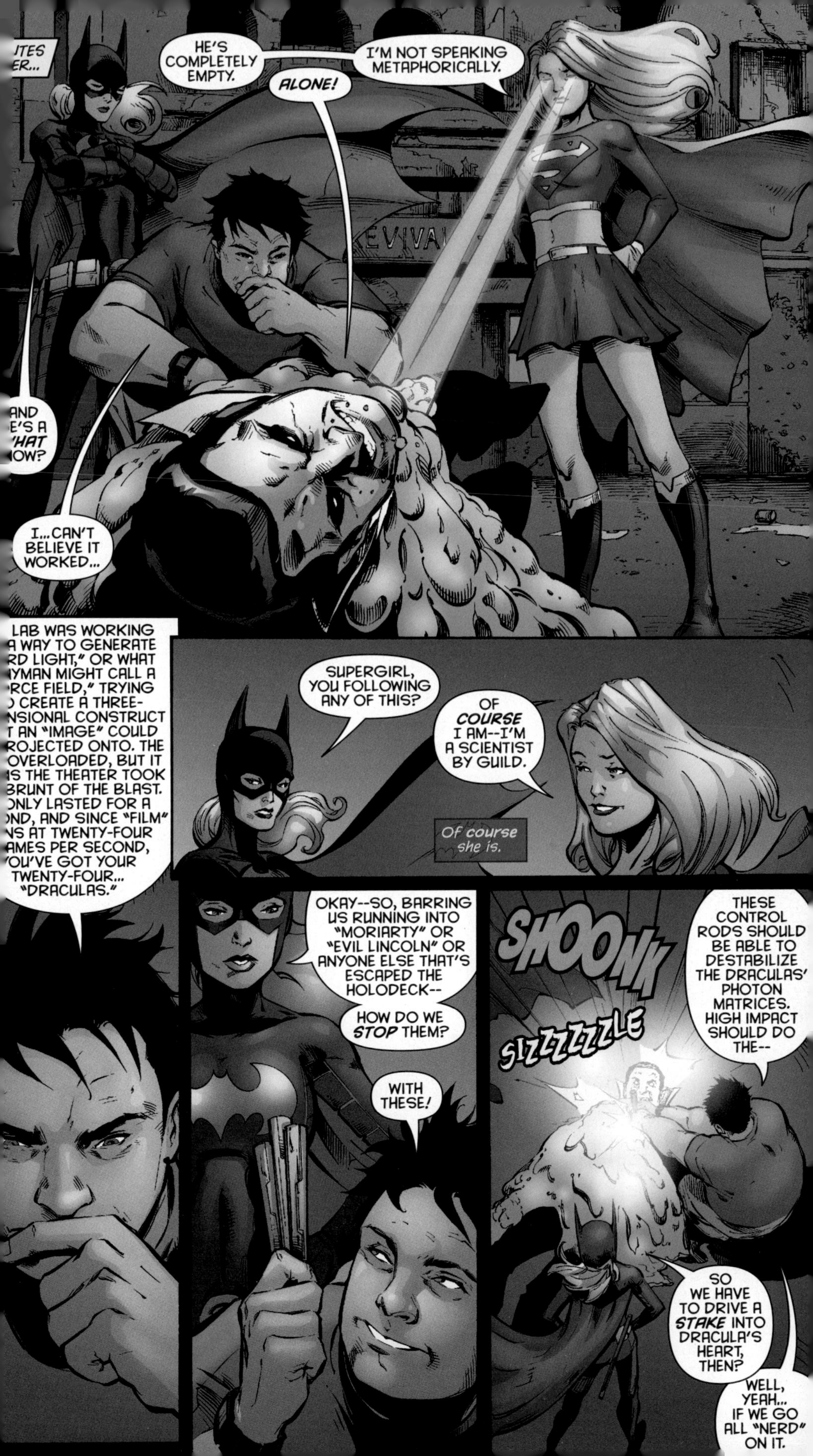
UTES ER...
HE'S COMPLETELY EMPTY.
I'M NOT SPEAKING METAPHORICALLY.
ALONE!
AND E'S A HAT OW?
I...CAN'T BELIEVE IT WORKED...
LAB WAS WORKING A WAY TO GENERATE RD LIGHT," OR WHAT YMAN MIGHT CALL A RCE FIELD," TRYING O CREATE A THREE-NSIONAL CONSTRUCT T AN "IMAGE" COULD ROJECTED ONTO. THE OVERLOADED, BUT IT S THE THEATER TOOK BRUNT OF THE BLAST. ONLY LASTED FOR A OND, AND SINCE "FILM" NS AT TWENTY-FOUR AMES PER SECOND, YOU'VE GOT YOUR TWENTY-FOUR... "DRACULAS."
SUPERGIRL, YOU FOLLOWING ANY OF THIS?
OF COURSE I AM--I'M A SCIENTIST BY GUILD.
Of course she is.
OKAY--SO, BARRING US RUNNING INTO "MORIARTY" OR "EVIL LINCOLN" OR ANYONE ELSE THAT'S ESCAPED THE HOLODECK--
HOW DO WE STOP THEM?
WITH THESE!
SHOONK
SIZZZZZZLE
THESE CONTROL RODS SHOULD BE ABLE TO DESTABILIZE THE DRACULAS' PHOTON MATRICES. HIGH IMPACT SHOULD DO THE--
SO WE HAVE TO DRIVE A STAKE INTO DRACULA'S HEART, THEN?
WELL, YEAH... IF WE GO ALL "NERD" ON IT.

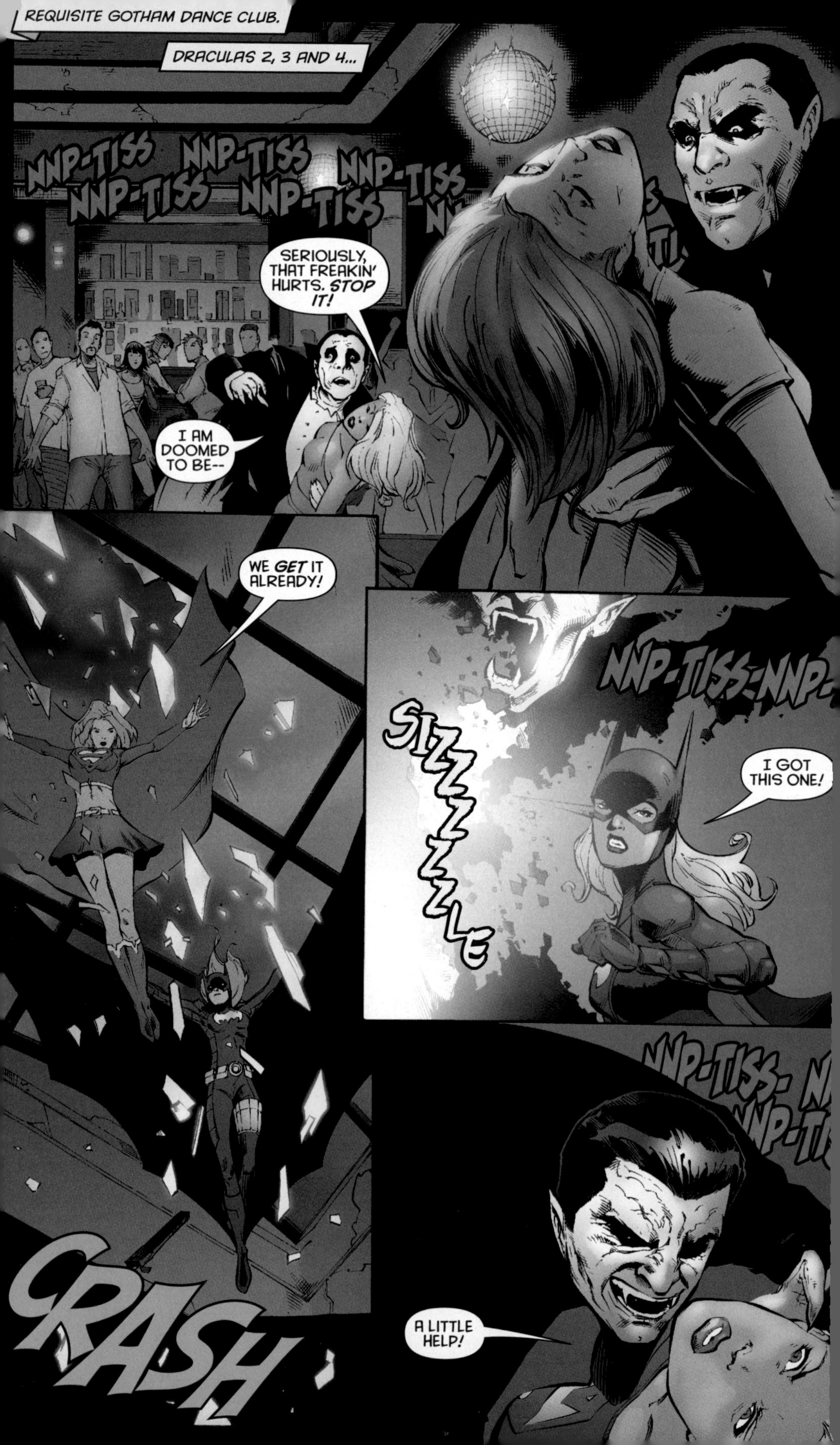

REQUISITE GOTHAM DANCE CLUB.
DRACULAS 2, 3 AND 4...
NNP-TISS NNP-TISS NNP-TISS NNP-TISS NNP-TISS NNP-TISS
SERIOUSLY, THAT FREAKIN' HURTS. STOP IT!
I AM DOOMED TO BE--
WE GET IT ALREADY!
NNP-TISS-NNP-
SIZZZZZZLE
I GOT THIS ONE!
CRASH
NNP-TISS-
NNP-TI
A LITTLE HELP!

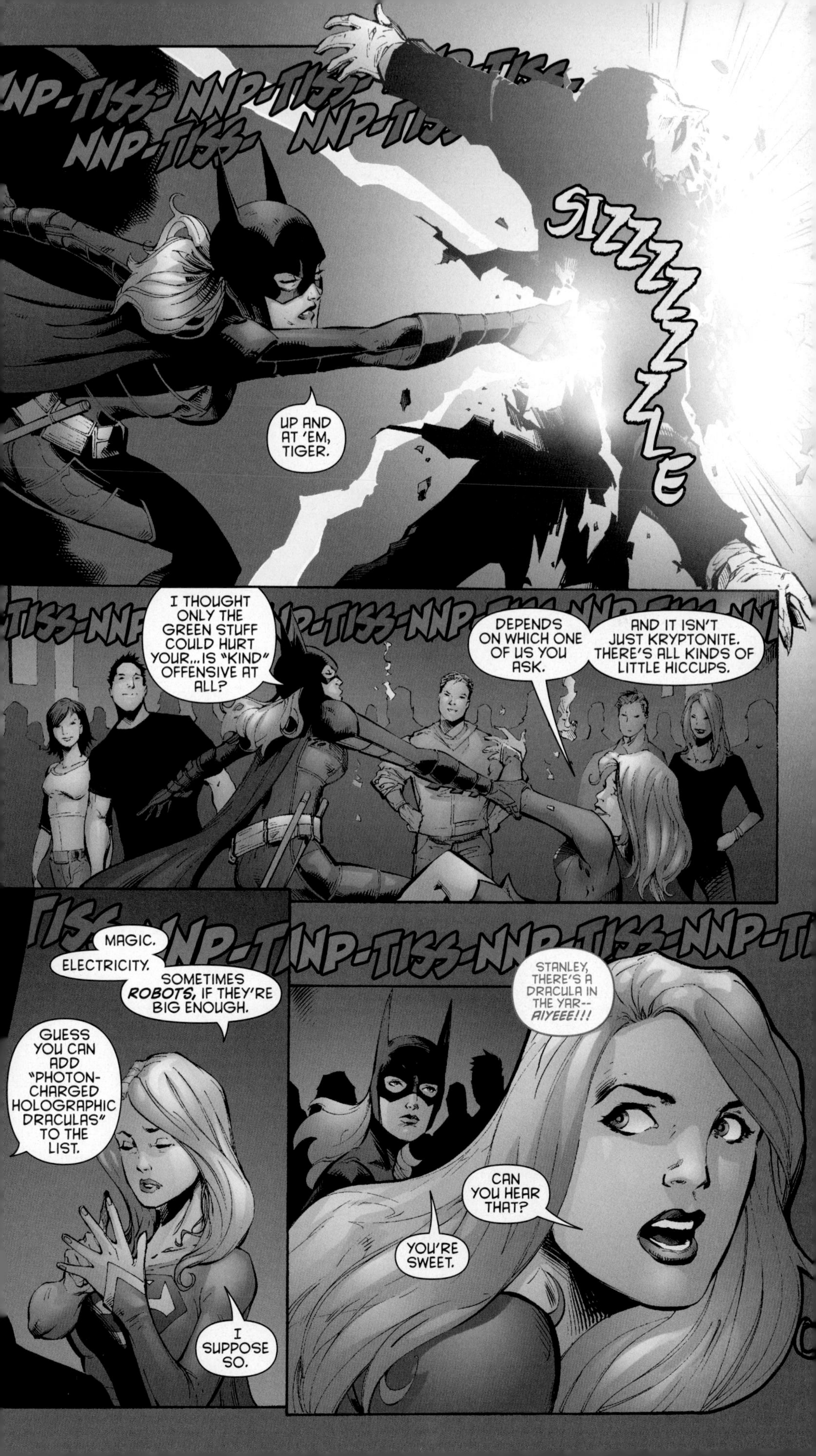
NNP-TISS-NNP-TISS-NNP-TISS-
NNP-TISS- NNP-TISS
SIZZZZZZZLE
UP AND AT 'EM, TIGER.
TISS-NNP-TISS-NNP-TISS-NNP
I THOUGHT ONLY THE GREEN STUFF COULD HURT YOUR...IS "KIND" OFFENSIVE AT ALL?
DEPENDS ON WHICH ONE OF US YOU ASK.
AND IT ISN'T JUST KRYPTONITE. THERE'S ALL KINDS OF LITTLE HICCUPS.
TISS-NNP-TNP-TISS-NNP-TISS-NNP-T
MAGIC.
ELECTRICITY.
SOMETIMES ROBOTS, IF THEY'RE BIG ENOUGH.
GUESS YOU CAN ADD "PHOTON-CHARGED HOLOGRAPHIC DRACULAS" TO THE LIST.
I SUPPOSE SO.
STANLEY, THERE'S A DRACULA IN THE YAR-- AIYEEE!!!
CAN YOU HEAR THAT?
YOU'RE SWEET.

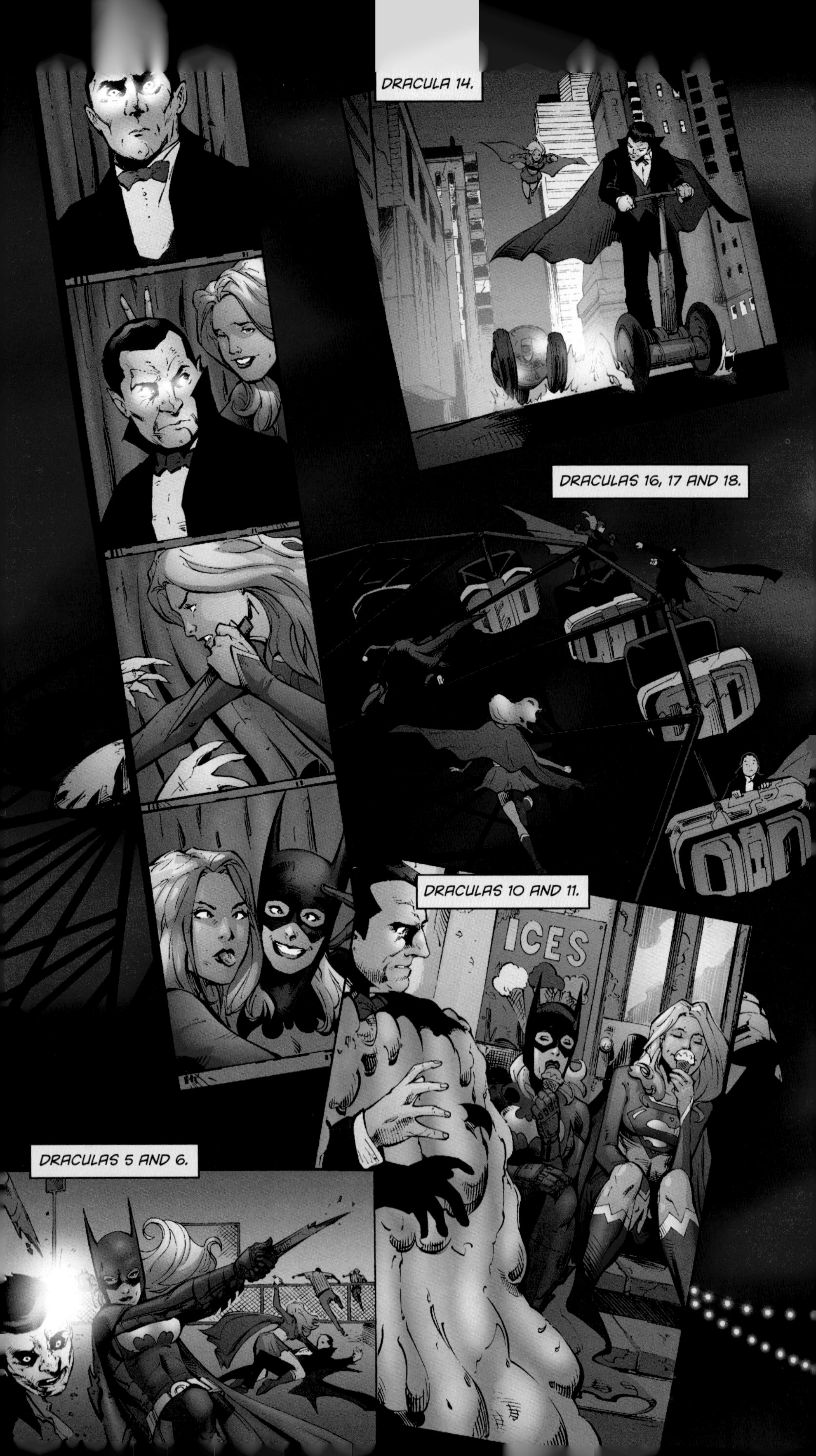
DRACULA 14.
DRACULAS 16, 17 AND 18.
DRACULAS 10 AND 11.
ICES
DRACULAS 5 AND 6.

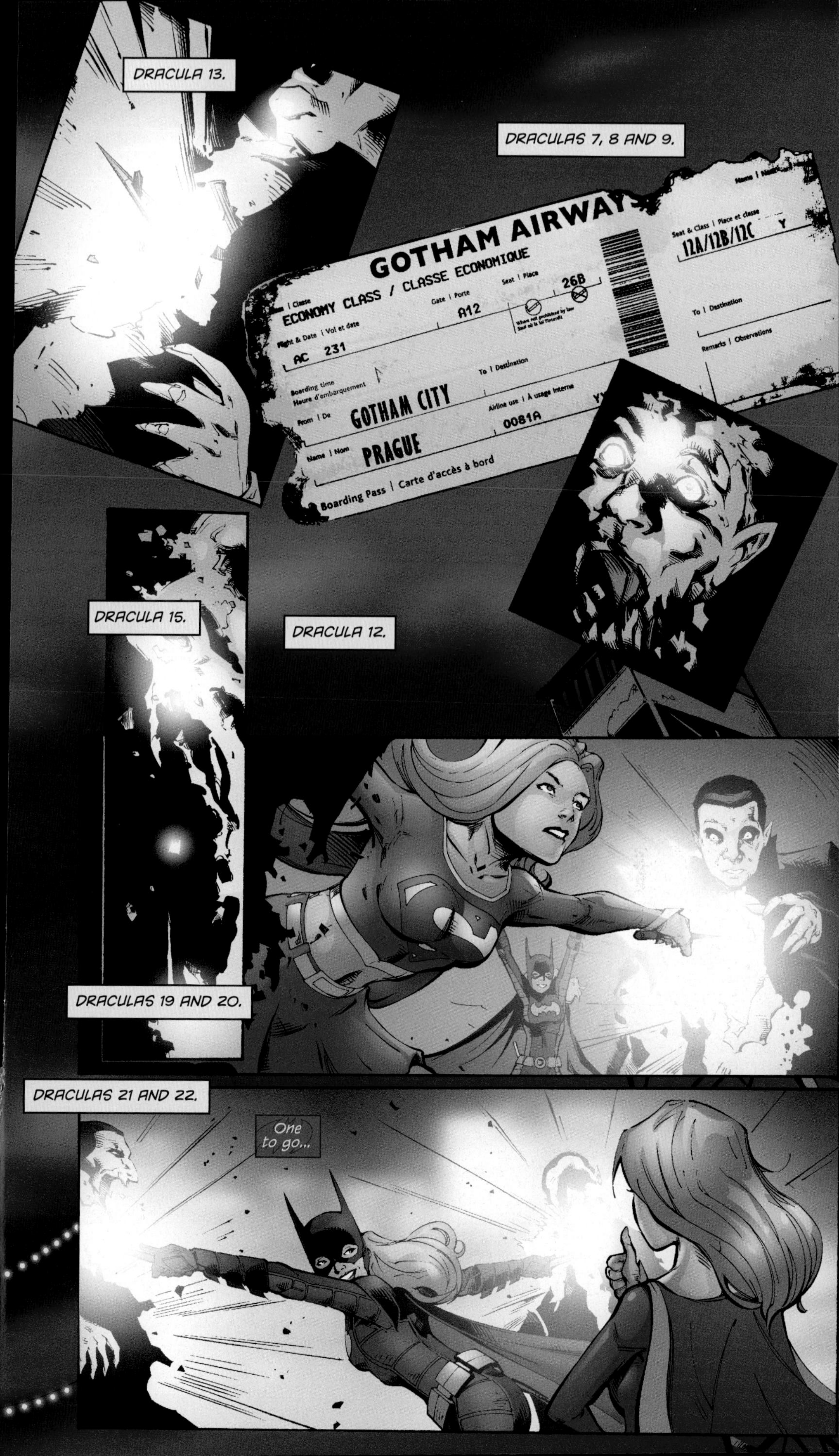
DRACULA 13.
DRACULAS 7, 8 AND 9.
GOTHAM AIRWAY
ECONOMY CLASS / CLASSE ECONOMIQUE
Flight & Date | Vol et date
AC 231
Gate | Porte
A12
Seat | Place
26B
Boarding time
Heure d'embarquement
To | Destination
From | De
GOTHAM CITY
Airline use | À usage interne
0081A
Name | Nom
PRAGUE
Boarding Pass | Carte d'accès à bord
Seat & Class | Place et classe
12A/12B/12C
Y
To | Destination
Remarks | Observations
DRACULA 15.
DRACULA 12.
DRACULAS 19 AND 20.
DRACULAS 21 AND 22.
One to go...

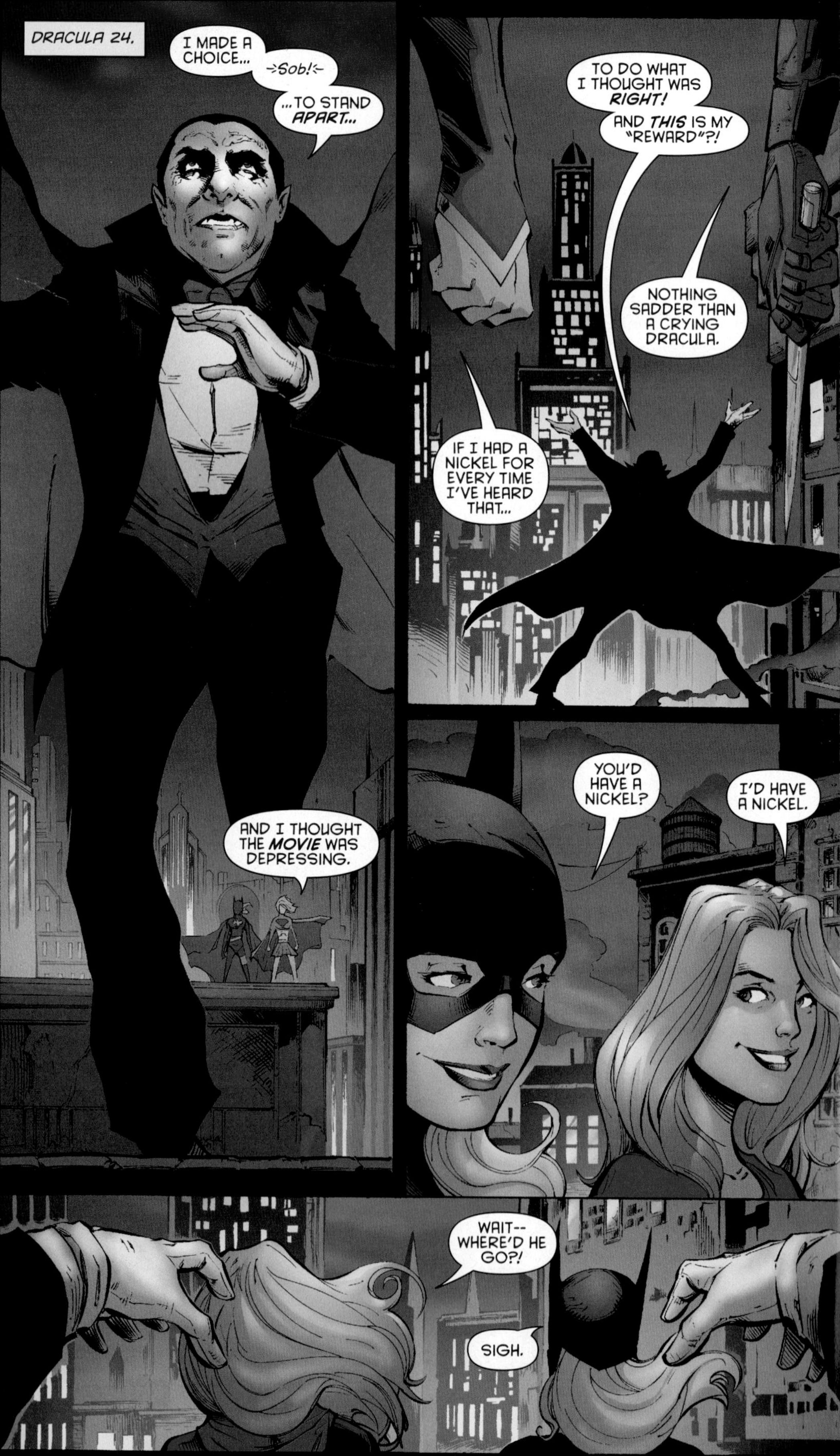
DRACULA 24.
I MADE A CHOICE...
>Sob!<
...TO STAND APART...
AND I THOUGHT THE MOVIE WAS DEPRESSING.
TO DO WHAT I THOUGHT WAS RIGHT!
AND THIS IS MY "REWARD"?!
NOTHING SADDER THAN A CRYING DRACULA.
IF I HAD A NICKEL FOR EVERY TIME I'VE HEARD THAT...
YOU'D HAVE A NICKEL?
I'D HAVE A NICKEL.
WAIT-- WHERE'D HE GO?!
SIGH.

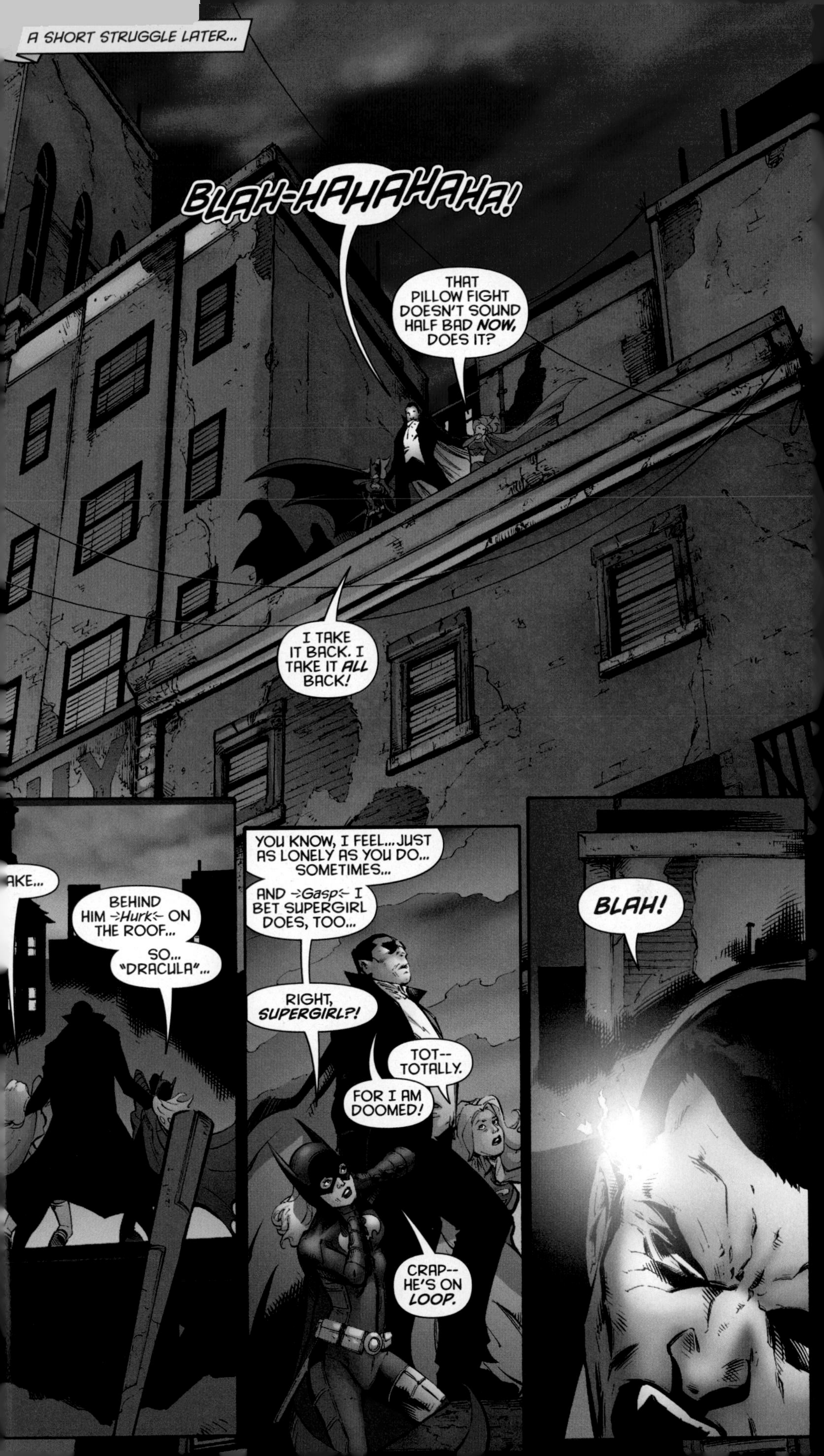
A SHORT STRUGGLE LATER...
BLAH-HAHAHAHAHA!
THAT PILLOW FIGHT DOESN'T SOUND HALF BAD *NOW,* DOES IT?
I TAKE IT BACK. I TAKE IT *ALL* BACK!
AKE...
BEHIND HIM ->*Hurk*<- ON THE ROOF...
SO... "DRACULA"...
YOU KNOW, I FEEL... JUST AS LONELY AS YOU DO... SOMETIMES...
AND ->*Gasp*<- I BET SUPERGIRL DOES, TOO...
RIGHT, *SUPERGIRL?!*
TOT-- TOTALLY.
FOR I AM DOOMED!
CRAP-- HE'S ON *LOOP.*
BLAH!

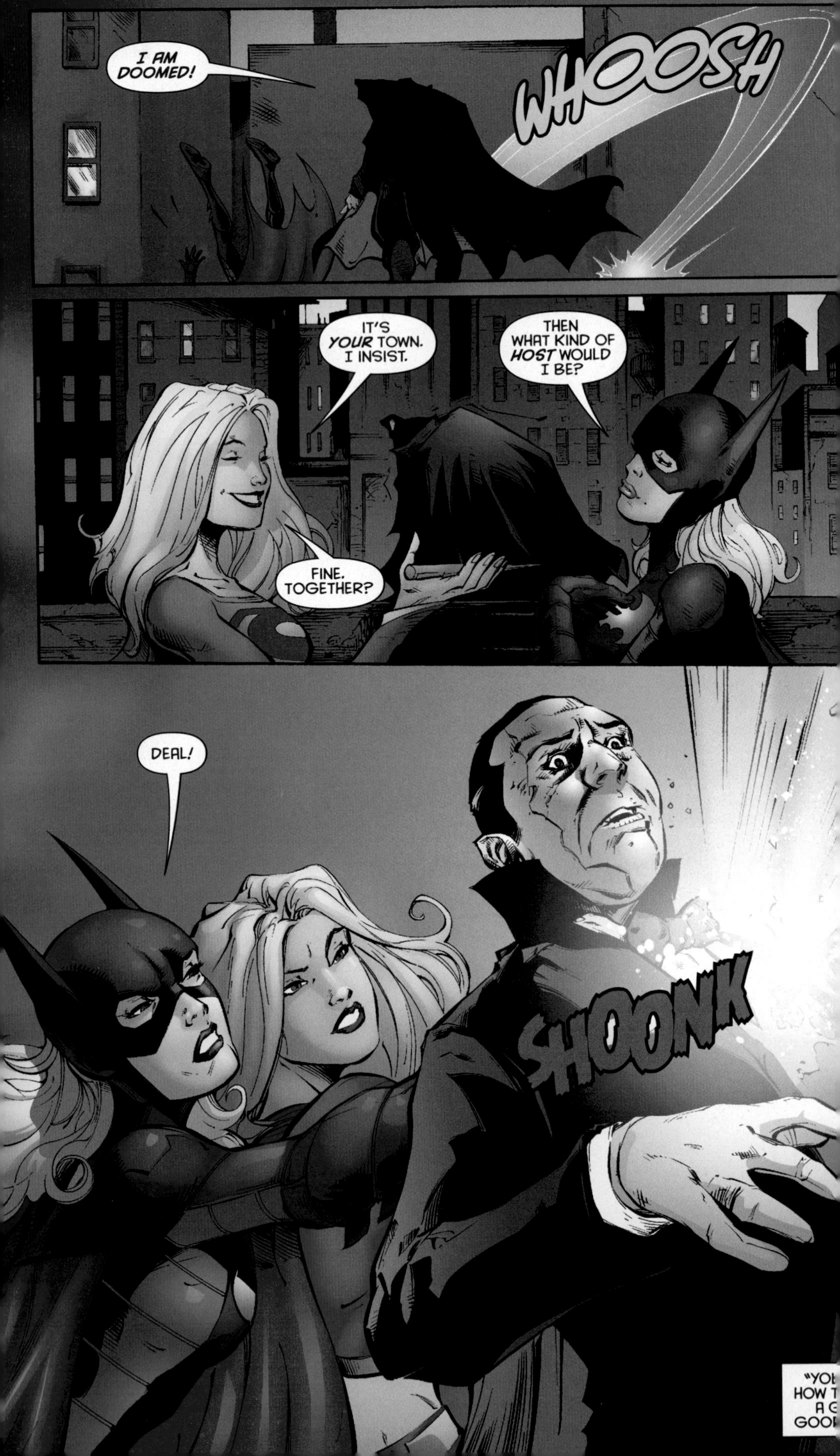
I AM DOOMED!
WHOOSH
IT'S YOUR TOWN. I INSIST.
THEN WHAT KIND OF HOST WOULD I BE?
FINE. TOGETHER?
DEAL!
SHOONK

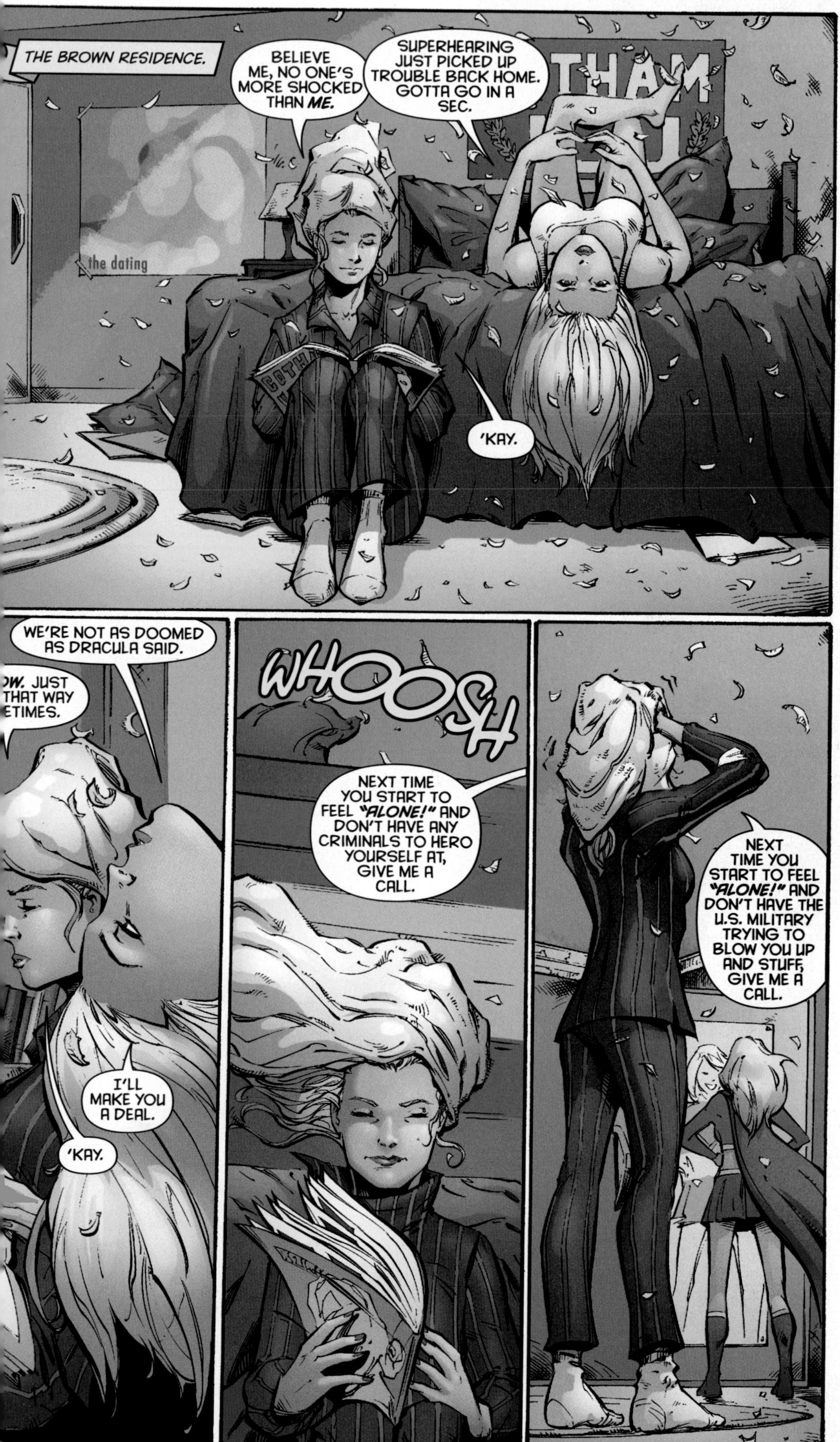
THE BROWN RESIDENCE.
BELIEVE ME, NO ONE'S MORE SHOCKED THAN *ME.*
SUPERHEARING JUST PICKED UP TROUBLE BACK HOME. GOTTA GO IN A SEC.
'KAY.
the dating
WE'RE NOT AS DOOMED AS DRACULA SAID.
OW. JUST THAT WAY ETIMES.
I'LL MAKE YOU A DEAL.
'KAY.
WHOOSH
NEXT TIME YOU START TO FEEL *"ALONE!"* AND DON'T HAVE ANY CRIMINALS TO HERO YOURSELF AT, GIVE ME A CALL.
NEXT TIME YOU START TO FEEL *"ALONE!"* AND DON'T HAVE THE U.S. MILITARY TRYING TO BLOW YOU UP AND STUFF, GIVE ME A CALL.

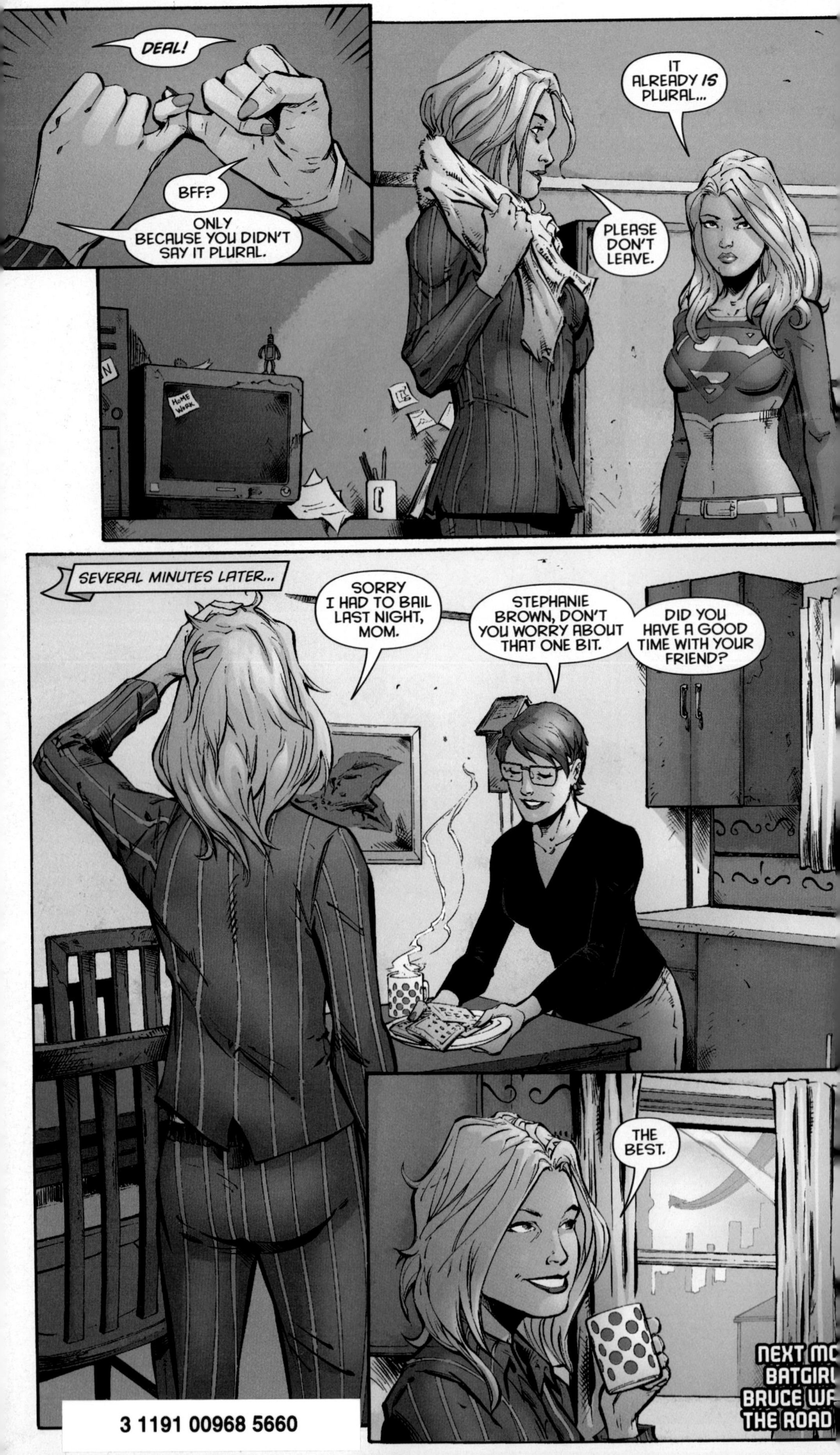
DEAL!
BFF?
ONLY BECAUSE YOU DIDN'T SAY IT PLURAL.
IT ALREADY *IS* PLURAL...
PLEASE DON'T LEAVE.
SEVERAL MINUTES LATER...
SORRY I HAD TO BAIL LAST NIGHT, MOM.
STEPHANIE BROWN, DON'T YOU WORRY ABOUT THAT ONE BIT.
DID YOU HAVE A GOOD TIME WITH YOUR FRIEND?
THE BEST.
NEXT MO
BATGIRL
BRUCE WA
THE ROAD

MORE CLASSIC TALES OF THE DARK KNIGHT

BATMAN: HUSH

JEPH LOEB
JIM LEE

BATMAN: UNDER THE HOOD
VOLS. 1 & 2

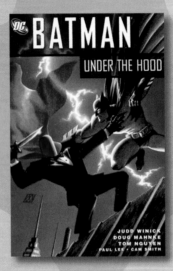

JUDD WINICK
DOUG MAHNKE

BATMAN:
THE LONG HALLOWE

JEPH LOEB
TIM SALE

BATMAN:
DARK VICTORY

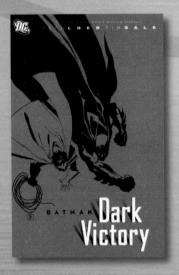

JEPH LOEB
TIM SALE

BATMAN:
HAUNTED KNIGHT

JEPH LOEB
TIM SALE

BATMAN:
YEAR 100

PAUL POPE